THE JESUITS'
ESTATES QUESTION
1760–1888

T0335322

CANADIAN STUDIES IN HISTORY AND GOVERNMENT

A series of studies edited by Goldwin French, sponsored by the Social Science Research Council of Canada, and published with financial assistance from the Canada Council.

THE JESUITS'
ESTATES QUESTION
1760-1888

A Study of the Background for
the Agitation of 1889

by
ROY C. DALTON

Bethel College
St. Paul, Minnesota

UNIVERSITY OF TORONTO PRESS

Copyright Canada 1968 by
University of Toronto Press

Reprinted in paperback 2015

ISBN 978-0-8020-3217-1 (cloth)
ISBN 978-1-4426-3968-3 (paper)

With Deepest Appreciation
to
Professor A. L. Burt

PREFACE

UNDER FRENCH RULE in Canada the Society of Jesus acquired, by grants or by purchase, well over half a million acres of land along the St. Lawrence River. The question of the disposition of its holdings was a knotty one for over a century after the British Conquest was recognized by the Treaty of Paris in 1763. Much of the trouble in later years arose from misinterpretation of the detailed history of the estates during the four decades immediately after the Conquest. The capitulatory articles of 1760 in favour of the proprietary rights of the Jesuits initiated the confusion. It became progressively confounded by the suppression of the Order by European Catholic rulers a decade before its suppression by the Pope in 1773; also by the British decision to suppress the Order and confiscate its properties, by the efforts of Jeffery, Lord Amherst, to secure possession of the estates, by strong efforts of the people of the province to have the estates devoted to education, and by the extensive provincial investigation of the estates.

Between 1800, when the last Canadian Jesuit died and the British government took formal possession of the estates, and 1832, the provincial government, after many vain efforts, finally got control of the revenues of all the properties, except the college, to be used for education. From 1832 to 1841 the Assembly continued to agitate for the restoration of the college, which was used by Imperial troops as a barracks, and made numerous protests against the management of the estates by a commissioner appointed by the executive and not responsible to the Assembly. The old college was not restored, but renewed pressure, after the reunion of Upper and Lower Canada in 1840, led to a decision in 1856 to use the revenues of the other estates exclusively for education in Canada East, a decision that might have been a lasting one had not the Order been restored by the Pope in 1814 and recalled to Canada by Mgr Bourget in 1842 to carry on its dual ministry of education and evangelization.

The financial needs of its newly established college, Collège Sainte-Marie, in Montreal made it urgent for the Order to secure the return of the estates or a monetary compensation for their loss. The Jesuits' attempts were blocked not only by successive governments but by a part of the Canadian Church hierarchy that stoutly maintained that the estates rightfully belonged to the Canadian Church after the suppression of the old Order. Rivalries between Collège Sainte-Marie, backed by a part of the hierarchy, and Laval University, supported by an even more influential part, compounded the difficulties involved in the question of the proprietorship of the estates.

When a government came to power, led by Honoré Mercier, that was sympathetic to the claims of the Jesuits and committed to a belated compensation for the loss of the estates, the disagreements within the ecclesiastical ranks of the Church in Canada made it necessary to accept the intervention of the Pope himself as an arbitrator regarding the receipt and distribution of the award. The "Act Respecting the Settlement of the Jesuits' Estates" was passed by the Quebec legislature in 1888 without any major dissent, but the matter did not end there. The large amount awarded and the Pope's role in its distribution aroused a political storm in the Dominion the following year which, as the Toronto *Globe* remarked, could have shattered the union of the provinces.

The agitation which the Act provoked was the evil fruit of misinformation, ignorance, and religious bigotry, and it did indeed seriously endanger the unity of the country. Vain efforts to secure disallowance through the Cabinet, the Dominion Parliament, the governor-general, and the British Crown itself were followed each in turn by mammoth protest rallies, furious political pulpiteering, threats of a third party, and a generous distribution of anti-Jesuit, anti-papal, and anti-Catholic tracts and pamphlets. Though voices of moderation ultimately prevailed, such phrases as these were repeatedly used: "insidious encroachments of Romanism"; "endowment of the Jesuits"; "Jesuit aggression in America"; "a foreign potentate"; "smashing of the Confederation"; "Roman Catholic briars and Jesuitical thorns"; "iniquitous measure"; "papal yoke" and "papal bondage"; "abject servility to the pope"; and "pandering to Rome by both our political parties." Protestant clergymen and other agitators repeated the question, "Which sovereign, the Queen or the Pope?" The agitation was not without a trace of humour, as in such advertisements as: "The Jesuit Question is Agitating the Public but the sensation of the day is how The Wonderful Cheap Man Can Sell a Man's All-Wool Suit Worth $8.00 for $3.90" and "The Jesuit Bill is for $400,000 but the Cluff Bill is only $2 for the Best Gents' Bal Cong or Button Boot in the City, or the Best Ladies' French Kid Button."

An Orangeman's song, entitled "Jesuitism versus Liberty" and sung to the tune of "Tramp, Tramp, Tramp," captured the spirit of the popular mood:

> In our own Canadian home, wrongful things are often done,
> And our dear old happy land has gone astray;
> In the Province of Quebec, British liberty's undecked,
> By the Jesuit Act of Popish Mercier.
>
> Wake up Briton's [*sic*] you are sleeping,
> Rouse up for the traitor's come;
> But beneath the Union Jack,
> We will keep the Jesuits back,
> And we'll live for freedom and a Briton's home.
>
> Dear old Protestants unite, party politics aren't right—
> Think of dear-bought liberty in days done by;
> Bury dirty party fight, cast your votes for truth and right,
> Leave our children something noble, grand and high.

The heat of the excitement produced by the Act and the efforts—not confined to, but emanating largely from, Ontario Protestants—to have it disallowed might soon have been dissipated had attention been focussed merely upon the constitutional character of the piece of legislation. However, its opponents coupled it with the Act of Incorporation of the Jesuits that had passed the year before with scarcely a murmur of dissent from Quebec Protestants, and they expanded their agitation to include the questions of separate schools, dual languages, racial and cultural interests, and other less clearly defined issues. In the context of the problems and difficulties that confronted the Canadian government and its people in 1889, the stormy Jesuits' estates agitation increased the tensions that militated against the creation of a sense of national unity and purpose.

When the Act of Settlement was passed in 1888 there was no balanced historical account of the Jesuits' estates. Two or three accounts existed (among them Reverend A. Rankin's and Father Braun's) but they were highly partisan. Nor, to the writer's knowledge, has there been any subsequent study that is even approximately satisfactory. The purpose of this book, then, is to provide the historical background of the controversial Act of 1888 in as full and unbiased a manner as possible. Such an account is essential to a judicious appraisal of the role of Mercier's government in its enactment as well as of the fury of the storm of protest that it unleashed. It is assumed that the repercussions of the Act are well known, however, and they are treated only in a very summary fashion in the introduction and at the conclusion of the study.

Chapter v, which is not strictly a part of the narrative of the period from 1760 to 1888, is, nevertheless, one of the most important parts of the background study because it contains an analysis of all the title deeds of the principal parts of the Jesuits' estates. Since the conditions under which the Jesuits received the estates in the seventeenth century remained the subject of heated controversy throughout the period from the Conquest to 1888, particular attention has been given to these details.

Bethel College   ROY C. DALTON
St. Paul, Minnesota

A*

CONTENTS

MAPS

TABLES

THE JESUITS'
ESTATES QUESTION
1760-1888

CHAPTER ONE

THE JESUITS IN CANADA
FROM THE CONQUEST TO PAPAL SUPPRESSION

BEFORE THE BRITISH Conquest of New France the members of the Society of Jesus had played such an important educational and evangelizing role in North America that one pictures great numbers of priests scattered throughout the country-side. An examination of the roll of Jesuit missionaries and teachers, however, reveals that an immense task was being carried on, particularly among the Indians, by a relatively few dedicated missionaries. A lengthy tribute might be paid to their endeavours prior to the Conquest, but this would be quite apart from the purpose of this history, which commences with the year 1759. At the beginning of that year there were thirty-one Jesuit priests, ten brothers, and three scholastics carrying on their tasks in the areas of Acadia, Quebec, Three Rivers, Montreal, the Great Lakes, and Illinois.[1] The City of Quebec, with its Jesuit college, was the focal point for their missions.

The "Articles of Capitulation" of Quebec included only a very general article regarding the question of religious rights and practices. Article VI provided for the maintenance and the free exercise of the Roman Catholic religion, for safeguards to all religious persons and to the houses of the clergy and the monasteries, and for the free exercise of the episcopal authority of the bishop of Quebec, all until the possession of Canada should be decided by formal treaty. In the case of the Jesuits, however, safeguards to the houses of the clergy gave way to military exigency. Necessity demanded military occupation of their college shortly after the fall of the city, an occupation which, though it may have been justifiable as a temporary measure, was to be a cause of considerable bitterness for decades to come.

The college, built on a six-acre tract and reconstructed about 1740, consisted of a large stone house that formed a quadrilateral. According to one contemporary, it surpassed the governor's palace in the nobility of its dimensions and of its architecture; it was about four times as large as the home of the governor and one of the most beautiful buildings of the city. The college, with its exterior chapel, received its share of shells during the fighting on September 13, 1759, but it was not set on fire or irreparably damaged.[2] General Murray justified its use as a storehouse for provisions on the ground that there was no other place in the town so proper, adding that "it was necessary to dislodge the Fathers the first Winter, less [sic] their turbulent and intriguing genius should prompt them to play some trick which might have proved fatal in the critical situation of affairs and which they could perhaps have easily compassed had they been suffer'd to reside in the House."[3] Murray notified the Jesuits of the need for taking possession and gave them permission to leave when they wished. Two priests and four brothers withdrew to join two other priests in the mission at Jeune-Lorette, not far from the city.[4] All the buildings of the college, including an exterior chapel, were then turned into a vast military entrepôt. A commissariat of rations was located there, which supplied not only all necessary provisions for the sustenance of the army but some of the needs of the Ursulines and the religious of l'Hôtel-Dieu as well.[5]

A year after the Capitulation of Quebec, Montreal surrendered (September 8, 1760) and all Canada passed into the hands of the British. The terms of surrender that related to religion were this time more detailed. Articles XXVII–XXXI of the Capitulation dealt particularly with the status of the Catholic Church as a whole, article XXVII providing for the full and free exercise of the Catholic religion in the customary manner.[6] Articles XXXII–XXXV were to have such an important bearing in the controversies to come that it is well to look at them in their entirety. The response of General Ahmerst to the French proposal is indicated following each of the articles.

ART. XXXII. The communities of Nuns shall be preserved in their constitutions and privileges; they shall continue to observe their rules, they shall be exempted from lodging any military; and it shall be forbid to molest them in their religious exercises, or to enter their monasteries: safe-guards shall even be given them, if they desire them. [Granted.]

ART. XXXIII. The preceding article shall likewise be executed, with regard to the communities of Jesuits and Recollects and of the house of the priests of St. Sulpice at Montreal; these last, and the Jesuits, shall preserve their right to nominate to certain curacies and missions, as heretofore. [Refused till the King's pleasure be known.]

ART. XXXIV. All the communities, and all the priests, shall preserve their moveables, the property and revenues of the Seignories and other estates, which they possess in the colony, of what nature soever they be; and the same estates shall be preserved in their privileges, rights, honours, and exemptions. [Granted.]

ART. XXXV. If the Canons, Priests, Missionaries, the Priests of the Seminary of the foreign Missions, and of St. Sulpice, as well as the Jesuits, and the Recollects, chuse to go to France, a passage shall be granted them in his Britannic Majesty's ships, and they shall have leave to sell, in whole, or in part, the estates and moveables which they possess in the colonies, either to the French or to the English, without the least hindrance or obstacle from the British Government.—They may take with them, or send to France, the produce of what nature soever it be, of the said goods sold, paying the freight, as mentioned in the XXVIth article; and such of the said Priests, who chuse to go this year, shall be victualled during the passage, at the expense of his Britannic Majesty; and they shall take with them their baggage. [They shall be masters to dispose of their estates and to send the produce thereof, as well as their persons, and all that belongs to them to France.][7]

Thus the Jesuits were refused, "till the King's pleasure be known," the same recognition of their constitution and privileges as was granted to the communities of nuns, and the right to nominate to certain curacies and missions. But article XXXIV granted the preservation of full proprietary rights to all the communities, and the Jesuits were specifically included in article XXXV which gave the various ecclesiastical groups the freedom to sell their holdings and to send or take the income to France.

During the months when Canada was passing from the control of the French government to that of the British, events were taking place elsewhere that were bound to have a bearing upon the future of the Society of Jesus in Canada. What was ultimately decided concerning the status and the proprietary rights of the Order there is closely related to what happened to the Order as a whole throughout the world, particularly in Europe.

In the second half of the eighteenth century, a keen hostility to the Jesuit Order arose in most of the European states, and repressive measures against them were begun by several governments. In 1750 Don Sebastian Carvalho (later Marquis de Pombal) became prime minister of Portugal. Carvalho was an enemy of the Jesuits, and soon laid severe restrictions upon them. Following an attempt upon the life of the King, Joseph I, on September 3, 1758, the Jesuits were accused. The King ordered the sequestration of all their estates in January of the following year and expelled them from the kingdom in September, 1759.[8]

In France, the Order also had many enemies. Their controversies with the Jansenists had aroused violent partisanship, and their great political and ecclesiastical influence had excited the jealousy of other religious orders. Jeanne Poisson, marquise de Pompadour, Louis XV's favourite, was bitterly hostile to them, and it was she whose influence had raised to power the Duc de Choiseul, the minister of foreign affairs from 1759 to 1780. Choiseul was opposed to clerical ascendancy at the court and he was supported by a large body of the enlightened thought of the era.

An airing in the courts of the commercial transactions of a Jesuit, Antoine de Lavalette, seems to have provided the occasion for the thoroughgoing investigation of the activities of the Order in France that led to their expulsion. Lavalette, procurator-general of the Jesuit mission in the Caribbean islands, had engaged in extensive commercial operations for the support of the missions. In 1753 he was ordered to France to account to his superiors and to the government for his conduct in these enterprises. Two years' absence from his affairs and the capture (1756) of some of his ships by English cruisers caused him such great losses that he was compelled to go into bankruptcy. His creditors brought suit against the entire Order, which refused to aid him on the ground that the Order could not be responsible for the debts of its several houses, each of these being individually accountable. Judgments against the Order were rendered by the courts, however. The Jesuits appealed from these decisions to the Parlement of Paris, which ordered them to pay Lavalette's debts in full within a year. Lavalette's superiors found him guilty of having engaged in trade, contrary to the rules of the Society, and expelled him from its membership in 1762.

The Parlement of Paris went beyond the question of Lavalette's indebtedness. It investigated the constitution of the Order, the *Institutum*, and in August, 1761, condemned many publications of the Jesuits to be burned by the public executioner. In April, 1762, the Parlement closed all the Jesuit colleges in its jurisdiction, and defied Louis XV in his efforts to annul its decrees. Four months later (August 6) the Parlement decreed the suppression of the Order and the confiscation of its estates. Other provincial parlements (except those at Besançon and Douay, and those in Alsace and Lorraine) quickly followed this example. Finally, a royal decree of December 1, 1764, dissolved the Order throughout the king's dominions, though it permitted individual members to remain as private citizens.[9]

All the Jesuits residing in Spain or in her colonies were suddenly expelled in April, 1767, and shipped to the Papal States. Naples and the other Italian states followed suit. The Society of Jesus had fallen upon evil days, and was soon (1773) to be suppressed by papal order.[10]

The suppression of the Order in France led to similar proceedings elsewhere. What might have been the fate of the Jesuits in Canada, had the country remained under French rule, is illustrated by what happened in Louisiana. The Superior Council of Louisiana expelled the Jesuits in July, 1763. According to the later report of François Philibert Watrin (one of the Fathers involved), a new Governor, D'Abbadie, came to Louisiana in June accompanied by a royal official who secured a decree from the Council for the expulsion and deportation of the Jesuits to France. They were charged with not having taken care of their missions, with caring only for the extension of their estates, and with usurpation of the powers of the vicariate-general for the episcopate of Quebec, the latter charge involving a quarrel between the Capuchins and the Jesuits regarding this dignity. Father Watrin denied the charges.

At New Orleans all the Jesuits' property, real and personal, was seized and sold at auction; their chapel furniture and sacred utensils were given to the Capuchins, and the chapel was razed to the ground. The Jesuit Fathers, except the Superior, Father Michel Baudoin, who was allowed to remain as the guest of a Louisiana planter, took refuge in Spanish colonies (from which the Order was not expelled until 1767). The decree of expulsion also embraced Kaskaskia (Illinois Country) and was carried out by the civil authorities there in the latter part of the year. The fathers were driven from their house, and all their property was seized and sold, despite protests from their French and Indian parishioners. The Jesuit priests were then sent to New Orleans and from thence they embarked for France.[11] The suppression of the Order in the Illinois Country is of particular interest because this area had already been ceded to Great Britain by the Treaty of Paris of February 10, 1763. The reason for the continued exercise of French authority was that the Illinois Country was not formally surrendered to the British until October 10, 1765, at which time Louis St. Ange de Bellerive delivered Fort Chartres.[12]

Meanwhile, the band of Jesuits in Canada had begun to diminish in numbers. At the end of December, 1760, there remained only twenty-five of the thirty-one priests who were there at the beginning of 1759.[13] Age was a telling factor against the survival of the Order, unless recruits could be gained. The average age of the Jesuits was 50·4 years—the highest among the various communities. At the end of 1760 their ranks included an octogenarian (Father Etienne Lauverjat) and two septuagenarians (Fathers René-Pierre-Daniel Richer and Jean-Baptiste St-Pé). Nearly half of them were over fifty years of age, while the youngest was thirty-five. Not one of the remaining Jesuits was of Canadian origin; all but one were French—a fact which made their position extremely delicate after the Conquest.[14]

During the next four years (1761–4), nine of the twenty-five remaining priests were lost. At the end of 1764 there were only sixteen priests and five brothers left to carry on the work for which the Society had become famous. In the period from the Conquest to the end of 1764 it had lost 48·4 per cent, or nearly half, of its effective membership. The average age of its members was now 52·7 years. There was not a single missionary in Acadia, only one under the government of Three Rivers, six under the government of Montreal, five under the government of Quebec, two in the Great Lakes region, and two in the Illinois region.[15]

For the British, the problem of permitting the mere exercise of the Catholic religion in its newly acquired possessions was a very thorny one, to say nothing of the problem of how to deal with orders that were embraced by the Catholic Church locally and internationally. The Treaty of Paris contained no specific provisions respecting the status or the proprietary rights of the religious orders. Article IV of the Treaty said simply:

. . . His Britannick Majesty, on his side, agrees to grant the liberty of the Catholic religion to the inhabitants of Canada: he will, in consequence, give the most precise and most effectual orders, that his new Roman Catholic subjects may profess the worship of their religion according to the rites of the Romish church, as far as the laws of Great Britain permit. His Britannick Majesty farther agrees, that the French inhabitants, or others who had been subject of the Most Christian King in Canada, may retire with all safety and freedom wherever they shall think proper, and may sell their estates, provided it be to the subjects of his Britannick Majesty, and bring away their effects as well as their persons, without being restrained in their emigration, under any pretence whatsoever, except that of debts or of criminal prosecutions: the term limited for this emigration shall be fixed to the space of eighteen months, to be computed from the day of the exchange of the ratification of the present treaty.[16]

In the light of the articles of Capitulation of Montreal, this article might well be interpreted as including the religious as well as lay persons, in so far as the sale of estates was concerned. Further information was obviously needed by the British government. In December, General James Murray, newly appointed governor-in-chief of the province of Quebec, received instructions to implement article IV and to supply an account of the nature and constitution of the religious communities, of their proprietary claims, and of the situation and revenue of the Catholic churches in the province. He was firmly instructed not to admit any ecclesiastical jurisdiction of the See of Rome, or any other foreign ecclesiastical jurisdiction in the province.[17]

Murray, as military governor, had already reached some negative conclusions regarding the Society of Jesus. Although there was no overwhelming evidence to warrant it, the Jesuits were suspected for several reasons. Attention has already been directed to the fact that they were almost entirely "foreign." In addition, their close affiliations with the savages when the savages were engaged in military exploits against the British constituted a strike against them. In 1759 Jesuits were mixed up in a live-stock raid on the grounds of l'Hôpital Général de Québec, though probably not as participants. Moreover, they were suspected of encouraging desertions among British soldiers. Such evidence, though perhaps very inconclusive, combined with a fair amount of rumour-mongering, did nothing to inspire confidence in their loyalty to the new régime.[18]

In his report on the state of the government of Quebec of June 5, 1762, Murray spoke of the "turbulent and intriguing genius" of the Jesuits. Though he paid tribute to their civilizing influence upon the Hurons settled at Jeune-Lorette, he considered the Jesuits to be neither loved nor generally esteemed and he thought that the Order might be easily removed whenever the government thought proper. Out of part of their estates provision might be made for bishopric and chapter, thus relieving the Crown of further expenses. It was, he thought,

not improbable that the Jesuits warned by their late disgraces in the dominions of these Potentates who seemed to favor them the most, and apprehending the like or worse treatment from those they stiled Heretics will chuse to dispose of their Estates and retire, as they might possibly find some difficulties to get purchasers the Government might buy their Lands at an easy rate and dispose of the same to many good purposes.[19]

Murray seemed to recognize certain proprietary rights of the Jesuits, though he questioned their continuance as an Order. In a letter to the Secretary of State, the Earl of Halifax, in October, 1763, he expressed the opinion that as the Jesuits had undergone a severe persecution in most of the Roman Catholic countries, those residing in Canada would not think it hard to be dismissed with a pension; they were but a few, some of them aged, and it would not require a very large sum to provide for all of them. Their estates might be put under proper management, and their unconceded lands might be leased to English farmers who would be encouraged to introduce better methods of cultivation and to mix with the people. Income thus derived could be used to meet the expenses of pensions and any surplus could be employed for other public needs.[20]

The Jesuits had already found a champion in the Grand Vicar, Jean-Olivier Briand, who, during the summer of 1763, addressed two memorials to the government in their behalf. One of these paid high tribute to the educational endeavours of the Jesuits in Europe and in Canada and urged that their college be sustained. Briand suggested that additional teachers could be secured from Savoy or Hungary if the British government had such a distrust of the French. In a special *Memoire concernant le Collège de Québec*, the Grand Vicar suggested four alternatives which the British might follow: (1) they could suppress the college, leaving no resource for the training of either clergy or laity; (2) they might oblige the seminaries to provide instruction for persons of both faiths; (3) they could ask Canadians, drawn from the seminaries, to maintain the college; or (4) they could allow the Jesuits to continue the college, the income from their estates being sufficient to finance it. In his opinion the fourth alternative was by far the best.[21]

In October, 1763, the clergy were apprised of a letter from the Earl of Egremont to Murray, dated August 13, in which Murray was instructed to discourage any regular clergy from repairing to Canada from elsewhere and to endeavour to prevent the filling up of any vacancies in the regular orders.[22] The instructions spelled disaster for the Society of Jesus. Two of the Jesuits, the Superior-General, Father Augustin-Louis de Glapion, and Father Marin-Louis Lefranc, immediately drew up an address to the king, in which they protested their loyalty and pleaded for permission to resume their educational work and for the reopening of their college. They also asked to be allowed to recruit sufficient staff members from Europe until they might be able to train them in the colony.[23]

No move was made by the government against the Jesuits' estates at this time, however, and with the exception of the seigniory of Sault-Saint-Louis, which Governor Gage removed from their temporal control for the benefit of the Iroquois, they continued to administer their estates as long as the Order continued its existence in the province. The records indicate that they enjoyed rents from various properties and that they in turn were generous in their almsgiving to other religious and charitable institutions.[24] There were, however, threats made upon their estates from perhaps unexpected sources. In 1764 an English merchant of Quebec, John Gray, made advances to Murray to obtain a part of the estates in favour of a London merchant, Robert Grant. The latter held letters of exchange, amounting to some 294,536 *livres*, that the procurator-general of the missions in the Caribbean islands had drawn on him to pay the debts of the enterprising Father Lavalette. Grant wanted the estates seized, any part of the Order being responsible, according to him, for the debts contracted by their members around the world.[25] Murray rejected this demand on the ground that it would not be reasonable to hold the estates of the Jesuits of the province responsible for the letters of exchange that had been drawn in Martinique. It was up to the French government to satisfy the creditors of the Jesuits under its jurisdiction. Murray argued, as the British government was to continue to do, that the estates had been given to the Jesuits for precise ends and that when the Society was no longer existent, the estates would revert to the Crown.[26] Shortly thereafter Murray expressed similar views to the Board of Trade, emphasizing his determination to prevent the estates from falling into the hands of anyone other than the Crown.[27]

One of the gravest threats to the income and to the existence of the Order came from one of its own, Father Pierre-Antoine Roubaud. Born of a Catholic father and a Protestant mother, Roubaud studied with the Jesuits and took the habit of the Order at fifteen years of age. He arrived in Canada in 1754 and was immediately assigned to the Abénaquis mission of Saint-François-du-Lac. He followed the savages during their military campaigns at Carillon and William-Henry, and at the siege of Quebec. After the Capitulation of Quebec, Roubaud returned to his mission. In April, 1760, he delivered a sermon in the church at Montreal that was derogatory to the French armies and their leaders. The officers were infuriated; Roubaud hid in his convent, then departed to take refuge at Sault-Saint-Louis.[28]

In the fall of 1760 Roubaud was again at Saint-François-du-Lac, from which he was recalled by the superior-general because of his loose living, a recall that was over-ruled by Colonel Ralph Burton, military governor of Three Rivers, on the grounds that it violated the articles of the Capitulation. From the beginning of 1762 Roubaud became the despair of the authorities, eventually leaving, without permission, the jurisdiction of Governor Haldimand in Three Rivers to go to Quebec. Having arrived in Quebec in mid-November, he at first lived in the college. However, his personal conduct and his relations with the English put him in conflict with the members of his Order. In the course of the summer of 1763, Governor Murray took him into his own residence and used his services, the exact nature of which is not known. They probably consisted in supplying information, building up false hopes that a number of Canadians were becoming Protestants, and spreading rumours regarding the non-celibate lives of other clergy (to justify his own conduct).[29]

After several months in Murray's home, Roubaud decided to go to Europe under the pretext of entering a convent to mend his ways and his *confrères* were obliged to provide for his needs during the trip to London. De Glapion reluctantly agreed to defray the costs of a five months' stay in London, during which it was expected that the General of the Order would take some decisive action.[30]

Murray's letters to various persons in England, however, fail to make any mention of Roubaud's intention of putting himself at the disposition of the General of the Jesuits. From three of these letters it appears that Murray was most desirous of having a man-on-the-spot to defend himself against a pressure group operating against him in the homeland. The renegade Roubaud was depicted in glowing terms as an authority on ecclesiastical and other matters in the province.[31]

Roubaud was in debt from the moment of his arrival in England. Hoping to capitalize upon the claims then being asserted by the creditors of Father Lavalette, Roubaud argued that he had as much right to the possessions of the Canadian Jesuits as they. Such hopes, however, were quashed by a ruling of the Court of King's Bench that neither Lavalette nor his creditors had any claim upon the possessions of the Canadian Jesuits.[32] Roubaud then resorted to an attempt to use his friendship with Governor Murray. Early in 1765 he sought Murray's approval of a letter of exchange for the sum of 3,000 *livres* sterling drawn on the College of Quebec. By this time, Murray had lost all patience with Roubaud; he showed the letter of exchange to Father de Glapion, and then promised to burn it. In Murray's opinion de Glapion owed nothing further to Roubaud. He did, however, hold the Order responsible for ten or twelve months' subsistence for him, instead of the five originally agreed upon.[33]

Roubaud remained in London and continued to indulge in an even more scandalous manner of living than in the colony from which he had come.[34] Failing in his efforts to get further assistance from Canada, he appealed to the king. Picturing himself the innocent victim of the unfavourable dispositions of the Quebec Jesuits, he asked the king to free him of all subjection to the Jesuits because of their disloyalty to the Crown.

He asked for a portion and a half of the possessions of the Jesuits, the half to compensate for the fact that, in leaving the Order, he would lose the right of inheritance from those who died. Complaining that the Jesuits had refused him his pension, he asked that they reimburse him at the rate of 150 *livres* sterling per year. Finally, Roubaud requested the right to become a British subject.[35]

When de Glapion was approached concerning the claims and charges of Roubaud, he presented a frank statement of his scandalous behaviour and of his disregard for his superiors. As to the complaint that he had received nothing from the Canadian Jesuits, the Superior-General remarked that they had receipts to show that they had disbursed 6,640 *livres tournois* on his account since his determination in June, 1764, to go to London. De Glapion vigorously denied the right of any Jesuit, after leaving his house, to receive an annuity.[36]

Roubaud failed in these efforts to secure further considerations for himself from the Quebec Jesuits. Guy Carleton, who became lieutenant-governor and administrator of Quebec in 1766 and governor-in-chief in 1768, substantiated de Glapion's estimates of Roubaud. In a succinct character sketch that includes the suggestion that the officials at home were toying with the idea of sending Roubaud back to Quebec, Carleton states:

I had heard of Mr. Roubaud before I left England, tho' I never saw him; Here he is very generally disliked and despised by all sorts of Men both old and new subjects; some that know him particularly well, talk of him as a Man of Genius, a fine Imagination, and a Masterly writer; but void of Truth, without one spark of Honor, or of Honesty; This is the best character I have been able to obtain of him, after which, should your Lordship still think it right to send him over, I shall make the best use of him I can.[37]

But Roubaud stayed in England for over twenty years instead of five months, attempting to gain favour there by proposing rigorous measures against his *confrères* in Canada, against the Sulpicians, against the Seminary of Quebec, and against the bishop.[38]

As late as 1786 the few surviving Jesuits had to defend themselves against an order from the home government to pay not only a pension of 126 *livres* sterling per year, which they had allegedly agreed to give Roubaud, but arrears since 1764 as well. They presented their case against Roubaud in much the same fashion as de Glapion had done in 1768, and so effectively that Governor Hope commended it to the home government for careful reconsideration.[39] Having failed to secure anything further for himself, Roubaud lent his services toward securing the Jesuits' estates for General Amherst, an effort to be discussed in the following chapters.

In the decade preceding the passage of the Quebec Act of 1774, the British government turned its attention on numerous occasions to ecclesiastical problems in Canada. Among the persons consulted was the Archbishop of York who in April, 1764, offered a number of suggestions regarding the Church as a whole, and a few that were specifically related to the Society of Jesus. The Archbishop proposed that no regular priests should be allowed except those who were then serving parishes. The Jesuits, in his opinion, had no right to expect greater indulgence than they would have had if they had remained under the French Crown. No Jesuit refugees from the European persecution ought to be allowed into Canada "because they were proved and declared Enemies to the safety of any State." If they continued to exist in Canada, it would be the asylum for the "most obstinate, the most violent, & the most artfull of that

Order; and their Missions to the Indians might easily, from their influence, endanger the Tranquility and safety of the British Empire in those parts."[40]

As to their estates, the Archbishop made a distinction between the Jesuits and other ecclesiastical bodies which he thought might sell their property according to the conditions of the Treaty. In his opinion, however, the property of the Jesuits should be under the same rule as in France and applied to public uses. If a bishop were allowed he might be paid from the surplus of the revenues of the seminary at Montreal or the Jesuits at Quebec. The Archbishop also called for the application of revenues to ministers of the Church of England and to schools, as well as to the Indian missions, which he thought should be instantly placed in British hands for the fear of their being used by Roman Catholics against the English. According to his proposal, there would probably be a sufficient number of churches and houses for use by the Church of England if the Recollects and the Jesuits were banished.[41]

The Board of Trade appears to have acted upon the suggestions of the Archbishop as the basis of a plan for the establishment of ecclesiastical affairs that they completed in May, 1765. According to this plan, the Jesuits were to be abolished and the other religious houses were to be starved out of existence by forbidding them to recruit. Out of the revenues of their establishments, the existing members were to be allowed subsistence until they died or were appointed to vacant cures. The property thus gathered was to be applied to the support of Protestant churches and schools.[42]

Although the plan of the Board of Trade was not applied at this time, it was revived and revised by a later administration, which seriously considered applying it.[43] As a matter of fact, on March 10, 1766, the Lords of the Treasury did instruct the provincial Receiver-General, Thomas Mills, that since the Jesuits' estates were, or would become, part of the Crown revenue, he should endeavour to take them into his charge, giving those who might have a claim upon them a suitable allowance. He was instructed to make certain that the properties did not become alienated from the Crown.[44] There is also an interesting report of a project for creating a grand lottery in order to rebuild the Cathedral of Quebec which had been burned during the siege. In order to attract the Lords of the Treasury, the Archbishop of Canterbury, the Bishop of London, and the Bible Society to this enterprise, a prospectus was sent to them which announced the design of seizing the estates of the religious. The Board of Trade is reported by Garneau to have appointed an agent to administer the Jesuits' estates.[45] All other evidence, however, indicates that the estates continued to be administered by the Jesuits themselves until 1800.

Shortly before the Board of Trade submitted its report of 1765, one of the most important of the early legal opinions regarding the Jesuits' properties was submitted by Advocate-General James Marriott in a letter of May 12, 1765, addressed to Attorney-General F. Norton and Solicitor-General William De Gray. Marriott concluded from his study of French documents relating to the Jesuits that the Order was not like the other communities. The Society of Jesus was an indivisible corporation, under the domination of the general, who resided at Rome. It had not been incorporated in France, but had merely been allowed to exist at the king's pleasure. In Marriott's opinion,

From all these premises, it seems conclusive that the titles of the Society passed, together with the dominions ceded to Great Britain (in which dominions those possessions were situated) attended with no better qualifications than those titles had by the laws and constitution of the realm of France, previous to the conquest and cession of those countries.—But it seems further to be clear, that those titles are now in a worse condition since the conquest and cession: for till that period they were only in abeyance, and suspended upon a principle of probationary toleration; but by virtue of the natural law of arms, and conquest of countries, confirmed by the acts of the law of nations, by solemn cession and guarantee, the possessions of the Society lost of course all civil protection by the fate of war, but much more so by the only power, whose authority and intervention could have preserved the property of those possessions to their supposed owners, having withdrawn its tolerance and protection, and deserted them as a derelict at the mercy and entirely free disposition of the Crown of Great Britain, by making no provision in the articles of cession, to serve the pretended rights of the community of Jesuits. . . .[46]

The Advocate-General then pointed out to the law officers that the Father General, never having been an inhabitant of Canada nor a subject of the king of France, could not retire and avail himself of the fourth article of the Treaty of Paris, nor sell his estates, nor withdraw his effects within the time limited.

In a few words, the Society of Jesus had not and cannot have any Estate in Canada, legally and completely vested in them at any time, and therefore, could not and cannot transfer the same, before nor after the term of eighteen months, so as to make a good title to the purchasers, either with or without the powers of ratification of the Father General, who as he could not retire, so he cannot retain any possessions in Canada, since the time limited for the sale of Estates there agreeably to the terms of the treaty, because he is as incapable of becoming a British subject, as he was of being a French subject; nor can the individuals of the communities of the Jesuits in Canada, take or transfer what the Father General cannot take or transfer, nor can they, having but one common stock with all other communities of their order in every part of the globe, hold immoveable possessions, to be applied for the joint benefit of those communities which are resident in foreign States; and which may become the enemies of his Majesty and his government.

He emphasized that the Canadian Jesuits must be regarded as trustees for the head and the members of an indivisible society which claimed a territorial jurisdiction independent of all civil authorities and whose members had no fixed residence. Such trusts, by the very nature of their constitution, were inadmissible by the law of nations and by all civil government. They were null and void because there was no legal community, civilly established, to make use of them, unless it be a sovereign foreigner and alien subjects, who were entirely incapable, by the very nature of their institution, of any civil existence.

The report of Marriott, Norton, and De Gray on the Board of Trade's plan for establishing ecclesiastical affairs in the province of Quebec has not been found.[47] On June 10, 1765, however, Norton and De Gray answered a request by the Lords Commissioners for Trade and Plantations for an opinion on the question of whether Roman Catholics in the province were subject to the incapacities, disabilities, and penalties to which they were subject in Great Britain. The law officers reported that they were not.[48] A contradictory opinion was given by Francis Maseres, who was appointed attorney-general of the province of Quebec early in March, 1766, in a document that he wrote before going to Quebec. Maseres concluded that the exercise of the Catholic religion could not, consistently with the laws of Great Britain, be tolerated in the province, although, he went on to say, "that it should be tolerated is surely very reasonable, and to be wished by all lovers of peace and justice and liberty of conscience."[49]

In spite of the opinion of the Advocate-General that the Jesuits' properties right-fully belonged to the Crown, and the suggestion of the Board of Trade that the Order itself be abolished, the British government did not act hastily in the matter. Lieutenant-Governor Carleton was asked to gather a detailed statement of the Jesuits' estates,[50] a task which he entrusted to the Superior of the Order. De Glapion's report, dated

April 7, 1768, consisted of a financial statement of the revenues and the expenses of the estates, along with the statement of the case of Pierre-Antoine Roubaud. A rumour had apparently been circulated by Roubaud that the Jesuits were sending money to Italy, a rumour which de Glapion now vigorously denied. De Glapion offered proof that the Order in Canada was not nearly so prosperous as some perhaps had imagined. The Jesuits did not have 300 *livres tournois* in cash, they were lacking a number of necessary provisions, and they owed 2,000 *livres* or more to a carpenter who had repaired their church.[51] Parenthetically, one might note that this is one of the earliest of many reports, in the subsequent history of the estates, which presented a much less optimistic picture of the income from the estates than they were popularly believed to afford.

Carleton was persuaded that de Glapion's statement of affairs was fair and just, and that the Jesuits had neither concealed nor misrepresented the value of their possessions. Though their estates were great, he informed Lord Shelburne, they were largely uncultivated, and their mills yielded their greatest income. Carleton believed that, considering what they had spent upon the repairs of their mills, the church, and the wing of the house they occupied, and the care they were taking of some of their aged brethren, they barely maintained themselves. He pointed out that the king of France had formerly allowed them 14,500 *livres* yearly for the maintenance of their missionaries, and that their college had had an income of more than 11,000 *livres* a year from an estate in France which shared the fate of all the other effects of the Society at the time of their general expulsion from that country.[52]

A major concern of the Jesuit fathers during these anxious years was the fate of their college. Though not a great deal is known of its pre-Conquest history, it was one of the oldest colleges in the New World, and the only college in the province. Its occupation for military purposes in the fall of 1759 has already been noted, its faculty having repaired to Jeune-Lorette. They were permitted to return to Quebec toward the end of June, 1761, and were allowed to occupy a third of their house.[53] The third included the small chapel of the Confrérie de la Sainte-Vierge, which they repaired for religious services; the exterior chapel was retained by the military.[54] Three of the priests who returned were over seventy years of age; Father de Glapion was really the only one capable of teaching. A limited faculty and very limited space ultimately precluded the continuance of anything except primary instruction. There was no room for boarding students, nor even a day school for classical students, private instruction being about the only possibility. Even the very limited space was encroached upon by the British officers for their housing needs.[55] With the departure of the three scholastics in 1760, classical instruction in the college was virtually suspended.[56]

The government's instruction to Murray, discouraging the filling up of vacancies in the regular orders, was a particularly hard blow for the Jesuits. Their pleas and those of Grand Vicar Briand on their behalf brought no favourable response. Primary instruction, in which one English layman took part, was continued in an English school which had been opened in October, 1765, in the college. However, further encroachments were to be made upon the Jesuits' limited facilities. On July 4, 1765, *La Gazette de Québec* announced that the remainder of the college must be converted into a barracks to lodge officers and troops.[57]

Father de Glapion appealed once again in 1766 to the Secretary of State, Lord Shelburne. He reviewed the history of the college and its importance to the colony during the past, as well as its sad history during the years since the Conquest. He also called attention to the hard, uncompensated use to which the facilities were being put by the military, and to the hardships imposed by the decreases in their ranks. This statement he concluded by requesting that the educational services of the Jesuits be continued, that the prohibition against their receiving either European or Canadian members be revoked, and that the college buildings be restored for their full use and enjoyment, with indemnification for their use by the military over the period of seven years.[58]

The efforts of de Glapion and renewed appeals by Briand, now bishop of Quebec,[59] were equally fruitless. In 1765 and again in 1771 Briand made efforts to secure the retention of the college and the application of the revenues from the Jesuits' estates to its maintenance.[60] Briand argued that it was in vain to grant the free exercise of the Catholic religion, while at the same time prohibiting the recruitment of foreign priests and depriving the colony of the facilities for training the clergy. Anticipating the argument that the Seminary of Quebec should be charged with the maintenance of a college in addition to the training of ecclesiastics, and having become aware of proposals to dissolve the Jesuit Order and to give its properties to General Amherst, Briand suggested that the largest parts of the Jesuits' estates be given to the seminary for that purpose. The lesser part might be used for such purposes as church extension, care of aged priests, aid to l'Hôtel-Dieu and l'Hôpital-Général of Quebec, and as an aid in providing a pension for the bishop. Briand warned Carleton of how public sentiment would be aroused if the estates were given to the General instead of being used for their original purpose.[61]

De Glapion, informed by the Governor of the failure of his request for the restoration of the college to its original purposes, was forced to curtail the educational functions of the Society. He discontinued the course of letters at the beginning of October, 1768, and kept only the primary school for the teaching of reading, writing, and the basic elements of calculus. The school lasted until 1776. In that year the college was closed by the military administration in order to convert all the classrooms into courtrooms, depositories of archives, storerooms for provisions, or quarters for prisoners. The military authorities had already taken the larger part of the facilities for lodging troops, leaving only the chapel and several rooms for the use of the last Jesuits.[62] Its continued occupation by the military was to serve as an irritant until its demolition in the second half of the nineteenth century.

In 1769 the Lords Commissioners for Trade and Plantations returned to the question of the Society of Jesus and its estates as a part of broader considerations regarding the government of Quebec. On July 10 a report was drawn up in which the position of the religious communities was thoroughly discussed, a discussion based in part upon their deliberations in 1765.[63] While admitting that by the terms of the Capitulation several of the religious communities were to be preserved, the Commissioners were inclined to regard the Capitulation as a temporary agreement between the officers of the two sides, subject to the final treaty. The Capitulation was now out of the question and everything depended upon the fourth article of the Treaty of Paris which granted nothing more than barely a free exercise of the Catholic religion so far as the laws of England permitted. This being the case, the legislature of Quebec ought to pass a proper law or laws for the reform of the religious orders. The Lords Commissioners recommended that the Jesuit Order be entirely abolished in Canada, and that all their possessions, except their personal property, be vested in the Crown for public uses in the interests of the colony. The remaining members of the Order should be given a pension for the remainder of their lives equal to the share each was then receiving of the revenue of the estates. The report also included similar recommendations concerning the Recollects.[64]

The foregoing report and that of Solicitor-General Alexander Wedderburn, of December 6, 1772, were part of lengthy fact-finding activity that preceded the Quebec Act of 1774.[65] Wedderburn, in his report, stressed the fact that article IV of the Treaty of Paris was of little effect because of the severity of the laws of England (though seldom exerted) against the exercise of Roman Catholicism. Canadians must, therefore, depend more upon the benignity and the wisdom of the British government for the protection of their religious rights than upon the provisions of the Treaty. Maximum rights could only include freedom to profess the worship of their religion and provisions for the protection and maintenance of their ministers. In considering the status of the regular clergy, Wedderburn was of the opinion that the establishment of the Jesuits and of the other religious orders, as corporations holding property and jurisdiction, was repugnant to the constitution that Canada must receive as a part of the British dominions. He thought that the monastic orders ought to be secularized entirely, but that so great a change should not be made at once. The Jesuits, however, and the religious houses in France possessing estates in Canada were thought to be on a different footing than the others:

... The establishment of the first [the Jesuits] is not only incompatible with the constitution of an English province, but with every other possible form of civil society. By the rule of their order the jesuits are aliens in every government. Other monastic orders may be tolerated, because, though they are not useful subjects, still they are subjects, and make a part of the community ill employed. The jesuits form no part of the community. They, according to their institution neither allow allegiance nor obedience to the prince, but to a foreign power. They are not owners of their estates, but trustees for purposes dependent upon the pleasure of a foreigner, the general of their order. Three great catholic states have, upon grounds of policy, expelled them. It would be singular, if the first protestant state in Europe should protect an establishment that ere now must have ceased in Canada, had the French government continued.[66]

Wedderburn proceeded to enlarge upon the potential menace presented by the continued existence of the Jesuits, then concluded that it was just and expedient to assert the sovereignty of the king, and to vest their lands in the Crown, allowing the Jesuits now residing in Canada liberal pensions out of the incomes of their estates.[67] In this report are found the essentials of the policy that was eventually adopted by the British government.

The Attorney-General, Edward Thurlow, in a report dated January 22, 1773, paid more heed to general principles than had the Solicitor-General. His statement concerning property rights rather clearly expressed what was generally considered by the secular and regular branches of the Catholic Church to be the just provision with reference to their properties, as well as to those of the lay inhabitants. Thurlow offered the following general principle as one that must be observed as the basis of any new laws to be made in Quebec:

The Canadians seem to have been strictly entitled by the *jus gentium* to their property, as they possessed it upon the capitulation and treaty of peace, together with all its qualities and incidents, by tenure or otherwise, and also to their personal liberty; for both which they were to expect your Majesty's gracious protection.

It seems a necessary consequence that all those laws by which that property was created, defined, and secured must be continued to them. To introduce any other . . . . tend [*sic*] to confound and subvert rights instead of supporting them.[68]

Such a report could be used later by the Catholic hierarchy to substantiate their claim that when the Jesuit Order was dissolved its properties should have reverted to the Catholic Church, rather than to the Crown. At least, the Attorney-General was not inclined to ignore the Capitulation of Montreal which had rather explicitly insured to the Jesuits, among others, their proprietary rights.

Several factors explain the gradual unfolding of an anti-Jesuit policy on the part of the British government. Some of these were already operating by 1770: a historic distrust of the Order, dating back to Elizabethan times, suspicions engendered by their associations with the Indians during the period of the Conquest, their betrayal by Roubaud, financial and military exigencies that caused their properties to be coveted, the extent and assumed worth of their numerous holdings, actions of European governments against them, as well as General Amherst's effort to secure their estates for himself (already lively by 1770, but reserved for later discussion). Their treatment by the Catholic powers of Europe was a most important influence, as is evident from the report of Wedderburn and others that preceded it. In view of the otherwise generous treatment of the Roman Catholic inhabitants during the period of the Conquest to the Quebec Act, the Crown might not have begun to entertain the idea of confiscating the properties, some of which were specifically dedicated to education, had it not had the example of predominantly Catholic powers to cite and fall back upon.

The prudence and wisdom of Governor Carleton, with reference to the practice of religion by the Catholics, is too well known to need lengthy documentation, though it must be mentioned because, as we shall see, Carleton probably did more than any other British official to delay a settlement of the Jesuits' estates question that would be adverse to the interests of the Catholic inhabitants. The Jesuit historian Rochemonteix has remarked that the Governor showed himself to be the friend and protector of the Canadians and that the bishop exercised his episcopal functions with the most complete liberty. Briand himself informed Cardinal Castelli that the British liked him (Briand), esteemed him, and respected him more than the Catholics themselves.[69]

To the influences that have already been noticed as operating in the determination of the ultimate fate of the Jesuits and their properties was added a conclusive one, their suppression by the Pope himself in 1773. On the death of the pro-Jesuit Pope Clement XIII (February 2, 1769), the Bourbon courts used pressure to bring about the election of Lorenzo Ganganelli as a means of procuring the dissolution of the Society of Jesus. No sooner was Clement XIV, as Ganganelli became known, on the papal throne than the Spanish court, backed by other members of the Bourbon "Family Compact," hopefully renewed the efforts they had vainly brought to bear upon his predecessor to get a papal suppression of the whole Order. Clement XIV skilfully stalled for a time, showing an inclination to force some reform of the Society rather than to suppress it. This was completely unacceptable to the Bourbons, who had decided that the Order must go. In the middle of 1772 Charles III of Spain sent a new ambassador to Rome who was not a cleric. The Ambassador, Don Joseph Moñino, afterwards Count Florida Blanca, was a strong, hard man. Under the threats which he applied, conjointly with representatives of the other Bourbon rulers of France and Naples, Clement XIV gradually gave way, and on July 21, 1773, he signed the brief, *Dominus ac Redemptor*, which needs to be examined fully because it was later much misinterpreted in the anti-Jesuit agitation of 1888–9.[70]

The brief of suppression opened with the following considerations:

Our Lord and Redeemer (*Dominus ac Redemptor*) Jesus Christ, who was pre-announced and revealed as the Prince of Peace, committed his office of atonement to the care of the Apostles and conveyed to them the power of the word, so that they, as emissaries of Christ, who is the God of peace and love, not of dissension, might proclaim this peace to the whole world and that all begot in Christ might form one body and one soul. Thus it is above all the duty of the Pope, who administers Christ's office of atonement, to secure the peace of the Church and in this cause to sacrifice even those things which are personally dear to him. Assuredly the religious Orders are the best means of ensuring the welfare of the Church, but if an Order ceases to fulfill the mission entrusted to it, the Pope must receive it, reform it, or dissolve it.[71]

This preface was followed by the body of the brief which was composed of three main parts: the first two were of a historical character intended to provide the grounds for the last one, which contained the actual enactments and the provisions made for their execution. Clement XIV cited a substantial list of precedents for the reforming or dissolving of religious orders, and noted that on all these occasions the Pope had not adopted any regular judicial procedure, which would only have provoked further dissension, but had acted on his own authority, decreeing the suppression without leave of appeal or defence.

In the second part of the brief, Clement XIV indicated that he had carefully studied the history and present state of the Society of Jesus. In his review of the record, the Pope bowed to the pressures of the agents of the Bourbons, to whose influence the brief was chiefly due. Everything good and favourable that could have been said about the Order was passed over in silence, whereas the accusations against it were proportionately accentuated. An attempt was made to prove that "at the very birth of this Society there germinated manifold seeds of dissension and jealousy . . . not merely within itself but also against other Orders, against the secular priesthood, against academies, universities, public schools, and even against the princes in whose States the Jesuits had been received."[72] A statement of charges against the Jesuits by a provincial council in Mexico is instructive: it included their wealth, their ambition, their false doctrines, their commercial dealings, their attitude in the ritual question, their secretiveness, their intrigues, political and otherwise, their participation in attempted assassinations and their consequent expulsion.[73] It should be noted that the brief was in accord with prior instruments of reform or suppression, in that it was an administrative measure, not a judicial sentence based on judicial inquiry. Those who engaged in a wholesale denunciation of the Order in the late nineteenth century were inclined to treat *Dominus ac Redemptor* as if it were the latter.

In an audience with Moñino, on September 6, 1772, the Pope had accepted detailed proposals for the drawing up of a bull of suppression. The provisions of this proposal dealing with the execution of the proposed brief of suppression were repeated in their entirety in the actual brief of July 21, 1773. The novices in the Society were to be dismissed and sent back to their families. Those who had taken simple but not yet solemn vows were to be released from every obligation and might choose another profession. Those who had taken solemn vows were also to be discharged and could either enter another Order or become secular priests obedient to the bishops in whose dioceses they resided. Priests who did not wish to leave the houses of the Society might remain for the time being, provided they dressed as secular priests and became obedient to the local bishop. In each diocese an account was to be made of the properties, revenues, and charges of all the Jesuit houses, college, and hospices. The revenues were to be used for the good of the bishoprics and for the maintenance of the members of the suppressed Society of Jesus, especially those who could find no employment or remained in their Order's houses for the reasons already stated. The Jesuit houses were to be used as the bishop thought fit, but only for religious purposes.

The purpose to which the Jesuit houses were to be devoted was to be decided as far as possible by agreement with the government and the Pope. The bishops were to use their discretion in assigning the duties of the ex-Jesuits. The more competent Jesuits might be employed in religious or lay education but they were not to direct any establishment. The Jesuits who remained in their houses were not to be replaced by others when they died or left the Society; the houses could thus be used for their new purpose as quickly as possible and it would be plain to all that the Society really had been suppressed. The powers of all the superiors of the Order were annulled for ever.[74] It is important to notice that by the brief the persons and the properties of all the Jesuits now came under the immediate jurisdiction of the local bishops. In all the subsequent history of the estates question in Canada this was to be a major contention by the hierarchy.

Mgr Briand learned with deep chagrin of the brief of suppression. Before carrying out the orders of the Pope, he conferred with Governor Carleton on the precise measures to be taken. According to the Bishop's own account, the Governor was deeply sympathetic. Following his meeting with the Governor, Briand called the Jesuits of Quebec together and told them that he had the brief and the order to make it known to them. He softened the rigour of the pontifical act as much as possible, as he later reported in a letter to Mesdames de Pontbriand:

> Our Jesuits still wear the Jesuit habit, still have the reputation of Jesuits, carry out the functions of Jesuits, and in Canada it is only the governor, I and my secretary, who know that they are no no longer Jesuits, they excepted. I am giving account to the sovereign pontiff of all my conduct . . . , notifying him that I have established the same superior and attorney who will administer the estates under my orders.[75]

The Bishop had obviously not carried out the provisions of the brief in their entirety. The brief stipulated that the Jesuits who remained in their houses and colleges were to have no administrative posts, that they would wear only the habit of the secular clergy, and that they would be entirely submitted to the ordinary of these places. In a letter to Cardinal Castelli, Mgr Briand sought to explain both his and the Governor's conduct of this delicate matter. Carleton, he said, had asked him not to make any outward changes in the present circumstances for three reasons: (1) the government was already being embarrassed by the opposition of the English inhabitants to the provisions of the Quebec Act that favoured Roman Catholics; (2) General Amherst was requesting the Jesuits' estates and the Governor was trying to keep them for the use of the Church in Canada; and (3) Carleton, having taken it upon himself to let the Jesuits die out without molesting them, thought it better to let the matter rest there for the moment. A desire to be in accord with the Governor, and the impossibility of filling the mission posts occupied by the Jesuits, caused the Bishop to ask the Pope's approval of his deviations from the procedure of suppression outlined in the brief and a confirmation of the indulgences and privileges accorded to the Jesuits' church. The Pope approved his conduct of the business and accorded all the favours asked.[76]

Though it was not carried out according to the letter of the law, the brief was none the less carried out. When the disposition of the Jesuits' estates became a matter of contention within the Church a century later, there were those who were inclined to argue that the Order had never been suppressed in Canada and that the members of the now restored Society who returned to the country in 1842 were possessed of all the privileges and properties that the old Order had exercised.[77]

Briand's mode of treatment of the remaining Jesuits was followed until the death of the last of them in 1800. Mgr Hubert, who assumed the responsibilities of the bishopric in 1788, addressed the following succinct report to the Holy See in 1794:

> At the time of the extinction of the Order of the Jesuits in 1773, the Bishop at that time, in order to keep for them their estates, of which they made an edifying use, obtained permission from the Holy See and from the government, for them to retain their old habit and remain under their Superior. The people perceived no change in their manner of existence and continued to call them Jesuits. There remained about a dozen of them. All have died, one after the other, while working for the salvation of souls. There remains only one, and what characterizes well the humanity and the liberality of the English government, is that this ex-Jesuit peaceably and tranquilly enjoys the revenue of all the estates which belonged to his Order in this country and gives immense alms from it.[78]

The statement that the last survivor continued to enjoy the revenue of their estates is significant because of the insinuations made later that the government enjoyed them and had made no accounting of how they were spent.[79]

During the long discussions leading up to the passage of the Quebec Act in 1774, a number of questions were raised concerning the question of religion in the colony of Quebec. Were all the religious orders and communities of the Church of Rome in Quebec to be abolished? Which, if any of them, were to be continued, and under what restrictions? If any were to be abolished, was the suppression to take effect immediately, or when the existing members of such communities had died? What was to become of the estates and revenues of the religious orders and communities which were to be discontinued? Were the secular clergy to have any episcopal superintendence over them? If so, by what authority, and under what limitations and restrictions was such power to be established?[80]

Carleton expressed a wish that he might be allowed as much discretion as possible regarding ecclesiastical arrangements. He had no objection to having the ideas of the government suggested in his instructions, but he disapproved the suppression of any religious communities except the Jesuits, and asked that he might use his own judgment "in that very delicate business."[81] The Governor's wish was honoured in the passage of the Act. Articles v–vii accorded a remarkable degree of freedom for the practice of the Catholic religion in Quebec. Article vii provided for an oath of allegiance which was specifically designed so that Roman Catholics could take it instead of the oath required by an Elizabethan statute, which they could not take. There was only one stipulation in the Act which affected the proprietary rights of the religious orders and communities. Article viii excepted them from the provisions for the enjoyment of proprietary rights that were granted to Canadian subjects generally.[82]

As Carleton had requested, the procedures for dealing with the ecclesiastical problems of the colony were outlined at greater length in the instructions to him of January 3, 1775. General provisions were included for the control and supervision of the freedom which had been granted to the Catholic religion. Specific orders were given that the Jesuits' Society be dissolved and suppressed and that their estates and other possessions be vested in the Crown. Provision was to be made, however, to satisfy their needs during the remainder of their lives.[83] Here, finally, was an official pronouncement from the British government on the fate of the Jesuits. The basic policy of these instructions was maintained until the death of the last Jesuit in 1800.

An identical instruction was given to Governor Frederick Haldimand on April 15, 1778,[84] and repeated to Carleton, now Lord Dorchester, in 1786.[85] The provisions of the Quebec Act and of the gubernatorial instructions were explicitly confirmed by article xxxv of the Constitutional Act, 1791, subject to provincial legislative amendment that received the approval of the home government.[86] The new instructions to Dorchester, pursuant to this Act, contained a repetition of the pertinent clause in the 1775 document.[87]

CHAPTER TWO

THE AMHERST CLAIMS: PRELIMINARY ENDEAVOURS

IT WAS NOT UNDERSTOOD that the Jesuits' estates embraced a total of nearly a million *arpents*[1] when General Amherst began to pursue his claims to them. According to a recapitulation of the principal estates, based on an *aveu et dénombrement* submitted by Father Jean-Joseph Casot in 1781, there was a total of 121,936 *arpents*.[2] "A Plan of Part of the Province of Quebec Shewing the Estates of the Late Order of Jesuits," drawn up by Surveyor-General Samuel Holland in 1790, indicated a total of 793,342 *arpents*. On the plan Holland called attention to a discrepancy between this total and that of 128,543 *arpents* indicated by records in the Council office.[3] A recapitulation of the principal estates which accompanied a report of the attorney- and the solicitor-general in 1790 showed a total of 125,909 *arpents*.[4] Some of the discrepancy between these figures is due to variations as to what was included in a list of the estates, but the greatest discrepancy is observed with reference to major parts of the estates, a fact that can be explained only by assuming that imperfect and incomplete surveys had been made in the earlier period. A report by the Commissioner of Crown Lands in 1858 indicates the following composition of the estates, the whole giving a total that is close to that of Surveyor-General Holland:

1.	Sillery	8,979 *arpents*
2.	St. Gabriel	119,720
3.	Notre Dame des Anges	28,224
4.	Belair	14,112
5.	Estate in Quebec	(not exactly known)
6.	Estate in Lauzon	2,140
7.	Batiscan	282,240
8.	Cap de la Magdeleine	282,240
9.	Isle of St. Christopher	80
10.	Fief Coteau St. Louis	96
11.	Fief Pacherigny	(about) 3
12.	Banlieu of Three Rivers	575
13.	Tadoussac	6
14.	La Prairie de la Magdeleine	56,448
	Total	794,863[5]

It is difficult to ascertain just when George III first promised to grant the Jesuits' estates to General Amherst as a reward for his military services. Kingsford states that the promise was made not long after the Capitulation of Montreal.[6] From Amherst's own testimony it would appear that it was toward the end of the decade after the Capitulation that he requested the estates, a request that was probably prompted by the legal opinions against the proprietary rights of the Order that had multiplied in that decade. Amherst first asked for a grant of the coal mines in Cape

Breton or a suitable grant of lands as a reward for his role in the Conquest. The coal mines were refused, but a mandamus was given for 20,000 acres of land in the newly acquired territory. However, Amherst's agent in Canada, Colonel James Robertson, advised him to refuse such a meagre grant. Robertson hinted that Amherst should ask for the Jesuits' estates, which he did in November, 1769. In the early part of 1770 he was pressing for fulfilment of the royal promise of the estates.[7]

Among those who served General Amherst in his endeavour was none other than the ex-Jesuit, Father Roubaud, who in 1770 produced a memoir to justify the royal grant of the Jesuits' estates to Amherst. The Jesuits had maintained: (1) that to despoil them of their estates would be a violation of the Capitulation; (2) that their estates were only conceded to them under the obligation of teaching Canadian youth free of charge; (3) that the king of England was not the master of the estates of his subjects, and the Order, by the cession of Canada, should enjoy the rights of subjects over the estates which belonged to it. Roubaud argued that the provisions of the Capitulation were merely temporary, and that there was no mention of the Jesuits in the Treaty of Paris. He argued further that they were positively condemned by the article in the Treaty which stipulated toleration "as far as the laws of Great Britain permit," since the laws of Great Britain positively proscribed the Jesuits. Roubaud stated erroneously that in no concession by the French Crown to the Jesuits was there any mention of the Canadian nobility or of the education of youth.[8] He argued still further that the Jesuits were not Canadian at all, since not one of them had been born in Canada. He hit upon a reason for there being no stipulation in favour of the Jesuits in the Treaty when he remarked that the French representatives could hardly have insisted on protection for the Jesuits in view of their government's actions against them just prior to its conclusion.[9]

In a further document Roubaud sought to supply sufficient information about the Jesuits' estates to enable the king to proceed with the grant to General Amherst. He warned that if the properties remained in the hands of the Jesuits, they would abuse them and allow the buildings and equipment to deteriorate. He insisted that only the Jesuits residing at Montreal and Quebec had a right to the estates because the College of Quebec and the house at Montreal had never contributed to the support of the Jesuit missionaries. He concluded that if Amherst received the estates on the condition that he should enjoy them only after the death of the last of the Jesuits, it was doubtful whether he or his heirs would reap any benefit from them since the few remaining Jesuits had decided upon a policy of enjoying the fruits of the estates to the utmost, without making any expenditures for improvements. There were members of the Order who might live for another thirty years. In addition to his assertion that there would be an inevitable deterioration under such disinterested management, Roubaud suggested that the surviving Jesuits would allow debts to accumulate which would ultimately be chargeable against the estates. Therefore Amherst ought to be given immediate possession of the estates, a pension should be provided for the remaining Jesuits, and they should be placed in Canadian parishes that had no priest. Roubaud's willingness to aid Amherst's cause is explained by the fact that he was destitute.[10]

Amherst eagerly seized upon Roubaud's arguments in his behalf. He optimistically informed Colonel Robertson that he might be able to send him a copy of the grant by the next packet. Roubaud's argument that only the Jesuits at Montreal and Quebec had a right to the estates Amherst thought to be useful because, according to his impression, there were only three of them. The General had also been verbally assured by Solicitor-General Wedderburn that he might gain the possession of the estates. Amherst was so optimistic that he wrote to Robertson at the end of March stating that he looked upon the grant as virtually secured, and he asked his agent to take the necessary steps to transfer the ownership of the estates from the Jesuits, while assuring them of an income for their lives.[11]

Delays were inevitable, however, and in early April Amherst was informed by George Ross, his agent in London, that those who were seeking to obtain the grant for him were ignorant of the cause of the delay. Ross suggested that Amherst see Lord Hillsborough since responsibility for drawing up the grant must lie with him. Yet, according to a note from John Pownall, under-secretary of state for the colonies, Hillsborough knew nothing of the proposed grant.[12]

Solicitor-General Wedderburn now submitted an opinion which pointed up some of the difficulties attending a grant of the estates. According to him, the principal difficulty arose from the fact that neither the status of the surviving Jesuits, nor the question of their proprietary rights, had been determined. If they had no rights, which the Solicitor-General argued would have been the case had Canada remained under the French Crown, then the estates were now the property of the British Crown and subject to no legal claim by the Jesuits. If the Society retained any rights to the estates, such rights extended only to those living in Canada because property belonging to the Society at large was inconsistent with the laws of England. Wedderburn advised putting an end to all the thorny questions by negotiating an agreement with the Jesuits that would secure an absolute conveyance of their estates to the British Crown without calling attention to the proposed grant to Amherst.[13]

Secrecy regarding the proposed grant was manifestly impossible. In the latter part of April Amherst received a note of congratulation from a New York acquaintance who suggested that a "great lawyer" there advised the General to secure immediately exact information regarding the estates to prevent any subsequent tricks by the Jesuits.[14] Colonel Robertson also wrote expressing his pleasure that Amherst had been granted the reversion of the properties and assuring him that they were a more valuable acquisition than any other the Crown could have given him in North America. So certain was Robertson of the grant that he had already taken steps to secure complete information about the estates, as well as to assure the Jesuits that they would be generously treated by Amherst.[15]

It was not until May 24 that the king actually referred Amherst's petition for the estates to the Committee of the Privy Council for Plantation Affairs.[16] The Committee referred the petition to the Board of Trade which reported in favour of the grant to Amherst on June 7.[17]

Murmurings against giving the properties to Amherst were already being heard in Canada. Attention was directed to article xxxiv of the Capitulation of Montreal, the article that granted the full proprietary rights of all the communities and all the priests. Certain individuals now began to argue that "communities" included the Order of Jesuits at large, and that those in Canada at the time of the Capitulation were not proprietors of any estates, but entrusted by the Order and accountable to it for the rents they received. Such being the case, the banishment of the Order from France did not affect their property rights in British colonies; these would remain until the entire Order might be dissolved.[18]

Such interpretations prompted Colonel Robertson to seek the advice of a distinguished New York lawyer, William Smith. Smith felt that it was important to determine whether the Jesuits' estates in Canada belonged to a religious community incorporated in France or to the Society of Jesus in all Catholic countries. Such a distinction being made, the thirty-fourth article of the Capitulation should be construed as applying only to the French corporation. That corporation having been dissolved, it was scarcely possible, in Smith's opinion, that Amherst would be disturbed by any claim from it. Smith went on to say that it was doubtful whether the Society of Jesus at large could take advantage of the capitulatory article, and whether they could build any stronger claim upon that basis than that of being preferred before all others in an application to the British Crown for a grant and confirmation of the estates. If this was all the security the Jesuits had, and the grant was made to Amherst, any litigation over the estates would be between the Jesuits and the Crown. Amherst would be a disinterested spectator, and the Jesuits would be over-matched in the controversy.

Smith recommended that a deed be secured from the Jesuits in Canada that would include a statement of pension provisions for them. Such an instrument would indicate that they had relinquished their claims; it might even include assertions, contrary to the pretensions of the Society at large, that would be useful to the Crown or Amherst in case of future litigation. As a double protection, this shrewd lawyer suggested that Amherst get an Act passed at Quebec, ratifying such a deed of contract and conveyance and including clauses extinguishing the claims and pretensions of all other persons than the General and his heirs. All claimants would thereby be obliged to petition the Crown, which would not be easily disposed to act contrary to Amherst's interests.[19] Robertson, however, was not overly optimistic concerning the possibility of getting the remaining Jesuits to sign such a conveyance. The only hope seemed to lie in a search of the original deeds to the Jesuits that would show that they had been granted to the houses in France. These being dissolved, the property would now be vested in the British Crown and might well be granted to Amherst, with only the stipulation that he provide for the Jesuits during the remainder of their lives.[20]

In a Privy Council meeting of July 5, 1770, the June 7 report of the Board of Trade was read.[21] A report and opinion of the attorney- and solicitor-general was also brought to the attention of the councillors. The law officers raised doubts about the power of the Crown to grant the Jesuits' estates. A discussion followed the reading, in which the general opinion seems to have been that the matter was fraught with great difficulties. Amherst's friend, General Conway, attempted to combat this opinion by arguing that the British Crown had as much power over the Jesuits and their estates as the French Crown had prior to the Conquest. Since the French Crown had now expelled the Order and confiscated all its estates, the British king might exercise the same power. Conway contended that the most liberal interpretation of the Capitulation, in the light of the British constitution, could mean nothing more than the guarantee of security to the present possessors for their lives. The Privy Council ordered that Amherst be informed of the various reports which it had considered and of the state of affairs relative to the grant. If he then thought it proper to persist in seeking the estates, the Council would again consult the law officers.[22]

In the deliberation of the Privy Council it had been argued that since the intention of providing for the Jesuits during their lifetime was not stated in Amherst's petition, the Council could not take it into account. Conway now advised Amherst to formally indicate his intentions concerning the remaining Jesuits as the best means of removing the only difficulty that seemed to cause doubt in the minds of the law officials. Amherst was informed that, although few lords were present at the meeting of the Privy Council, those present were favourably inclined. The Bishop of London had mentioned the need of the chapel and a dwelling for the use of the Protestant minister. Some notice was also taken of the other buildings which were being used for lodging the troops and other public purposes.[23]

In the days that followed the meeting of the Privy Council, Henry Davidson, who acted as Amherst's agent during Ross's absence from London, sought to assure Amherst that the objections to the grant were more insignificant and fewer than he had at first imagined. Cognizance had to be taken, however, of certain problems involved in securing the estates. A second reference to the law officials would cause delay. The Privy Council might meet again soon, but Davidson feared that unless Amherst were personally represented nothing would be done to hasten his cause. There was a strong inclination in the different departments to avoid any direct approbation of the grant, each trying to throw the responsibility for decision on the other. Amherst's petition was thus being thrown into the circuit of a common application rather than being directly considered by the Crown. If a second reference were made to the attorney- and solicitor-general regarding the expediency of the grant, the powers of the Crown, and the mode of granting, they would likely plead insufficiency of materials upon which to make a judgment. Davidson remarked about the "frightening influence of publick Censure," though he was still persuaded that everyone wished Amherst to have the grant.[24]

Amherst found it difficult to understand the official delay and the misgivings that were being encountered by his agents. The Board of Trade reports of 1765 and 1769 might have raised some doubts as to the right of the Crown to make a grant of the estates, but these reports preceded his request. He was convinced that there had been a shift of opinion and that the right of the Crown to make the grant at present was not doubted. Additional information had been received from Francis Maseres, attorney-general of Quebec now returned to London. Amherst was confident that sound legal counsel was on his side. He felt that he had given ample assurances with regard to the needs of the Jesuits during their lives. As to the chapel or church and a dwelling for the use of the Protestant minister, he would readily give them up for the public good.[25] Davidson had to inform him, however, that there appeared to be no likelihood of a meeting of the Privy Council to deal with private business before winter. It now seemed certain that the securing of the grant would prove a "tedious business."[26]

In addition to agents like Ross and Davidson in England and Robertson in Canada, Amherst seems to have made every effort to secure the services of the most important legal authorities in England. To what extent these officials were influenced in their official opinions, some of which were important in the formulation of the Quebec Act, by their desire to serve him is a matter for considerable conjecture. Outstanding among those who spoke in his behalf was Alexander Wedderburn, who became solicitor-general in 1771. His official report, in connection with the information-gathering that culminated in the Quebec Act, had already been considered. Wedderburn expressed himself more fully in a letter to Davidson concerning the tactics to be pursued in the attempt to secure the Jesuits' estates for Amherst. He frankly stated that the difficulties with which Amherst was confronted were not to be removed by any opinion he could send him. The law officers had quite properly reported in 1768 that they lacked sufficient information concerning the estates to be able to give an opinion regarding a plan proposed in 1765 for giving them to the Society for the Propagation of the Gospel. The same argument would surely apply with reference to efforts to secure them for Amherst. The Board of Trade had suggested that the Quebec legislature pass a law abolishing the Society of Jesus, vesting its real property in the Crown and providing pensions for the remaining Jesuits. Wedderburn was uncertain as to what bearing these reports might have either for or against the granting of the estates to Amherst.

Wedderburn anticipated some difficulty in the mode of preparing the proper instruments for granting the estates, but it seemed to him by no means impossible to overcome. As the existence of the Order of the Jesuits in Canada was totally inconsistent with the government of the country as a British colony, the estates of the Order either belonged to the remaining Jesuits as individuals incapable of succession, or were presently vested in the Crown, although no act declared the king's title. If the properties still belonged to the Jesuits, Amherst, by being authorized to treat with them, might acquire the estates and subsequently a regular title from the Crown. If they were vested in the Crown, directions might be given to the governor to take the proper measures for declaring the king's title and to have a grant passed with such reservations in favour of the remaining Jesuits as should be thought proper. The report of the Board of Trade had suggested a third method to Wedderburn, that of recommending to the legislature of Quebec that it pass a law vesting the estates in the king for the purpose of granting them to Amherst. It was Wedderburn's opinion that if the legislature could pass an Act for purposes not defined, it seemed very clear that there could be no objection to their passing one for a purpose plainly expressed. He was convinced that the members of that legislature would think the purpose of granting the estates to Amherst a very laudable one. Should the question come before the Attorney-General, Wedderburn volunteered to appear on Amherst's behalf, not to argue whether a grant should be given or not but to submit his ideas upon the mode of making the grant. He expressed the hope that the more recent report of the Board of Trade, of June 7, 1770, would guide the Council in its decision.[27]

While the grant to Amherst was being delayed in London, the Jesuits had become aware of the intended grant. Robertson informed Amherst on August 20 that the Jesuits had told him that some of the inhabitants, without their permission, had sent a petition to the king not to give the estates of the Jesuits to any private person, but to preserve them for the uses for which they were originally intended, namely, for the education of their children and for the conversion of the savages. According to Robertson, Governor Carleton was bringing the petition to England.

Robertson had been busy trying to convince the Jesuits that their estates would soon belong to Amherst and it would be for their interest and security to accept pensions equal to the value of the estates, which might increase under Amherst's management. He had expressed the hope to de Glapion that they would not decline an act that would benefit Amherst and would also secure them from depending on Amherst's heirs, who might not be so generous as he. De Glapion's reply to these overtures was that he must depend upon the goodness of the Crown and on that of Amherst. He was forbidden by his general to convey any part of the estates which he thought, by the Capitulation, was payable to the last father who should remain alive. Robertson reported that he had discovered that companies in England had applied to the General of the Jesuits at Rome to purchase the estates. The Jesuits in Canada, however, entertained hopes of the restitution of their Order, the favour of the administration, and the success of their petition to the British government. They were not disposed to listen to Robertson's proposition.[28]

Robertson sent Amherst copies of such papers as might give a clear idea of the nature of the grants to the Jesuits. According to his account, the chief justice and the best lawyers in Quebec thought that the fathers (those who were actually such at the time of the Conquest) could be entitled only to their respective proportions of the estates during their lives. Cramahé, charged with the government of Quebec during Carleton's absence, and the provincial secretary had been engaged by Robertson to prevent the making of any new fathers or the taking of any new mortgages on the estates. Three fathers had actually been ordained since the surrender, and a mortgage had been taken on one of the estates for 20,000 *livres*.[29] Amherst's agent had been told that the Jesuits had offered to convey their estates to the government in exchange for pensions and that Murray had made the proposition to the government but had received no answer. He was certain that their interests would induce them to renew their offer whenever they thought themselves in danger.[30]

Meanwhile, Amherst was trying to remedy the objections of the Privy Council by supplementing his petition with extracts from his correspondence with Robertson to prove that he had no intention of depriving the Jesuits of a suitable livelihood. Other necessary papers further to substantiate his claims to the grant were being assembled for the Council's consideration. The General's hopes were high, and he again expressed the hope to Robertson that by the next packet he might have authority to tell him that the grant which had been promised so long ago was at last made.[31]

Robertson fanned Amherst's hopes with a report which he made toward the end of September regarding the situation in the province.[32] An annual income from all the estates of £1,200 sterling was predicted. Mills might be erected at a small expense which would greatly increase that figure. Though the Jesuits believed that the petition of the inhabitants and Carleton's favourable representations would prevent the grant from being executed, Robertson thought they would be more pliable when they found themselves depending on Amherst's goodwill. In the meantime, he was doing his utmost to allay their fears and to prepare them to accept the anticipated *fait accompli*.

Robertson was hard put to stifle a notion, which he thought might have an ill effect if believed in Canada and published in England, that the Capitulation was going to be broken. He warned Amherst that Governor Carleton was carrying a petition against the grant to England, in which the grant was represented as being disagreeable to the Canadians. Robertson, however, assured Amherst that even the petitioners did not expect that the estates would be kept in possession of the Order of the Jesuits at large, but wished at most that those who were actually in Canada at the Capitulation might enjoy them for the remainder of their lives. If Amherst could get possession of the estates and pay each Jesuit the proportion he was then receiving, for life, he (Amherst) would still have a good income immediately. That part of the house at Quebec which the Jesuits did not possess could be leased for £150 a year; that at Montreal for half that sum. The Jesuits had complained to Robertson of the use of their house in Montreal as a jail; Amherst might well curry their favour by indulging them in this matter.

As the year was drawing to a close, new representations regarding the grant were made to a member of the Privy Council. Amherst appears now to have reconciled himself to the conclusion that if he were not the successful recipient of the estates, they would, nevertheless, be granted to someone else who might ask for them.[33]

The renegade Roubaud was still in London. On October 31 he wrote to Amherst, informing him (erroneously, of course) that he had just learned at the Colonial Office that the Crown had accorded Amherst full possession and enjoyment of the Jesuits' estates in Canada. After some very flattering remarks, Roubaud revealed his purpose in writing. He hoped that Amherst's generosity and friendship for him would distinguish him from the other members of the Society. He had only a small pension from the government which had come only after he had become debt-ridden. The Jesuits, he falsely asserted, had accorded him a pension of ten guineas per month when he left Quebec. This, to the disgrace of Murray, who had witnessed the event, they had refused to pay. Roubaud, after mentioning his financial straits, assured Amherst of his willingness to do everything possible to assist him in acquiring the Jesuits' estates. He indicated that he had several instructions to give Amherst concerning the securing of the estates.[34]

The Lords of the Committee made their report to the Privy Council on November 2. They suggested that the attorney- and solicitor-general should be directed to prepare a draft of the proper instrument for granting the Jesuits' estates to Amherst. The Jesuits' colleges and chapels in Quebec, Montreal, and Three Rivers should be reserved for public uses to be determined by the Crown. Such a document should also insure that Amherst engaged himself to provide for the remaining Jesuits who were in possession of the estates at the time of the Conquest. The Committee's report was approved and an order was issued to the attorney- and solocitor-general which included its recommendations.[35]

On the other side of the ocean, Robertson was seized with another brain-storm. He had suggested that since the Board of Trade had judged it equally politic and proper to vest the estates of other orders as well as those of the Jesuits in the Crown, Amherst should try to get the Sulpicians' estates which were worth £3,500 sterling a year, while those of the Jesuits were worth only about £1,200. Though he continued to try to further the objective of obtaining the Jesuits' properties, he was to come back again and again to this belated inspiration, berating himself for not having suggested it sooner.[36]

Robertson made no progress in his efforts to convince the Jesuits to accept a point of view favourable to the interests of his employer. The Jesuits considered themselves as only agents for the Order at large, and, while the Order existed, they thought Amherst's Capitulation entitled it to the estates. They staunchly proclaimed that they were "children of obedience" and could do no act without the approval of their general. To Robertson's contention that the word "community" meant the community of the Jesuits in Canada, they replied that they considered the whole of the estates to belong to the longest survivor. Robertson was upset by a suggestion from de Glapion that, upon his death, the general of the Order would replace him, in which case, Robertson reasoned, the Jesuits would keep the estates for ever. Amherst was repeatedly advised by his agent that, in order to prove his good intentions towards the Jesuits, to get rid of all contests with the fathers, and to benefit from the estates, his petition should request that the properties be vested in him immediately. He also advised that each of the Jesuits be given a lifetime pension equal to the share he was presently receiving from the revenue, or a thirteenth part of the income of the estates as reported by de Glapion.[37]

The attorney- and solicitor-general reported on December 14 that since they had no authentic account of the nature and description of the estates in question, they were not able to prepare a grant which would be legally valid.[38] Amherst attempted to meet this objection by calling for the acceptance of an affidavit by General Murray, containing an account of the nature and description of the estates. The law officers, however, refused to accept this document as containing an authentic account of the estates. This refusal prompted a further petition to the Privy Council by Amherst in March, 1771, in which he submitted an account and description of the estates based on the registers of the intendant's office and those of the pre-Conquest Superior Council of Quebec.[39]

During the months of delay, Robertson repeatedly warned Amherst against accepting a mere reversion of the estates. The General must get immediate possession, while personally assuming the obligation of paying a pension to the remaining Jesuits. Robertson deplored the proposed reservation of the Quebec and Montreal facilities to the Crown because this would result in a loss for Amherst of about £200 a year.[40] He was optimistic concerning the possibilities from a careful management of the estates. In good hands the income might be £1,500 sterling a year. By building mills and by making additional concessions of lands, the yearly value might be raised immediately to £2,000. As the allowance to the remaining members of the Order should be based upon the valuation which they themselves had put upon the income of the estates, Amherst would have immediate possession and a handsome income that would be augmented as the members died one after the other. On the other hand, Robertson pointed to a mortgage of 20,000 *livres* on one of the Jesuit properties in Montreal to illustrate what would happen if Amherst did not get possession of the estates until after the death of the last of the Jesuits.[41]

The proposed grant to Amherst was now stymied. One may reasonably conjecture that the reason for this was the preoccupation of the British government with the broader considerations regarding the future of Canada, which culminated in the Quebec Act of 1774. On July 2, 1772, Maseres, who contributed to the fact-finding in connection with these considerations, sought to explain the delay of the grant to Amherst. He wrote that it was a maxim of English law that in making grants of land from the Crown to any subject, the king must have precise information regarding what was to be granted. For this purpose, the Crown ought to procure authenticated copies of the original grants and other title deeds of the Jesuits' estates and evidence that the Jesuits were in possession of specified lands at the time of the Conquest of the country in 1760, and proof that they were still in possession of the same. Without that information, the grant would not be valid, and the Crown might subsequently void it upon the ground that the king had been deceived into making it by a misrepresentation of the extent and value of the lands.

Maseres pointed out another, and greater, objection to the grant. The king could grant nothing but what was certainly his own, either in possession or reversion. If he was in possession of it he might grant it immediately; if he was clearly entitled to the reversion of it after the deaths of certain persons, he might grant the reversion of it. If, however, there was only a chance of the king's becoming possessed of a piece of land, he could not grant it. This would be called a mere possibility, and could not be granted. In the opinion of Maseres, who knew French as well as English law, such was the case with the Jesuits' estates, of which the king was not in possession. The Jesuits had been allowed to keep them and might even sell them, by the express words of the articles of Capitulation in 1760 and the Treaty of Peace of February 10, 1763.

B*

The king was not clearly entitled to the reversion of the estates after the death of the present Jesuits because it was not certain that they would not fill up their numbers and continue on for ever since there had been no proclamation, order-in-council, or ordinance of the province that forbad them to do so, or declared that their Society should be at an end in the province after the death of the remaining members.

Maseres was convinced that the king's interest in the Jesuits' estates was a mere chance or remote possibility until an act of state for fixing the period of their Society should be passed. Consequently, the estates could not be granted. Maseres showed some familiarity with the diversity of means by which the Jesuits had secured their properties when he argued that if the remaining Canadian Jesuits were all to die in one day, all their lands would still not revert to the Crown, but only such as had been granted by the French king. Those granted by other lords would belong to the heirs of the persons who gave them to the Jesuits. Maseres concluded that a positive act of state, such as an order-in-council or an Act of Parliament, seemed necessary to fix a certain period for the existence of the Society in the province and to vest the reversion of all their lands in the Crown before it could grant them to any other person. This order-in-council, in addition to an order to the provincial governor to secure the necessary papers, Amherst was advised to undeavour to obtain, if he desired the grant of the Jesuits' estates.[42]

Though expressing total incomprehensibility as to the reasons for delay, Amherst decided to act according to Maseres's advice.[43] He proceeded to the task of securing the papers which Maseres had advised him to procure.[44] Extracts relative to the Jesuits' estates were taken from the registers at Quebec and transmitted to Amherst by Robertson in April, 1773. Robertson again warned Amherst of accepting a mere reversion of the estates because such deterioration of the estates would take place before the last Jesuit died that their value would be greatly impaired.[45] In January of the following year, Amherst wrote to Lord North, requesting that if an Act of Parliament were passed to regulate the affairs of Canada, a clause might be included in the Act which would overcome the difficulties raised by the king's law officers and thus effect the grant of the Jesuits' lands to himself.[46]

Sometime during 1774 Amherst expressed his reactions to the delay in a summary statement of what had transpired relative to the grant. It appeared to him that the potential value of the Jesuits' estates had created some doubt and objection to the completion of the grant. If this were the case, he remarked, it was quite new to him and might easily be removed. The estates were small in income and large in extent of waste acres. Any part of the latter might be withdrawn if there was any reasonable objection to the quantity. Should any difficulty arise from the estates having already been given to him by the resolution of Council of November 2, 1770, he would give back any part accordingly. He reasoned that the Jesuits' estates would not produce any income for his benefit. The income, exclusive of the colleges, was reckoned at £800 a year, which he would be bound to divide among the remaining Jesuits. It was therefore not probable that he would receive from the estates even the expenses he had incurred in obtaining the grant. He was hopeful, however, that they would produce an income for his heirs. The present grant would appear as some reward for his services in America. To further emphasize their small value, Amherst wrote that he had been informed that if the grant of the Jesuits' estates was put up at auction, it would not produce half the sum that had already been offered for the smallest of the two grants lately given to two general officers who served under his command in

America. It appears that Amherst actually drafted a clause and proposed its insertion into the forthcoming Act of Parliament, in which the Crown was said to have become vested of the proprietary rights of the Jesuits, Amherst's services were reviewed, and the lawfulness of a potential grant to him was sustained.[47]

It is not known to what extent, if any, Amherst pressed the matter of making provision for the grant in the Quebec Act. If he tried, he was doomed to disappointment. It will be recalled that article VIII of that Act excepted the religious orders and communities from the provision for the enjoyment of property and possessions.[48] The disposition of the Jesuits' estates was prescribed only in the instructions which were sent to Governor Carleton on January 3, 1775. The twelfth clause of article XXI called for the suppression and dissolution of the Society of Jesus and the vesting of all their rights, possessions, and property in the Crown for such purposes as it might think fit. It was stipulated, however, that the existing members of the Society, as established at Quebec, should be allowed sufficient stipends and provisions during their natural lives.[49] One might well assume that Governor Carleton's presence in London during the deliberations leading up to the passage of the Quebec Act helped to prevent any stipulation in it which might have secured to Amherst a grant of the Jesuits' estates. Carleton had disapproved of the suppression of any religious communities except the Jesuits, and had asked that he might be left at liberty to use his discretion in the matter.[50]

During the negotiations of the first phase of the Amherst claims, several obstacles had appeared to thwart the granting of the estates to him. The uncertain status of the Jesuit Order, as well as that of their estates, militated against the estates being granted immediately upon Amherst's request. Inadequate information regarding the estates made it impossible to draw up a grant that would be legally acceptable, assuming that the king had a right to make such a grant. Compared to the mass of documentary evidence which was to be submitted later, the evidence submitted by Amherst was paltry and piecemeal. The first-named obstacle was removed by the Quebec Act and by the subsequent instructions to Governor Carleton, but the second remained to prevent any grant being made. During the period from 1774 to 1779 little or nothing seems to have been done by Amherst to forward his claims. One may reasonably assume that this was due to the intense preoccupation of the British government with the revolt of the American colonies, and the continuing uncertainty as to whether the province of Quebec would remain under British control. It is not unreasonable to assume that Amherst, in addition to the patriotic motivation of not pressing a personal claim during the time of crisis, was wary of the possibility that the estates might not rest finally in the hands of the British Crown at all. At any rate, there was an interlude of inaction before the claims were again pressed in 1779.

CHAPTER THREE

THE AMHERST CLAIMS: PROVINCIAL INVESTIGATIONS

IN MARCH, 1779, Lord Amherst[1] asked the government to renew its former order to the attorney- and solicitor-general for the preparation of a draft of a grant, after they had considered some further evidence regarding the estates. His petition was accordingly referred to the law officers by an order-in-council of March 9, 1779.[2] Again there was a long delay, for which Amherst himself was partly responsible. When, several years later, he finally laid before the law officers an account of the estates sent from Canada by the clerk of enrolments, and the affidavit of General Murray, he explained that he had forborne to submit this information "by Reason of the Troubles which then [1779] and for some Years afterwards subsisted in North America."[3]

Not until July 6, 1786, did the law officers submit their report. In it they pointed out that the additional evidence presented by Amherst consisted of a copy of an instrument dated May 12, 1678, in which Louis XIV had confirmed certain grants of lands and buildings to the Jesuits prior to that date by the governors and by the Company of New France. This document described the extent of the lands and their local situation, but without sufficient precision. In addition to the confirmation of 1678, the law officers had also received short extracts of certain other grants made by the French Crown and by private donors. This evidence was even more unsatisfactory than that contained in the confirmation. The attorney- and solicitor-general reported, therefore, that they were unable to ascertain the various particulars which they thought the Crown must be aware of before a grant might be made. More information was necessary concerning the nature and quality of the lands, the existing titles by which they were possessed, the persons by whom they were possessed, their present value, the nature and extent of the rights of the seigniory, the nature of the tenures by which they were held, their exact local situation, the state of their culture and population. and whether any claims were made by the heirs of the donors of the lands that were given to the Order by private persons. The law officers offered the opinion that the necessary information might best be ascertained by an inquiry to be instituted in the province. Such an inquiry might be made by commissioners appointed by the governor, or by some other method that would be in keeping with the laws and customs of the province.[4]

Thereupon Lord Amherst, taking his cue from this report, presented a further petition. After referring to the fact that much time had been lost because the evidence which he had hitherto been able to procure had not proved sufficient, he asked that to avoid further delays and obstacles to his enjoyment of the estates, the suggestion of the law officers be carried out immediately. Amherst indicated a willingness to have excepted from the desired grant such parts of the estates as the governor of the province might report to be necessary for public uses.[5]

On August 11 the Lords of the Committee of the Privy Council for Trade and Foreign Plantations acted on the report of the law officers of July 6, as well as the further petition of Amherst. To avoid further delay, the Committee advised that an order-in-council be issued to carry out the suggestion of the law officers. They recommended that any grant which might follow the proposed investigation should be subject to the reservations and conditions previously stipulated in the Order-in-Council of November 9, 1770, namely, the exception of the Jesuits' colleges and chapels from the grant, and provisions for the survivors of the Order.[6]

The report of the Committee was approved on August 18 by the king-in-council. An order-in-council was accordingly issued, approving the Committee's report and ordering the governor of the province of Quebec to carry out the proposed investigation promptly.[7] Guy Carleton, now Lord Dorchester, had been again commissioned governor of Quebec on April 11, and the instructions issued to him on August 23 repeated the words of the 1775 instructions relative to the suppression of the Society of Jesus.[8] The Order-in-Council of August 18 was transmitted to Dorchester by Amherst himself. Later, on receiving a letter from Quebec, Amherst had some reason to fear that Dorchester might think he had not received the Order-in-Council in proper form. He therefore requested that the Privy Council send a duplicate of the Order to the Governor. The duplicate was sent on February 5, 1787, but Dorchester was informed, with reference to private orders-in-council, that no other form than the delivery of an order by the party or parties concerned was usual or necessary.[9]

It was not until May 31, 1787, that Dorchester laid before his Council the pertinent clause of his instructions and the duplicate of the Order-in-Council of August 18, 1786.[10] At a meeting of the provincial Council on June 2, it was decided that the Order-in-Council should be referred to the Attorney-General for a report to the Governor on the steps necessary for its execution.[11] Four months later, Attorney-General Monk submitted a draft of the commission for making the investigation as directed by the Order-in-Council.[12] On October 30 the Attorney-General's draft was read at a meeting of the Council, along with another that had been drawn up, and it was decided that both be submitted to the Attorney-General for an opinion as to which was more acceptable.[13] Monk submitted his choice on November 1 and suggested that the king's Order-in-Council of August 18, 1786, which included several important reports, should accompany the commission.[14] He suggested that the commission be composed of Kenelm Chandler, Thomas Scott, John Coffin, Gabriel Elzéar Taschereau, Jean Antoine Panet, George Lawes, James McGill, Quinson de St. Ours, and Jean Bertel de Rouville.[15] On November 1 the Council approved the Attorney-General's choice of a patent of commission, as well as his suggestions for its membership, substituting, however, a M. Descheneaux for Panet. A copy of the minutes of this meeting was to be sent to Chandler, who was represented as Amherst's agent. Chandler was asked to confer with the other nominees regarding the expenses that might be incurred in the investigation and to communicate the results to the Council.[16]

Chandler reported to Dorchester on November 30. The nominees residing in Quebec, except Taschereau, who was absent on private affairs, and Descheneaux, who had declined the nomination because of ill health, had met on November 19. The others, Chandler, Scott, Coffin, and Lawes, were convinced that a thoroughgoing investigation of the Jesuits' estates would be very costly, involving expenditures for surveying the lands, the services of a clerk, travelling and other expenses in connection with the collection of papers and examination of public records, legal opinions, postage and publications, a business office, and contingencies. The nominees therefore felt that they should receive the allowance usually made to commissioners appointed for the purpose of dividing Crown lands in England.[17] The Montreal nominees, McGill, de St. Ours, and de Rouville, meeting on November 26 for the same purpose, concurred in this conclusion.[18] On December 4, Chandler reported upon the meetings of the two groups of nominees to the Council, which ordered that a commission be issued those who had agreed to serve and that they proceed to carry out the commission at Amherst's expense.[19]

Rumours of an impending grant of the Jesuits' estates to Lord Amherst stirred alarm among the inhabitants of Quebec, and, on November 19, a petition signed by 195 persons whom Dorchester characterized as "respectable inhabitants"[20] was presented to the Governor. The petition was considered by the Council on December 4, and it was decided that the clerk should inform Lord Amherst's agent, Kenelm Chandler, of its contents. It and a supporting memorial were, in the meantime, to be tabled for further consideration.[21]

The petitioners dwelt upon the want of education among them since the Conquest, which they felt was all the more lamentable because of the continued occupation of the college at Quebec by garrison troops.[22] Their memorial opened with an admirable discourse on the dangers of neglecting the education of the subjects of a state.[23] A long historical and legal argument followed,[24] the main intent of which seems to have been to show that the College of Quebec was a lay corporation, and that the town had the right to employ the funds of the college. Regardless of the fate of the Jesuits, the college and its attendant properties could not be confiscated. The memorialists insisted that the Jesuits were only the administrators of the college and that the civil law of the province and the laws of England provided that the conduct, debts, or condition of a person managing the estates of a community or corporation established for the public good could not destroy the establishment or the intent of the founder.[25] Simply put, the argument was that the Jesuits were merely "benevolent and temporary Rectors or Managers" of the college and its dependent estates; the Canadians were the real owners.[26]

These "respectable inhabitants" admitted that the Quebec Act of 1774 had excepted the religious orders and communities from the provision for the enjoyment of proprietary rights, but they concluded that the Act was a law which, far from altering the Capitulation (which had stipulated in favour of the proprietary rights of the religious orders and communities), confirmed it in favour of the Canadians who were the true proprietors of the College of Quebec and its dependent estates. Although the Quebec Act had not by the exception expressly confirmed the proprietary rights of the religious orders and communities, the exception had not confiscated their property or their possessions.[27]

In the second part of the argument,[28] the principal causes that had deprived the Canadians of their education in the College of Quebec since the Conquest were reviewed. Attention was called to the use of the college as a barracks since 1776. Though justifiable for a short period of time, its continued use as a barracks no longer appeared to be so urgent. The complaint was expressed that "the neighbourhood, composing the most elegant Quarter and the Most frequented, receive a foetid Air, and are continually mixed with the Troops."[29]

In part three of the memorial, the means of restoring their educational facilities to the Canadians was discussed. As the memorialists considered the citizens and inhabitants of Canada to be the true corporation in which the property rights to the Jesuits' estates were vested, the Jesuits being merely trustees, it was proposed that the inhabitants of each parish should assemble to elect persons for the management of the estates belonging to it.[30] Nothing more seemed to be required than to dislodge the troops and to allow an assembly of the natives or residents in the province to elect representatives for the purpose of managing the college and its estates. It was thought to be in order that a portion of the revenue of the estates should be used as an allowance for the surviving Jesuits.[31] On January 9, 1788, Dorchester transmitted the petition and the accompanying memorial to the home government without comment.[32]

On December 29, 1787, a patent of commission for the investigation of the Jesuits' estates was finally issued to nine commissioners: Kenelm Chandler, Thomas Scott, John Coffin, Gabriel Elzéar Taschereau, Jean Antoine Panet,[33] George Lawes, James McGill, Quinson de St. Ours, and Jean Bertel de Rouville. In view of the objections which were raised at the end of the investigation by Panet and Taschereau concerning the majority report of the commissioners, the functions of the investigators as defined by the patent of commission must be carefully noted. They were to determine: (1) what lands and estates were held, possessed, and claimed by the Jesuits within the province, and the manner and ways by which they had acquired them; (2) what parts of the estates had been alienated and exchanged; (3) what parts were now vested in the Crown and might be legally granted; (4) the nature and quality of the properties and the present titles by which they were possessed; (5) their present value; (6) the nature and extent of the rights of seigniory; (7) the nature of the tenure by which they were held; (8) their exact local situation; (9) the state of their culture and population; and (10) whether any claims were made by the heirs of the donors of lands that had been given to the Jesuits by private persons.[34]

The commissioners held their first meeting in Chandler's home on January 23, 1788. After the routine business of organizing for their task, they decided to inform the superior of the Jesuits of their commission in order to secure copies of the title deeds of the estates and to obtain other useful information from the Jesuits.[35] Having been approached by Taschereau and Panet, Father de Glapion, superior, and Father Casot, attorney of the Jesuits, assured the commissioners that they would submit their plans and titles and all other information possible to a notary chosen by the commissioners. Charles Voyer was chosen as the notary, and after some hesitation by John Collins, the deputy surveyor-general, a certain McCarthy of St. Thomas agreed to serve as surveyor.[36]

For the district of Quebec, Scott and Taschereau were assigned the task of examining the titles which the Jesuits produced, of getting from the public registers such titles as the Jesuits would not produce, of putting those titles in order, and of preparing reports on them to be considered by all the commissioners. If they met obstacles or extraordinary difficulties in the course of their work, they were to report such to the president so that he could call the commissioners together.[37] De Rouville and de St. Ours were chosen to do the same at Montreal. Taschereau, Scott and Lawes were selected to consider the best means of surveying and making a *papier terrier*, or land roll, of the Jesuits' estates in the district of Quebec; and McGill, de Rouville, and de St. Ours were to do the same for the district of Montreal.[38]

Difficulties were encountered almost at once. On March 31 the Quebec commissioners were informed by those at Montreal that Father Well would not give them the information which was required for fulfilling the commission. Father Well had judged it proper to refuse all papers relative to the Jesuits' estates in that district except an authentic copy of the original concession of the seigniory of La Prairie. Such evidence was clearly insufficient, and the Montreal commissioners thought Well ought to be required by a notary to supply the plan of the seigniory, the *papier terrier*, and contracts given to the Jesuits when they acquired certain property in Montreal.[39] The Montreal commissioners, anticipating the persistent refusal of the Jesuit Father, asked for a copy of part of an *aveu et dénombrement* which had been submitted to Governor Haldimand in 1781[40] to enable them to draw up a *papier terrier*. Should the tenants refuse to give further necessary information, the commissioners suggested that the Council be consulted as to whether there were any means of forcing them to consent.[41]

Chandler and Coffin consulted the chief justice, who advised that the Montreal commissioners write a very polite letter to Father Well informing him of the documents needed. This letter should be sent to him by a notary and a convenient time for a reply be allowed. If any difficulty still remained, Dorchester should be notified and he would probably take the necessary measures to obviate it and any other difficulties that might arise in the future.[42]

Anticipating difficulties, Taschereau had introduced on March 17 a motion that a request be made to the Governor for a proclamation requiring the tenants and farmers of the fiefs and seigniories to exhibit their titles and papers in order that the commissioners might have all the necessary information. A delegation was appointed to seek such a proclamation from the Governor.[43] Panet went further and submitted a draft of a proclamation on March 18, proposing that it be included as part of a provisional report to the Governor. Action on Panet's proposal was deferred because of Dorchester's indisposition.[44] Framing of a provisional report was deferred once again on April 2, pending word from Montreal concerning Well's refusal to co-operate. That was finally received on April 17 and it was as had been anticipated.[45]

Panet and Taschereau stuck to their contention that a proclamation was necessary in order to get the co-operation of tenants in the fact-finding assignment of the commissioners. In reviewing the motion to seek a proclamation from the Governor, Panet explained on April 17 that according to the laws and customs of Canada only the king had the right to cause *lettres de papier terrier* to be expedited and published. Without a proclamation equivalent to the old *lettres de papier terrier*, the tenants would not be obligated to declare and exhibit all their titles. A multitude of refusals would result, causing difficulty and delay.[46]

On April 19 the commissioners agreed upon a temporary report to Lord Dorchester which informed him that they had located the principal title deeds of the fiefs and other Jesuit properties and authentic copies had been made. It also stated that they were now ready to make out a *papier terrier* of the estates but would not complete it until after a proclamation equivalent to letters patent, called *lettres de papier terrier*, was issued and published.[47] The commissioners argued that a proclamation was essential because (1) they were directed by commission to proceed without delay and in due form of law; (2) the laws that were in use in the province before the Conquest were applicable; (3) according to the laws and customs of the province, only the king had a right to cause *lettres de papier terrier* to be issued and published; (4) without a proclamation equivalent to these *lettres*, the vassals and tenants would not be legally obligated to provide the needed information; and (5) since the Conquest, particularly in 1777 and subsequent years, the governors of the province had issued several proclamations for the purpose of making land rolls for the Crown lands.[48]

The question of the advisability or necessity of a proclamation was considered in Council on May 14 and then referred to the law officers of the province for a report and the necessary draft of a proclamation.[49] Attorney-General Monk and Solicitor-General Williams reported on June 24 that they considered the Society of Jesus to be incapable of any civil existence in the province. In their opinion, the Jesuits' estates and any rights pertaining to them had fallen to the Crown. Such being the case, the commission of December 29, 1787, based on the Order-in-Council of August 18, 1786, appeared to them to fulfil every purpose that might be fulfilled by a *lettre de papier terrier*. A proclamation could be expedient only to announce to all interested persons the appointment of the commissioners; these persons might then be prepared to perform their duties when called upon to do so.[50] Those who then refused to assist the inquiry might be compelled to do so under penalty of the law. The Attorney- and Solicitor-General emphasized, however, that the Crown should be in actual possession of the estates before any such proclamation was issued.[51]

In a statement of observations to the commissioners, the law officers again emphasized that a proclamation was expedient only for the purpose indicated above. It was their opinion that the title deeds of the fiefs and other properties possessed by the Jesuits should be certified at large to become a matter of record, and they felt that the *right* of the king to the estates was clear, for, they stated:

> By the conquest of Canada and the Treaty of Paris in 1763, the Estates which were of the Community or order of Jesuits in this Country fell to the King; and by the Act of the 14th of His Majesty, ch. 83, and the Inquest to be certified in the manner abovementioned, we conceive His Majesty becomes vested in the Possession of all those Estates, without any formal Entry. The proposed Proclamation may Issue for the aid of The Commissioners in their Inquiry for ascertaining the particulars required—for His Majesty's Instructions, with propriety and Strict legality.[52]

Here it will be recalled that the Jesuits, along with the other religious orders, were confirmed in their proprietary rights by the Capitulation of Montreal. Furthermore, the Treaty of Paris had contained no specific reference to the Jesuits' estates (or the Jesuits), but had contained an agreement that the French inhabitants, or others who had been subjects of the French king in Canada, might within eighteen months of the ratification of the treaty retire with all safety and freedom, wherever they should think proper, *and might sell their estates and take the proceeds with them*. It was not until the passage of the Quebec Act (14 Geo. III, c. 83), that the religious orders were specifically excepted from the general provision for the enjoyment of proprietary rights. The first official announcement that the Jesuits were to be suppressed and their properties confiscated was in the instructions to Governor Carleton, of January 3, 1775, but even these instructions did not indicate that the confiscation was by right of conquest.

The report of the Attorney- and Solicitor-General, with the draft of the proclamation, was read in Council on July 22 and referred to a committee which was given the task of determining the proper procedure for the carrying out of the Order-in-Council of August 18, 1786.[53] This special committee was composed of Hugh Finlay, Thomas Dunn, Adam Mabane, J. G. Chaussegros de Léry, William Grant, Paul Roc de St. Ours, and Charles de Lanaudière.[54] The first meeting of the committee was held on August 21, 1788, at which time papers relating to the proposed grant were laid before it. Grant moved that a copy of the Governor's Order-in-Council of July 22 be sent to the king's law counsel, to the commissioners, and to Father de Glapion. They were to be informed that the committee would meet on September 15 to receive any information which they might think proper to offer in consequence of the Order-in-Council.[55]

Grant's motion was carried at a subsequent meeting on August 25, over the objections of Mabane and de Léry, objections which were rather important. The two argued that the sole purpose of the committee was to report to the Governor on the due course required by law for carrying out the Order-in-Council of August 18 1786. If the committee could, after considering the papers at its disposal, point out that course, there was no need for seeking further information. They further contended that the proclamation applied for by the commissioners could not legally or expediently be issued until the Governor had suppressed the Jesuits within the province and had taken their estates into the possession of the Crown. The commissioners might then, if necessary, be more fully authorized to try to get additional information from the *censitaires* of the estates.[56] Father de Glapion was notified that he would be heard at the September 15 meeting of the committee if he had anything to offer concerning the matter which had been referred to it. Commissioners Chandler, Coffin, Scott, and Taschereau, as well as Attorney-General Monk and Solicitor-General Williams, were likewise notified of the forthcoming meeting.[57]

De Glapion replied by letter on September 10. He assumed that the English governors who had commanded in the province would attest to the fidelity and obedience of the Jesuits. He than pointed out that their estates had come to them as gifts from the kings of France and other individuals or had been purchased by the Order itself. The majority of the fathers had ceased to devote themselves to the charitable works for which the estates were acquired only when they died. Those who survived were engaged in the same work, and intended to continue in it until their deaths—which, in the course of nature, could not be very far distant. De Glapion emphasized that all their title deeds, which were properly recorded in the record office of the province, showed that all these estates had always belonged to them in full ownership, and they had always managed and administered them as their own without opposition. He reminded the committee that the Jesuits' property had been fully recognized in the Capitulation of September 8, 1760, and he referred to article xxxv which specifically permitted them "to dispose of their estates and to send the produce thereof, as well as their persons, and all that belongs to them, to France." "In any case," he concluded, "we are in his Majesty's hands, and he will decide according to his good pleasure. But subjects and children without reproach can look forward to nothing but a favourable . . . decision from so benevolent a Monarch and so kind a father as his Majesty George III."[58]

The law officers were present at a meeting of the committee on September 15, but asked for additional time to prepare a written report. Panet, on behalf of the commissioners, again urged the necessity of issuing a proclamation in accordance with the request of the commissioners in their temporary report of the previous May.[59]

When the committee met again on October 16, Grant called attention to a number of public documents relating to the establishment and possessions of the Jesuits in Canada and moved that such of the documents as were not of public notoriety might be selected from the records of the province and entered in the minutes and report of the committee. The chairman was authorized to obtain such of the necessary papers which were to be annexed to the committee's report.[60] Here there was obviously duplication by the committee of some of the work assigned to the specially appointed commissioners.

The committee, having examined various public and private documents which came before it on October 18, concluded that in order to effect the king's intentions toward Lord Amherst and the public, an act of the provincial legislature, suppressing the Jesuits and taking possession of their estates for the Crown, would be required. Under the Quebec Act, the legislature of the province had full power, in the opinion of the committee, to make laws, statutes, and ordinances for the welfare and good government of the province, and consequently for the execution of royal instructions to the Governor of August 23 and the Order-in-Council of August 18, 1786.

The committee did not perceive the propriety and legality of issuing a proclamation as requested by the commissioners. When an ordinance was passed suppressing and dissolving the community of Jesuits and giving the Crown possession of their estates, they could no longer be deemed the seigniors or administrators of them, or hold suits in the king's courts. Thus reunited to the domain of the dominant lord, the king, the vassals and *censitaires* would be compelled to render their feudal obligations to the king or his appointed officials. Such an ordinance was necessary because possession of the estates was still retained by the Jesuits under the sanction and eye of the government, and under diverse approbative, if not confirmative, acts of its ministers.[61]

In a proposed committee report submitted by Grant at the meeting of the 18th the following statements were included:

That the estates of a society which had not a legal existence even in the dominions of France, vested in His Majesty at the conquest of the Country, cannot, nevertheless be admitted into doubt.

The Laws of England were then as now, equally inamicable [sic] to the Institutes, Constitutions and Doctrines of a body of Men who acknowledged no head or superior under Heaven, but a Despotic General & the Bishop of Rome.[62]

At a subsequent meeting on October 21, it is significant to note that on a motion by Dunn the two statements just quoted were struck out of the draft report.[63]

The committee also called attention to the *arrêts* and edicts of the French government which clearly indicated the legal means adopted in that kingdom to do justice to the Crown, to the public, to the Jesuits, to its creditors, and to other individuals. Adequate provisions were made for the future administration of the estates and the continued use of the revenues for the purpose of education. All parties concerned were heard in person or by their representatives before the proper authorities of the realm. Proper legal documents were issued from time to time as the business of the suppression proceeded and as the particular cases required.[64]

Mabane dissented from the report, proposed by Grant and adopted by the committee, because it was, in his opinion, contradictory to the royal instruction of August 23, 1786, to the Governor, which did not require the interference of either the legislature or the Privy Council for its execution. Mabane offered an alternative draft of a report at the meeting of October 18, but this was voted down on October 21. He would have had it that the committee was of the opinion that the proclamation applied for by the commissioners and recommended by the law officers should not be issued, as they did not consider the king to be in possession of the estates in question. The commissioners had received sufficient information to enable them to report without a proclamation being issued. Mabane wished the committee to recommend that the Governor in the meantime carry into operation the royal instruction relative to the suppression of the Jesuits.[65] Grant, however, moved that as the season was advanced and the last ships were soon to sail for England, the clerk of the Council be requested to select authentic copies of the papers referred to in the minutes of the various sessions of the committee, and to present them to Lord Dorchester in support of the conclusions reached by the majority of the members. In the meantime, the chairman would report to the Governor.[66]

The report and papers from the committee of the Council were now submitted to Chief Justice William Smith who advised that the king, as conqueror, became not only the proprietor of the country but the lawgiver as well. The conquered Canadian subjects retained only those rights to which they were entitled by the law of nations under the articles of Capitulation. It was his opinion that the Quebec Act, by excluding the religious orders and communities from the provision for the security of the property and possessions of other inhabitants, left the persons and property of those orders and communities as much subjected to the Crown's sovereignty and legislative authority as they were at the moment of the Conquest. On the basis of the governor's commission and instructions following the Quebec Act and also of Dorchester's present commission and instructions, it appeared that a royal grant of the estates would be valid and that such portions as the Crown might not grant would remain at its disposal.

It was the view of the Chief Justice, however, that a distinction must be made between estates alienated by the Jesuits before the dissolution of the Order and the ungranted residue. Those to whom lands had been alienated appeared to be entitled to all the security given to the Canadians in general by the Quebec Act. The dues of those still retained by the Jesuits could not legally be withheld from the Crown, but they must be exacted in due form of law, and that would not be the case, in Smith's opinion, if a mere proclamation was issued in accordance with the commissioners' recommendation. If Lord Amherst had the grant of the estates, he would be entitled to use *lettres de papier terrier* in accordance with French law. However, according to the letter of the royal order, no such grant could be passed until the previous information concerning the estates, mentioned in the order, was obtained. The Chief Justice called attention to the broad administrative and legislative powers which the French intendants had exercised, particularly with reference to matters of land tenure. It was his opinion that no act or declaration of the Crown, standing only upon the right of conquest, would have the force of a law upon such as held parts of the Jesuits' estates. Nothing short of the authority of Parliament, or of the Legislative Council established by Parliament, would suffice to enable the commissioners to acquire all the information necessary to make a proper grant to Amherst.

In the light of these observations, Chief Justice Smith suggested that the commissioners ought to be directed to report all the information they had been able to acquire, with a statement of the obstacles which prevented the completion of their work and with suggestions as to how these might be overcome. The law officers should then submit to the Governor a draft of such an act as might be required. Lord Amherst ought to be kept fully informed of what was taking place to facilitate any further applications to the Crown which he might have to make.[67]

Meanwhile, the specially appointed commissioners seem to have accomplished little or nothing. A few months later, however, Chandler's prodding brought some activity. At a meeting on March 25, 1789, he proposed that because Father Casot of Three Rivers had refused to deliver the *livre terrier,* some of the commissioners be sent to Three Rivers and elsewhere to investigate the obstacles which were hindering the completion of their work. Taschereau and Panet obstinately held to their view that the commission could do nothing further without a proclamation. Lawes and Coffin, however, agreed to assist Chandler. Shortly thereafter, Scott having joined them, they proceeded to Quebec, after which they went to Sillery, Belair, and Three Rivers, where they obtained the needed information without any further difficulty. This done, Chandler expressed to Taschereau the hope of getting his report before the commissioners.[68]

In view of the assurances from the law officers and the Council that a proclamation was not really necessary to the work of the commissioners, it is extremely difficult to resist the conclusion that throughout the whole of their proceedings the two French members, Taschereau and Panet, deliberately sought to delay the final report of the commission as long as possible. At a meeting of the commission on April 23, Taschereau reminded the other members that they had been ordered by the commission of December 29, 1787, to inquire concerning any claims which might exist among the heirs of private persons who had given parts of the Jesuits' estates. Chandler therefore proposed that the commission, or the relevant part of it, be published immediately, to the end that all parties having claims to the estates might have an opportunity to present them.[69]

Apparently this was not done; an omission that may be explained, at least partly, by the pressure the Council now put upon the commission. In accordance with a resolution of the Council, adopted on April 22, an order of the Council was presented to the commissioners at their next meeting on April 25, calling for a report to the Governor as to (1) how far the commissioners had been able to execute the trust committed to them; (2) what remained to fulfil the same; (3) what obstacles were in the way; and (4) by what means they thought the obstacles might be removed and the intention of the commission fulfilled.[70] It was then decided that each member of the commission would draft a general report to be considered at the next meeting. Panet submitted such a draft on May 2, and Chandler presented his on May 7.[71] In the light of what followed, it is important to keep in mind that Chandler was the agent of Lord Amherst as well as one of the commissioners.[72]

The next session of the commission was convoked on June 17, at the request of Taschereau and Panet. At this session, Chandler's draft was, in a certain sense, "railroaded" through the meeting, over the objections of Taschereau and Panet, who felt that the Montreal commissioners should be summoned to join the rest in Quebec. It was decided, however, Taschereau and Panet dissenting, that Lawes should carry the proposed report and the substantiating documents to Montreal for the perusal and signatures of the commissioners who resided there.[73] Lawes reported the result at a meeting on June 29. A letter from the Montreal commissioners, dated June 20, indicated that, because of insufficient time in which to examine the papers and draft report, they could not sign it. Though expressing their confidence in the commissioners at Quebec who had signed, they raised a question concerning the fact that no public notice had been given to possible claimants to the Jesuits' estates, and consequently that the commission would have failed to carry out one of the objects of the inquiry. They thought that Lord Dorchester should be reminded of this. The Montreal commissioners expressed their regret that since Rouville and St. Ours had been prepared to come to Quebec when the draft report was submitted for adoption, this mode of operation had not been followed. Well might the Montreal commissioners complain that there had not been adequate time for a satisfactory perusal of the schedule of the estates, the report, and the titles and plans thereof. Lawes, according to his own statement, left Quebec on Thursday, June 18, at 4 a.m., arrived at Montreal on Friday, June 19, at 5 p.m., departed from Montreal on Saturday, June 20, and arrived at Quebec on Tuesday, June 23, at 2 p.m.[74]

Taschereau and Panet were given four days in which to say whether they would sign the various documents which the other Quebec commissioners were going to sign and submit to Lord Dorchester. At a meeting on June 29, when asked if they were ready to sign, Taschereau answered that he had not engaged himself to answer within four days, while Panet admitted saying that in so far as he might be able to understand the English in which the documents were written, he would strive to examine them within four days in order to decide whether he would sign or produce reasons to the contrary. He pleaded that the materials had been held four days by those who had signed, and that he and Taschereau needed additional time in which to make up their minds to sign or to furnish their objections. This request, along with another that the Montreal commissioners be asked to come to Quebec, was voted down, and it was decided that the report be given to Lord Dorchester the next day, June 30, by Chandler, Coffin, and Lawes. A further request that the two French commissioners be permitted to attach a dissenting petition to the majority report and that they be permitted to accompany the other three when they presented the report and their petition was likewise rejected.[75] Panet and Taschereau did, however, submit a paper of observations, dated June 30, stating their objections to having the report and the proceedings of the other four Quebec commissioners considered as representative of all nine of those who had been appointed.[76] Their specific objections will be considered after the principal conclusions of the other commissioners have been examined.

The report of the commissioners was accompanied by a general extract of the titles of the Jesuits' estates.[77] In answering the question as to what parts of the estates had fallen to the Crown, the general conclusion of the commissioners, as it appeared in the tabulation of the estates, was: "Le tout, tel qu'il nous paroit."[78] The commissioners admitted in the report that they had not fulfilled the part of the commission which called for the determination of whether there were any claims on the estates by heirs of private persons who had given parts of them. Two things remained to be done to fulfil the commission: (1) to notify those who might have claims upon the estates to indicate them in writing; and (2) to obtain, by due process of law, the information from the tenants which was needed for making a land roll. Therefore the commissioners proposed to insert an advertisement in the appropriate places so that all who were interested might be informed.[79]

The key question in the commission had been: "What are the parts or portions of the Jesuits' estates with which His Majesty is presently invested, and which he is able to give and to concede in the manner requested by Lord Amherst?" The commissioners found as to effective and actual possession, that from the Conquest until 1776 a part of the College of Quebec had been occupied by the provisions of the king, and that since then the troops garrisoned at Quebec had occupied the major part of the college as a barracks. Fathers de Glapion and Casot enjoyed the use of the rest of the college, and the church belonging to the Order. It was publicly known in the province that de Glapion and Casot had continued to receive the revenues from the mills and lands situated in the district of Quebec. It was also known that the income of a part of the fief of St. Gabriel and of the mill of Jeune-Lorette were received by Father

Girault, a Jesuit missionary maintained by the College of Quebec at the church and mission of Jeune-Lorette for the village of the Hurons. Father Well was occupying part of the house at Montreal, the other part being used by the government for a civil prison. Well was still receiving the revenues from the mills and lands situated in the district of Montreal.

In answer to the part of the question concerning what might be given to Lord Amherst, the commissioners reported that they were unable to say, until opportunity had been given to all possible claimants to present their claims against the estates. They concluded, however, that there was no doubt that the king, because of the conquest of the country, had rights of sovereignty over all the estates of the Jesuits, as well as over those of his Canadian subjects.[80]

The objections of Panet and Taschereau must now be considered. In their written observations to the Governor, they set forth nine objections to the report which had been submitted without their signatures. The first was that the report did not answer fully the four questions which the Council had posed by its order of April 22. The second was that the four commissioners who had signed had not proceeded in due form of law, according to the commission. Their third objection was against the statement in the report that all the estates might be legally given and granted to Lord Amherst. Panet and Taschereau protested that this point was "extremely delicate and of great importance to His Majesty's loyal Subjects in this province," and had never yet been officially proposed or debated at any meeting to which they and the commissioners at Montreal had been called.[81] The two French commissioners objected, fourthly, that the commission had not adequately ascertained the nature and quality of the Jesuits' estates, it having been impossible for them to make a land roll because of their failure to obtain a proclamation to enable them to get the required information. Their fifth objection was that the words in the schedule establishing that no claims had been made to the commissioners by the heirs of the donors were added only the day before: "because neither the commission nor any advertisement for that purpose had been published." The merits of that point, they maintained, had never been discussed in any meeting at which they and the Montreal commissioners were present. Only the day before the report was submitted, there had been added to the schedule the mention of a letter from Pierre Panet of April 17, 1789, giving notice of a claim, which letter they never saw among the papers of the commission or elsewhere. Furthermore, the four commissioners, though well aware of the petition and memorial of the citizens of Quebec presented to the Governor on November 19, 1787, had paid no attention, in their report or in their schedule, to that claim.

Panet and Taschereau entered a sixth objection to the effect that the commissioners had not really determined whether there had been alienations or exchanges of the estates after the Conquest, though the report did include a statement of such as had been made under French rule. It was pointed out in a seventh objection that the Order-in-Council of August 18, 1786, had never come to the official knowledge of the commissioners, although it was mentioned in the endorsement on the back of their commission. The eighth objection of the dissenters was that the report and schedules purported to establish that all the Jesuits' estates had fallen to the king, without having officially shown the proofs or discovered the nature of the claims known to have been made previously by the Jesuits themselves, and without reference to the fact, publicly known, that the Jesuits still possessed all the lands of which the schedules made mention. They had voluntarily exhibited the titles of these lands to

Scott and Taschereau, alleging that these were the titles of their property, and that they were in peaceable, effective, and actual possession. The two French commissioners further observed that by different judgments of the courts of justice in the province the Jesuits had been maintained in their rights, and that they continued to possess all their properties, except a part of the College of Quebec now occupied for the king's provision store and barracks for part of the garrison.

Finally, Panet and Taschereau noted that they had offered to submit their dissenting views with the report and schedules, but had been refused the liberty to do so. They asked for an authentic copy of all the various materials which had been submitted to Dorchester and suggested the necessity of ordering the president (Chandler) to call a meeting of the nine commissioners in order to draw up a true and just report, whether of a provisional or a final nature, to present officially to the Governor.[82] It will be noticed from all the foregoing observations that the basis of the difficulty concerning the status of the estates seems to have been the fact that there had never been an official, legal entry into possession of them by the Crown, and the consequent assumption that the Jesuits, who were permitted to enjoy the fruits of the estates by an act of generosity on the part of the king, were in real and full possession of the estates.

The law officers of the province, Gray and Williams,[83] in their report of May 30, 1790, considered all the materials submitted by the commissioners to the Governor, along with the dissenting observations of Panet and Taschereau. Before noting their conclusions on the report, it would be well to observe their answers to the objections of the two French commissioners. It appeared to the law officers that the commissioners' report contained the best possible answer to the four questions raised by the Council in April, 1789. Gray and Williams could see nothing contrary to law in the proceedings of the commissioners and no reason for doubting that the estates had been vested in the king, and that he had the legal right to grant them as he wished. Concerning the claims of the petitioners of November, 1787, they reported that, having compared the citizens' petition and the supporting memorial with the titles of the several estates, they did not find any just, legal, or well-founded ground to support the petitioners' claims. The law officers concluded that it

... no where appears that these Estates were given to or accepted by the Jesuits for uses and upon trusts that can Support any Claim whatever, either by the Heirs of the Donors or the Inhabitants of the Province; The great object in the Several Grants to the Jesuits in the last Century seems to have been the Conversion of the Savages to Christianity. Most of them are in consideration of Past services in that way, and in the great use they had been of in establishing the Colony. None of the Grants impose any conditions that can give rise to a claim from any quarter at this day [.] [O]n the contrary some of the Titles are anxiously explicit in freeing them from burdens that never existed or were meant to be imposed; and the General Maxim of their Institution alluded to in one of the Title Deeds of the Estate and Seigniory of Notre Dame des Anges, shews how different were the Ideas regarding them of these days and those now maintained. ....[84]

The objection that the report and the schedules did not establish the nature and quality of the lands, the law officers admitted, might in some degree be well founded, as the nature and quality of the soil had not been particularly adverted to by the commissioners. In answer to the objection that potential claimants against the estates had not had ample notice of the proceedings, Gray and Williams observed that "nothing could be better known throughout the province than the proceedings respecting the Jesuits' Estates," which was fully proved by the petition of the citizens of November, 1787, by the research continually being made by the commissioners themselves, by the proceedings of the Council upon the business, and by other circumstances of public knowledge. The claim of Pierre Panet could hardly come within the sphere of inquiry, since it was a mortgage on one of the estates for money lent, and not a claim by the heir of any donor.

The law officers were convinced that since the Conquest the Jesuits had not alienated, nor could they legally alienate, any part of the estates. In support of this conviction they cited the objections of Panet and Taschereau to the effect that it was publicly known that the Jesuits themselves were still in possession of the whole of their estates and had maintained their rights except in part of the college. The two French commissioners were then accused of inconsistency, if not contradiction, for having raised the question of alienations since the Conquest when they had insisted that the Jesuits were in possession of all the estates.[85]

The Attorney- and Solicitor-General did not know whether Panet and Taschereau had had official knowledge of the Order-in-Council of August 18, 1786, or what they meant to infer from the want of such knowledge. The commission was their direction. As to the eighth objection, concerning the continued possession of all the estates by the Jesuits, the law officers did not understand the objection raised unless it was that Panet and Taschereau meant to find fault with the style of the commission and its denial of the existence of the Jesuits as a body. That idea the other commissioners had very properly held throughout their proceedings and in their report and the accompanying schedules. It appeared to the Attorney- and Solicitor-General that the two French commissioners seemed to consider the Jesuits' continued possession of the estates, by the grace of the king, as evidence of the civil and political existence of the Order. Neither that, however, nor any other circumstance which had come to the knowledge of the law officers, would warrant such a conclusion.[86]

As to the dissenters' complaint concerning the refusal of the other four commissioners to annex their written observations to the report, the refusal of the French commissioners might perhaps be accounted for by a review of the nature and tone of the observations. The law officers were silent on this objection, however, because of the lack of information from the commissioners as to their particular reasons for such conduct.[87]

It is now appropriate to ask what the conclusions of the law officers were on the report of the commission as a whole. They agreed with the commissioners that the seigniories were vested in the Crown and might consequently be legally granted to Lord Amherst, his heirs and assigns, subject to the conditions of the Order-in-Council.[88] The law officers remarked that though a great deal was said by Panet and Taschereau regarding the Montreal commissioners, there was no countenance given by the latter to the objections of the former, nor did it appear from the commission that all nine commissioners must necessarily have met together and reported upon the business of the commission, since any three were competent for that purpose. A report of so great a majority as four out of six appeared to the Attorney- and Solicitor-General to be reasonably sufficient and decisive, especially in a case where information alone had been sought.[89]

It was the opinion of the law officers that any legitimate claims upon the estates might be made *after* the grant to Amherst had taken place. But it was also their opinion that there could be no individual claimants to the lands and estates which they had considered. The claim of the petitioning citizens of Quebec, however proper for the Governor's consideration and the grace of the Crown, could not be considered as a legal claim which might interfere with the right of the king to dispose of the estates as might seem fit. The Jesuits had held their estates in the province on the same basis as they held estates in France. Upon the basis of the proceedings in France and the judicial acts of tribunals in that country, the estates in Quebec would have fallen naturally to the king and have been subject to his unlimited disposal. Moreover, the Crown's rights were assured by the suppression of the Order by the Pope. As derelict or vacant estates, the king had become vested in them by the clearest of titles—if the right of conquest alone was not sufficient.[90]

The Attorney- and Solicitor-General disagreed with the special committee of the Council, which had reported on October 21, 1788, that a law or ordinance of the provincial legislators was necessary to carry out the royal instructions for the suppression of the Jesuits and the annexation of their estates, as well as the Order-in-Council providing for a grant of the estates to Amherst. The ground upon which the committee had adopted this opinion was the continued possession of the estates by the Jesuits. The law officers argued, however, that nothing had been done or countenanced by the government to change the footing upon which the Jesuits of Canada stood at the time of the Conquest or since. It was true that they had been permitted to remain in possession of the estates and that Governor Haldimand, in 1781, had received from them an *aveu et dénombrement* of the estates which they possessed in the province,[91] but there was an express understanding that such reception should not injure the rights of the Crown.[92] Neither continued possession, supported by the indulgence of the Crown, nor the act of submitting an *aveu et dénombrement* could be considered as approbative or confirmative acts.[93]

Gray and Williams concluded that a law was not needed to obtain possession of the estates "long fallen to and vested in His Majesty by every rule of Public or private, Civil or National Law and practice." It would be the Governor's business to make a grant to Amherst effective. If, prior to the grant, possession as well as title was thought necessary to be vested in the Crown, there was nothing to prevent if from being effected. Whatever the Governor's decision regarding the grant to be made or the parts to be reserved for public uses, the law officers could "entertain no doubt about carrying the wishes of Government into legal Execution under the present proceedings."[94]

In the final analysis, the law officers of the province held that the king's right to the estates rested not upon mere outright confiscation but upon the right of conquest, he having taken over what the French king would have taken had he remained in control over Canada, and upon the right of escheat, the land having fallen into his hands by virtue of the dissolution and suppression of the Order by the Pope. It occurs to the present-day observer that there would have been less confusion and misunderstanding concerning the estates had the suppression been far more public and had the representatives of the Crown formally taken legal possession of the estates and then exercised the magnanimity of the Crown towards the surviving members of the Order.

Though the Order-in-Council of August 18, 1786, had stipulated that upon return of information by the commissioners, the Governor was to cause a proper grant to be made to Amherst, reserving certain parts of the estates for public uses, Dorchester did not do this. Instead, on November 10, 1790, he sent all the relevant material concerning the estates to the home government, including a plan of the surveyor-general, which indicated that the estates exceeded by some 664,799 *arpents* the amount of land indicated in the commissioners' report.[95] Dorchester's reason for not complying with the Order-in-Council may be inferred from his covering letter. He pointed out that the prevailing sentiment in the country was that the Jesuits' estates ought not to be diverted from public uses. There were different opinions on these uses, he noted, but the general wish was that they might be applied to the great object of education. Some advocated that the estates be used to support religious instruction and missionaries among the Indians, and that their management be placed in the hands of the Roman Church. Others argued that they be used for various purposes of the Church of England. But the most enlightened wished to see such parts as were not wanted by the government appropriated for the support of a university for teaching the liberal arts and sciences on a plan that would avoid every occasion for religious disputes by the exclusion of all theological tuition.[96]

Dorchester himself thought that the buildings, gardens, and grounds occupied by the Jesuits in the towns of Quebec, Montreal, and Three Rivers should be reserved in the hands of the Crown for public uses. The churches or chapels of the Order at Quebec and Montreal, with a portion of their grounds in the town of Three Rivers, he thought, should be set apart for Protestant worship. The revenues of the estates should be applied to compensate the Crown for its support of the surviving members of the Society and for the maintenance of the necessary Roman Catholic missionaries among the Indians of the province of Quebec and in Nova Scotia.[97]

Dorchester reminded the home authorities that a part of the Jesuits' college at Quebec had, since the Conquest, been used for barracks, and another as a court-house for the Common Pleas jurisdiction and as a place of worship for the Protestants of the Church of Scotland. A part of the Jesuits' building at Montreal had served for a considerable time as the common jail of the district. An adjacent unfinished chapel, which had been used as a magazine, had recently been equipped and used by the Protestants of the Church of England for worship. The remainder of their buildings in both towns, with the whole of the estates, he reported, continued in the possession of the surviving members of the Order. It was his opinion that the buildings of the Jesuits at Montreal appeared to be suitable for the residence of the governor-general (he was anticipating the establishment of a general government for the British North American colonies under a governor-general) because that town enjoyed a central location with regard to the immense country in the West and communication with the United States. With this in mind, he thought that it would be proper to reserve a portion of the unsettled lands of the Jesuits in the country, to be exchanged for lands in the vicinity of Montreal which would remain inalienably attached to the king's domain, for the use of the governor-general, with a similar reservation near the town of Quebec for the use of the lieutenant-governor of Lower Canada.[98]

Dorchester's letter brought the second phase in the prosecution of Amherst's claims to the Jesuits' estates to a close. When the Governor failed to issue the grant under the provincial seal, Amherst petitioned the Crown once again but he was destined to get no satisfaction during the remainder of his life. In the meantime, Dorchester and his successors were to be subjected to a mounting pressure in the colony to prevent the grant and to secure the revenues of the estates for the public use of the Canadian people. In the next chapter it will be necessary to get a glimpse of certain developments which had been taking place concurrently with the closing stages of the investigation required by the Order-in-Council of August 18, 1786.

CHAPTER FOUR

THE AMHERST CLAIMS: PROVINCIAL MANŒUVRES

At the end of 1764 there were only sixteen Jesuit priests and five brothers in the province of Quebec.[1] Bishop Briand attempted to prolong the existence of the Order by ordaining three of the brothers. Jean-Joseph Casot and Jean-Baptiste Noël were ordained on December 20, 1766, and Alexis Maquet was ordained on September 11 of the following year. Unfortunately, Noël died prematurely in 1769 at the age of forty-one. Several other deaths ensued before the brief of suppression of 1773: P. Claude Godefroy Coquart, July 4, 1765; Frère Pierre Gournay, December, 1767; P. René-Pierre-Daniel Richer, January 17, 1770; and Jean-Baptiste St-Pé, July 8, 1770. One of the Illinois missionaries, P. Jean-Baptiste Aubert, returned to France in 1765. At the time of the suppression of the Order, therefore, there were only fourteen priests and one brother remaining.[2] During the period when the most serious deliberations regarding their estates were taking place, there remained only four of the Jesuits —de Glapion, Well, Girault, and Casot.[3]

In the last decade of the eighteenth century the provincial government gave more and more attention to the idea of using the Jesuits' estates for the purposes of education. What first aroused this public interest was the receipt, early in 1787, of the royal Order-in-Council of the previous August. Dorchester laid this document before the Quebec Council on May 31, 1787, and, at the same meeting, he appointed a committee of the Council to report on education in the province. It was to consist of Chief Justice William Smith, chairman, and eight other members, equally divided between old and new subjects—Thomas Dunn, Adam Mabane, Henry Caldwell, William Grant, J. G. Chaussegros de Léry, Paul Roc de St. Ours, François Baby, and (Jean Baptiste?) Lecompte Dupré.[4]

Two years and a half elapsed before the committee got to work on its assigned task. Smith was first engrossed by a sweeping investigation into the administration of justice in the province which the Governor had just ordered him to conduct;[5] and then he wisely waited for the political storm over this investigation to subside before he called the committee together. While waiting, however, he was working on the problem himself, with results that appeared at the first meeting of the committee on November 26, 1789. He then disclosed a rather comprehensive programme of investigation into the existing state of education, the causes of its imperfections, and possible remedies for its inadequacies. A Canadian lawyer, Jean Antoine Panet, had been detailed to solicit information, but, up to the time of the meeting of November 26, he had not reported. Baby was then appointed to confer with him and to assist in carrying out the inquiry.[6]

Smith, however, had himself prepared an elaborate report which he submitted at this meeting and the committee adopted unanimously. It was a long document setting forth the sad state of education in the province and proposing a plan for free primary and secondary schools supported by local assessments and for a non-sectarian university endowed in part by some of the Jesuit estates.[7] According to a French-Canadian historian's account, some emigrant loyalists from New England conceived the idea of founding such a university in the province and of using the Jesuits' estates revenues to finance the institution, whose purpose would be to de-Catholicize the Canadians. Dorchester and the bishop of Quebec's coadjutor, Mgr Bailly, are said to have done their best to favour the loyalists' scheme.[8] The evidence, however, seems to indicate that the project of a non-sectarian university originated with, and was fostered by, Chief Justice Smith.[9] Smith had sought the advice of Mgr Hubert, bishop of Quebec,[10] and his coadjutor, and he presented the objections raised by the former of these ecclesiastics.

Hubert opposed the idea of what he called a "mixed university." He doubted whether there would be enough students to justify such a university, observing that it presupposed the existence of several colleges and that even France did not get the University of Paris until the twelfth century though the kingdom of France had existed since the fifth. But his chief objection seems to have been that the university was to be administered by persons without religious prejudices. If there were such persons, he said, they would have no religious or moral convictions. He went on to insist that the time had not yet come for the founding of a university in Quebec, and he urged that everything possible should be done to encourage the studies already being carried on in the College of Montreal and in the Seminary of Quebec. He also thought it essential that a third place of instruction be secured for the youth of the province by the restoration of the Jesuits' college in Quebec, which might in time be developed into a university. He suggested that the administration of the restored college be headed by de Glapion until his death, and then by such person as the bishop might appoint. He justified his proposal by the familiar argument that the Jesuits' estates should be dedicated to their original purpose.[11]

A month after the committee approved Smith's report, it was submitted to the whole Council, which thereupon ordered that it be printed in both languages and circulated throughout the country by the magistrates and the clergy.[12] Publication brought into the open a sharp conflict between the Bishop and his coadjutor. Charles François Bailly's election as coadjutor had been at the suggestion of Dorchester, with whom he was on very good terms. It had been against the better judgment of Briand, who had resigned the see in 1784, and of Bishop Hubert, both of whom, however, were unwilling to offend the Governor by refusing his suggestion, in view of his favourable treatment of the Catholic Church.[13] On April 5, 1790, Bailly sent the committee a letter in which he pretended to believe that Hubert's letter was a forgery, and, with biting sarcasm, he tore its arguments to pieces. He twitted the writer for having suggested that the ultimate administration of the Jesuits' estates should be under the authority of the bishop of Quebec or his appointee. He concluded with an enthusiastic endorsement of the idea of a university.[14]

Dorchester's report to the home government noted that Bailly's letter came too late to be inserted in the report of the committee of the Council. It was, however, included in a subsequent report of the committee, which advised that it be published in the same manner as that of Hubert. Dorchester deemed in unwise for the government to become the channel for airing religious disputes, and had reason, he reported, to believe that there was a much wider breach between Bailly and Hubert than could be occasioned by a diversity of opinion on the subject of education. He had tried to reconcile them without success, but he noted that the clergy in general seemed inclined to side with Hubert.[15]

Such behaviour on the part of the coadjutor could not go unnoticed by the Bishop, and Hubert consequently addressed himself to Lord Dorchester. Explaining that Bailly could not pretend that the episcopal letter was a forgery because he had seen it beforehand and therefore knew it was genuine, Hubert bitterly complained of the coadjutor's conduct, which he ascribed to jealousy at not having succeeded Bishop Briand in 1784.[16] Briand, who was still living, also wrote to Dorchester, upholding Hubert and severely criticizing Bailly.[17] In October, 1790, Bailly published his offending memoir and put it on sale in the libraries. Only on his death-bed in 1794 did he seek Hubert's pardon.[18]

After reviewing Hubert's letter against the immediate establishment of a university, the Chairman of the education committee, Smith, was inclined to agree that the project of a university comparable to those of Europe would be extravagant for the province of Quebec. He thought, however, that there should be a college or academy in which theology would not be part of the curriculum. He therefore proposed that a corporation which would include Protestant and Catholic clergymen be created to promote such an institution; the Crown would have the right of inspection, and the use of funds for sectarian purposes would be legally barred. He reminded the committee that the Bishop of Quebec was not alone in suggesting that a part of the Jesuits' estates could be used for financing an educational institution. Amherst had accepted the Crown's reservation of part of the estates for public purposes, and there was nothing to discourage the possibility of other Crown lands being used.[19]

The committee concluded its work with several resolutions. One stated that it would be advantageous to establish a collegiate institution for the teaching of the liberal arts and sciences and that instruction in theology should be left to the respective communions. Another called for the incorporation of a society to establish such a school, whose charter would provide against sectarian teaching. There was, however, no resolution concerning the Jesuits' college or their estates.[20]

At the beginning of December, 1789, Lord Dorchester was informed by members of the Quebec hierarchy that a petition to the Crown asking for the appropriation of the Jesuits' estates revenue for provincial uses was being projected. The remaining Jesuits were represented as being willing to surrender them for that purpose. Hubert and Bailly informed the Governor that they had been asked to support the petition, but, though strongly impressed with the justice of the claim, they had hesitated to give their support without having first consulted him. Lord Dorchester informed the clergymen that various petitions respecting the Jesuits' estates had already been presented, and that all the papers on the subject were in the hands of the Attorney- and Solicitor-General, with orders to make a digest of their contents. He refused to offer any opinion on the subject until the law officers had reported and until all claimants to the estates had had an opportunity to be heard. On the following morning, Dorchester suggested to Hubert that the clergy state the whole business fully to Attorney-General Gray and take his advice upon it.[21]

Hearing no more about the petition, the Governor supposed the idea had been dropped. Towards the end of December, however, he was privately informed that the Jesuits were on the verge of making a formal alienation of their estates to certain individuals in the town. He immediately inquired of Hubert concerning the truth of this information, and the Bishop confirmed it. Dorchester therefore directed the Attorney-General to take proper measures to secure the rights of the Crown and to inform the hierarchy that the manœuvre would be markedly disapproved. He was then assured that the design would be immediately abandoned. Antoine Panet, who seems to have been one of the chief agents in the project, declared to the Governor that it was intended to submit the whole plan to him for the king's approval.[22]

The Attorney-General informed Dorchester that he had unsuccessfully sought to obtain a copy of the proposed deed of cession. The Governor, in reporting the scheme to the home government, found it difficult to reconcile such conduct on the part of the clergy with their protestations of loyalty and submission. Certain individuals had been named to him as the persons who were to become trustees of the estates for the public. But "some of the better sort of the inhabitants were much displeased at the presumption of these gentlemen in setting themselves unauthorized as representatives of the public."[23]

A document, such as that reported by Lord Dorchester, was in fact drawn up on December 31, 1789, and signed by de Glapion. It was in the form of a letter addressed to Louis Germain Langlois, Jr. After briefly reviewing the history of the grants and concessions and noting that the four remaining Jesuits were no longer able to fulfil the stipulated obligations of instructing the savages and young Canadians, de Glapion renounced all ownership and possession of the Jesuits' properties and transferred them to the Canadian citizens, in order that, under the direction and authority of the bishop of Quebec, provision might be made for the instruction of the savages of Canada and of Canadian youth. This renunciation was followed by a statement of generous provisions for the maintenance and comfort of the four remaining Jesuits.[24] One historian of the Canadian Jesuits, Rochemonteix, states that de Glapion had consulted with Bishop Hubert and had received his prior approval of the letter of cession. Rochemonteix admits, however, that no document proves that the donation was accepted, and he points out that the donation could not have been legally or canonically executed.[25]

It will now be recalled that at the close of the extensive investigation in the province, Dorchester had not caused a grant of the estates to be given to Amherst, but had simply transmitted all the information concerning them to the home government. Consequently, in June, 1791, Amherst presented another petition, renewing his plea that the provincial authorities might be ordered to effect the long-delayed grant. This petition was referred to the Lords of Committee of the Privy Council for Trade and Foreign Plantations, but it does not appear to have been taken up during the life of Lord Amherst, who died in 1797.[26]

In the meantime, of course, a new constitution had been instituted for the governing of the country, which was then divided into Upper and Lower Canada, each with an elected assembly in addition to a legislative council. When the Lower Canadian Assembly met in 1793, public instruction was one of the first questions to be debated.[27] This consideration of the broader question of public education was probably sparked by the introduction of a petition on the subject.[28]

This petition of March 2, 1793, with some 250 signatures, was introduced into the Assembly by Philip Rocheblave. The petitioners reminded the House of the deplorable state of education for the past thirty years, and they called attention to educational facilities which had existed previously but were now being used for other purposes. They then reviewed the grants to the Jesuits for education and recounted that, since the dissolution of the Order, the Canadian Jesuits had generously offered all the property and funds of their college for the use of the public to which they really belonged. The province, however, had not been able to secure the use of these resources, apparently because the nature of the titles and the foundation of the college had been misrepresented in Europe. Thus the province had been deprived of public education since the Conquest, although it was encouraged in every other part of the British Empire. The petitioners were therefore convinced that the Crown desired to be informed of those titles and that it wished to reserve whatever property might be needed for public education. According to the petition, the revenues of all the Jesuits' estates were needed for education in the province and ought to be claimed for it. The argument, like that in the petition of November 19, 1787, was that the Jesuits had been merely trustees of the properties for the inhabitants of the province.[29]

The Assembly considered the petition at length.[30] In a committee of the whole House, William Grant proposed several resolutions which were defeated because the first of them read: "That the estates of Corporate Bodies created and endowed by the Crown, upon their dissolution revert to the Crown, and are subject to His Majesty's disposition agreeable to Royal prerogative."[31] Such a forthright recognition of the Crown's rights to the properties of the suppressed Jesuits was unacceptable to the majority of the Assembly who were inclined to the view that the estates properly belonged to the Canadian inhabitants, the Jesuits having been mere trustees. The other resolutions called attention to the fact that the Order would soon be extinct in the province and that it was the duty of the Assembly to ask the Crown for the use of the estates for education. The vote against Grant's proposals was thirty-two to one.[32]

After the defeat of Grant's resolutions, it was proposed that an investigating committee of nine members be appointed to compare the actual titles of the estates with the references to them in the petition. This proposal was likewise defeated on March 20, by a vote of twenty to eighteen.[33] Panet then moved for the appointment of a committee for the purpose of drafting an address to the Crown, in which the educational needs of the province would be emphasized and the Crown would be asked to abandon all rights which it might have to the estates of the Jesuits after their death. In the course of the debate on this motion,[34] John Richardson moved an amendment which recognized implicitly the Crown's right to dispose of the estates.[35] Richardson's motion was carried by a vote of twenty-one to sixteen, despite the efforts of P. A. Debonne and Joseph Papineau to have it amended to include a recognition of the provincial claims to the revenues for the purpose of education. The amendments, which failed by very close vote, emphasized the original designation of the revenues for the education of youth.[36]

A committee was selected to draft a petition in accordance with Richardson's proposal.[37] A draft was introduced on April 3 and adopted April 11.[38] After expressing gratitude for the advantages and blessings of the British constitution and noting the deplorable state of education in the province, the petition proceeded:

In contemplating this subject, we have been naturally led to look forward to the reversion of the property now and heretofore possessed by the Jesuits in this Province, as capable of greatly contributing to so desirable an end.

We therefore most humbly beseech Your Majesty, to be graciously pleased, upon their extinction or demise, to order such measures, as to Your Majesty in Your Royal Wisdom and Justice shall seem meet, to secure and apply the same to the Education of Youth in this Province, by the re-establishment of a College therein: a purpose apparently congenial to the original intention of the

Donors, most benevolent in itself, and most essentially necessary for the promotion of Science and useful Knowledge.[39]

The House sought the concurrence of the Legislative Council in this petition.[40] and the Council referred it to a committee.[41] The upshot was a message to the Assembly that the Legislative Council had decided to submit a separate address on the subject of education.[42] A committee of the Council was appointed to draft such an address, and, upon their report, it was approved on April 22.[43] This address differed markedly from that of the Assembly in that there was no mention at all of the Jesuits' estates.[44] The petition of the Assembly was submitted to the king, along with the proceedings of the commissioners, which had been forwarded earlier.[45] The king referred the whole matter to the Privy Council, which did not report until April, 1799.[46]

Between 1793 and 1798 the question of the disposition of the Jesuits' estates does not appear to have figured in public affairs in the province. After the death of Jeffery, Lord Amherst, his nephew and heir, the second Lord Amherst,[47] petitioned the king on May 9, 1798, reviewing the history of proceedings to date and requesting that a grant might now be prepared for his benefit.[48] His petition was referred to a Privy Council committee, which recommended that the Crown make the grant but with the special reservation that when yearly profits of the estates should exceed £2,400 sterling, Lord Amherst should account to the Crown for the surplus, after having been allowed certain sums for settling, cultivating, and improving the estates and for the expenses incurred in securing the grant. It was recommended that the attorney- and solicitor-general prepare an appropriate grant, to be passed in the province, which would reserve to the Crown certain parts of the estates, as well as the surplus profits, for public uses. The report of the committee was approved on January 23, 1799, and an order was issued to the law officers accordingly. They prepared a draft of grant but pointed out that because the lands to be granted were in Lower Canada and because they lacked information regarding the tenures and a proper description of the estates, the provincial law officers might be more competent to prepare a proper grant. The Lords of the committee, to whom the report and draft of grant was referred, recommended that the draft be approved but suggested that before it was passed by the province, the governor should submit it to the provincial law officers for their consideration.[49]

An order-in-council to effect the recommendation of the committee of the Privy Council was made on April 12, 1799, and was forwarded to Governor Prescott on April 13, along with a draft of patent.[50] The order and the draft were submitted to the provincial law officers, who reported on November 15, raising certain objections. These were based mainly on the fact that the law officers in England had failed to understand many of the finer points of feudal tenure as practised in Canada.[51] One point was raised, however, which harked back to the petition of the inhabitants of Quebec of November 19, 1787. The draft contained a grant of all the lands possessed by the Jesuits at the cession in 1763, but an exception reserved

what the Governors of the Province have actually applied for erecting Hospitals, Barracks or for other public uses, and the Gardens, Yards, and other Grounds in the said Towns of Quebec, Three Rivers and Montreal, and their Suburbs respectively adjoining to the said Colleges, Chapels, and other Buildings or—*in any ways appertaining to them.*[52]

The law officers doubted if, by the law of Canada, the exception would operate against a prior and formal grant, and they observed that the exception itself was not clear.

C

If it was the king's intention to reserve from the grant all that property which in any way appertained to the College of Quebec, and if the petitions which had repeatedly claimed the whole of the Jesuits' estates for the college were well founded, the description of the property to be granted was wholly erroneous; if well founded in part, the description was erroneous to that extent and ought to be omitted.

Having raised an interesting problem, the law officers were obliged to say: "On these points, however, we are respectfully silent as we conceive that we are not called upon for any opinion beyond the form of the proposed Letters Patent." They warned, nevertheless, that the exception ought to be more explicit. If it was the king's intention to reserve certain parts of the estates for educational purposes, it would be neccessary to ascertain more precisely what parts were to be so reserved before the grant to Lord Amherst was made.[53]

Immediately upon receipt of this report of the provincial law officers, Lieutenant-Governor Milnes asked them to prepare a statement of the claims of the province to the Jesuits' estates and the steps which had been taken to support these claims. The law officers were to specify what property had been claimed as appropriated in any manner to public purposes.[54]

The attorney-general reported again on November 28. He pointed out that property possessed by the Jesuits at the time of the Conquest had been acquired by grants from the kings of France, by grants from the Company of New France, by gifts or donations from individuals, and by purchase. The first claim of the province was to the whole of this property, however acquired. If this could not be supported, then the claim was to those parts of it which were acquired by purchase, or by other means, for the purpose of education. The vow by which the Jesuits dedicated themselves to the instruction of youth was urged to be a sufficient explanation of the intention not only of the Jesuits themselves but also of every donor, whether public or private, to dedicate all the properties to the purpose of education. It had been further argued that the Jesuits, having vowed perpetual poverty, were able to hold property only in trust for others, and were by their constitution declared to hold all property whatever in special trust for the uses of their several schools and colleges.[55]

The second claim of the province was to all parts of the Jesuits' properties which were acquired by purchase or had been destined in any manner for education. To support this claim, it was asserted that the Jesuits had erected a college to enable them to fulfil their educational objectives. This college, it was claimed, was built in great measure from the voluntary contribution of the inhabitants of Canada, numerous grants and gifts of real property having been made for its support, many of them before the college had been actually built.[56]

Replying to the question of what property had been appropriated in any manner to public purposes, the attorney-general said that, excepting a few acres at Tadoussac given for the erection of a church and parsonage, he did not know of any Jesuit property that had been originally appropriated to any other public service than education. To substantiate this assertion, he included a table showing the Jesuits' estates which had been claimed by the province as property especially appropriated to the purposes of education, how they were acquired, the quantity and location of each, and the grounds on which the claim was founded.[57]

The attorney-general reviewed the history of the suppression of the Jesuits in France to show that even though the dissolution in that country had been very arbitrary, provision *had* been made to retain the Jesuit colleges and their attendant properties for the instruction of youth. The French king had specifically exempted from the Society's debts all property appropriated for education.[58]

The attorney-general noted that a number of the grants had been made for the instruction of savages. Broadly interpreted, however, the grants were for the education of the native youth of the country, and the present Canadian youth were equally natives with the Indians. From this interpretation it followed that the Canadians ought to participate in the revenues and profits from the property particularly granted for the use of the savages. If such a broad interpretation was not permitted, there were enough Indians remaining to justify the retention of the estates for their education. Some of the properties had been purchased by the Jesuits specifically for the support of the college. Since the Jesuits had declared by their constitution that whatever they acquired was in trust for education, it followed that even those acquisitions which had not been made specifically for the college were made and had been held by the Order to support education in Canada, and therefore might be claimed by the province.[59]

The attorney-general reported a current argument that the province ought to be compensated for the Imperial government's use of the college as a barracks. This compensation should come, he maintained, from the property of the Jesuits which had not been particularly appropriated to the purposes of education. It was also urged, according to this report, that whatever doubts might be entertained as to the other parts of the Jesuits' estates, it must be admitted that the college was unquestionably to be used solely for education.[60] It is obvious, as the attorney-general admitted in his conclusion, that this statement of the case for the province was taken from the various petitions which had preceded it, and from the arguments used in the Assembly in support of an address to the king.[61]

On December 5, 1799, Father Jean-Joseph Casot, the only surviving Jesuit in the province, addressed a memorial to the Lieutenant-Governor, asking permission to surrender to the Crown the actual possession of the estates and property of the Jesuits' college and expressing the hope that the Lieutenant-Governor would provide for the fulfilment of the pious wishes of its founders.[62] The memorial was referred to the attorney-general who promptly reported his opinion that it would be necessary to make an actual entry into every part of the Jesuits' estates in order to make the king's possession of them publicly known. For this purpose three special commissions should be issued, to one person or more, in each of the districts of Quebec, Montreal and Three Rivers. The attorney-general thought it would also be advisable to issue a proclamation in support of the commissions.[63]

On December 24 all the documents relating to the proposed grant to Lord Amherst since the Order-in-Council of April 12 were brought to the attention of a committee of the Executive Council.[64] Deliberation on these documents was postponed until January 21, 1800. On examining the documents, the committee advised that the passing of the grant be suspended until all the documents had been transferred to the home government. They did not foresee any problem in accepting the offer made by Father Casot and taking the Jesuits' estates into the actual possession of the Crown. Though they concurred with the attorney-general's report of December 7, they were not convinced of the necessity of issuing a proclamation. If, however, a proclamation was deemed expedient, they thought it advisable to allay all suspicions by indicating that it was adopted as a result of the voluntary offer by Father Casot. The committee concluded with a suggestion of how the surplus revenues of the estates might be secured to the province.[65]

At the end of January, Milnes transmitted all the various documents, including the report of the Executive Council, to the Duke of Portland. In his accompanying letter, Milnes observed that he had purposely avoided asking the Executive Council for any opinion on the policy of the intended grant. Individually, he reported, the members of the Council had expressed their opinion that it would be a most unpopular measure, and he, too, feared that when the grant was actually passed, it would cause very great dissatisfaction throughout the province. He then reviewed the history of the claims of the province, as the provincial law officers had done, noting that had the colony remained under French rule, provision had been made to preserve the properties for education, and that the inhabitants appeared to expect that an equal attention to their interests should be shown by the British government.[66]

Milnes appears to have become thoroughly convinced that the estates should be devoted to education in the province. He dwelt upon the need of giving every possible encouragement to an establishment in the province for higher education, calling attention to the fact that many families were forced to send their children to colleges in the United States because there was no college in the province, the ill effects of which, he remarked, were very obvious. A solution, thought the Lieutenant-Governor, would be to give Amherst only part of the estates and to reserve the remainder for such public purposes as the Crown might direct. Milnes concluded by announcing that actual possession of the estates would be attained, provision would be made for the sole surviving Jesuit, and the rents would be allowed to accumulate pending provision for their disposal by the Crown.[67]

Shortly afterwards, Milnes wrote again to the Duke of Portland, informing him that he had had an opportunity on a trip to Montreal and Three Rivers to learn more about the actual value of the Jesuits' estates, and that he now had reason to believe that the whole of them could not, for a considerable time, be made to produce more than £2,400 a year plus an amount equal to the expenses incurred by Lord Amherst. He felt that this information would eliminate the proposal he had made earlier to divide the estates—he had believed them to be much more capable of immediate improvement than they actually were.[68]

Once again the Assembly took up the provincial claims to the estates. On March 12 Joseph Planté moved that the House resolve itself into a committee of the whole to consider the most proper means of obtaining information concerning the rights of the province to the College of Quebec and its estates. John Young, a member of the Executive Council, rose in his place and said that he was authorized by the Lieutenant-Governor to inform the House that he, upon the advice of the Executive Council, had given orders to take possession of the Jesuits' estates for the Crown. On March 14 the House went into a committee of the whole,[69] which, on the following day, recommended that an address be sent to the Lieutenant-Governor asking for all available information on the estates. This recommendation was adopted by a vote of fifteen to eight, and a committee was appointed to present the address.[70]

Milnes's reply, reported on March 18, stated that the whole proceedings under the commission of December 29, 1787, and the Assembly's petition of April 11, 1793, had been submitted to the king; that the king had referred the matter to the Privy Council, whose recommendations, and an order-in-council thereon, had been sent to the provincial government in April, 1799, and that, in consequence of this action by the home government, commissions had been issued to take possession of all the estates for the Crown. Milnes also said:

After reflecting on these circumstances, should the House of Assembly continue to deem it advisable to persist in their proposed investigation, I shall comply with their request, to allow them access to those Papers which have already been made public, and shall in that case give orders that all persons duly authorized by the House of Assembly, be at liberty to take Copies of all Titles, Documents, Reports, Papers, and all Proceedings under the Commission mentioned, which were returned into the Council Office, on or before the 25th of August, 1790.

But, after the information I have now given, the House of Assembly will certainly deem it incumbent on them to consider whether it is consistent with that respect which they have hitherto uniformly manifested towards their Sovereign, to reiterate any application on the subject.[71]

When the House took the Lieutenant-Governor's answer into consideration on March 21, William Grant proposed an address to the king, reviewing the history of the estates under British rule and the deplorable state of education in the province, and requesting that the estates, if not already disposed of, be appropriated to the purpose of education in Lower Canada. If the estates were already alienated, the king would be asked to make other provision for education—the surest means of obtaining the devotion of the inhabitants to the British constitution. Planté moved, and Papineau seconded, an amendment to substitute the following for Grant's proposal: "This House ought to postpone to a future time the enquiry into the Rights and Pretensions which This Province may have upon the College of Quebec and the Estates dependant [sic] thereon." The amendment was adopted by a vote of eleven to three on April 22, and then the House passed it as a resolution.[72]

Milnes sent a copy of the Assembly's address of March 15 and his answer of March 18 to the Duke of Portland. According to his covering letter, he thought the Assembly would not do anything further regarding the estates except submit a petition to the Crown. However unpopular the measure might be, said Milnes, he now believed that the grant to Lord Amherst might be carried into effect without any further opposition from the Assembly. It appeared to him, however, that although the estates were not likely to produce more than £2,400 a year for a considerable time, a division of the property might still be worth considering. It might be to the advantage of Amherst to give him unconditional possession of a certain portion of the estates, reserving for the use of the Crown the parts most liable to litigation if they were diverted from the original object of the donations.[73]

Milnes, however, was not willing to see the estates granted to Amherst unless some provision was made for the needs of education in the province. He announced that the estates would be put in commission on April 15, the day fixed for the sheriffs to make their return. It was advisable, then, to defer the grant until he was able to transmit a more certain report from the commissioners as to the real value of the property. He warned the Duke that the want of the means of a liberal education was so severely felt that it would be very "grating" to the Canadians to see so large a property converted to other purposes, and that it would considerably lessen their dissatisfaction if measures were at the same time adopted for the establishment of a college. Some Crown lands and whatever might be reserved from the Jesuits' estates, he suggested, might be set aside for its endowment. He emphasized the need to encourage the English language throughout the province, it having made little or no progress among the Canadians—so little that there were but one or two English members in the House who spoke English there, because of the certainty of being unintelligible to the majority.[74]

On March 8 and 17, letters patent were issued to the respective sheriffs of the districts of Quebec, Montreal, and Three Rivers to take possession of the estates and the property that had belonged to the Jesuits.[75] Shortly after mid-March Father Casot, the last of the old Canadian Jesuits, died at Quebec, having willed his personal property and the church plate to the Catholic Church.[76] On May 21, a commission was issued for the management of the estates at last in the possession of the Crown.[77] Named as commissioners were Chief Justice Osgoode, Executive Councillors Baby and Dunn, Deputy Paymaster-General John Hale, and a Canadian lawyer, Berthelot Dartigny. The appointment was purely honorary, these gentlemen having accepted it without salary or other emolument. The selection of paid agents in the three districts was left to the commissioners. Milnes expressed the hope to the Duke of Portland that the commissioners would soon be enabled to form an accurate estimate of the value of the estates and recommended that, meanwhile, the grant to Lord Amherst be postponed.[78]

In July, Portland wrote to Milnes that his letters of January 31, February 13, and April 5, and accompanying documents, had been submitted to the Privy Council and that he would communicate the result as soon as possible. The Duke also approved the preparatory measures Milnes had taken and agreed with Milnes's views on the need for educational facilities in the province. The Lieutenant-Governor was authorized to appropriate sums from the provincial revenues to pay the salaries of masters of free schools to be established for teaching the English language. One or two schools for higher learning, comparable to the English public schools, might also be established for the encouragement of the study of classical languages. It was thought that the accomplishment of that much would be sufficient for the present, although in due time foundations of a more comprehensive nature would be needed for the promotion of religious and moral training and for the study of the arts and sciences. Milnes was directed to consult the members of the Executive Council and then to report to the home government in what manner and to what extent it would be proper to appropriate part of the Crown lands or revenues from them for the purpose of education.[79]

Early in 1801 Milnes forwarded the first report of the commissioners appointed to manage the Jesuits' estates. This report indicated that the annual revenue of the year 1781 had amounted to £1,245 5s. 4d., exclusive of the property situated in Quebec and Montreal, and that concessions since that time had increased the annual revenue to the sum of £1,358 13s. 4d. In Milnes's opinion, though the property was capable of great improvement under better management, and the unconceded lands amounted to more than 500,000 acres, the value of the estates, considering all the circumstances, would not warrant a division of the property as he had suggested earlier. He noted that the grants in general were twenty leagues in depth, but not more than one to two leagues in front (that is along the River). A great part of the estates extended back into mountainous country and, consequently, were not likely to be conceded for many years.[80]

The Lieutenant-Governor assured the Secretary of State that if the king decided to make the grant to Lord Amherst, the present moment was peculiarly favourable. The grant must always be considered as an unpopular act that would create much dissatisfaction, but he believed there would be infinitely less dissatisfaction now than at any former period. The announcement concerning the establishment of a suitable number of free schools had had "the happiest effect in setting aside all reference to the Jesuits Estates." The Assembly, he reported, instead of pursuing the subject of the Jesuits' estates, were now preparing a bill for the purpose of erecting schoolhouses in the different parishes and under the control of the executive government. Milnes thought that the buildings and town lots formerly belonging to the Jesuits in Quebec and Montreal, which were to be reserved for the use of the Crown, might be considered as more than an equivalent for the expense of establishing free schools.[81]

In April, 1801, the Privy Council informed the British attorney-general of the proceedings that had taken place in the province concerning the proposed grant to Lord Amherst. The attorney- and solicitor-general were directed to consider the original draft of the grant and the report of the law officers in Canada, and to report whether the proposed alterations and amendments should be adopted. If they concurred with the provincial law officer, the Privy Council wished to know whether a new draft would have to be prepared, or whether the governor might be told to have the alterations and amendments inserted in the instrument already prepared.[82]

In their reply, the law officers offered objections to the provision under which Amherst was to hold the lands and be made accountable for the surplus profits of the estates beyond £2,400 *per annum*. Such a provision, they thought, would make Lord Amherst a public accountant and would expose him and his sub-tenants to endless difficulties and perplexities. It would operate as a deterrent to the full improvement of the estates and consequently to the revenue to be derived from them for the Crown.[83] These objections led to another two years of delay.

Finally, early in 1803, the home government inquired of Milnes whether there would be any objection on the part of the province to an arrangement with Amherst whereby the seigniory of La Prairie de la Magdeleine would be vested in him upon the condition of his giving up all claims to every other part of the Jesuits' estates. Alternative parts of the estates were to be suggested, if there were objections to La Prairie.[84] Milnes replied that the seigniory of La Prairie was worth more than all the rest combined.[85] If it was the king's intention to use the Jesuits' estates revenues to assist the cause of provincial education, the other estates would not prove adequate for that purpose. Milnes expressed the hope that if the estates should become the property of Amherst, an established annual sum in lieu thereof might be appropriated by the Imperial government for the foundation of a public seminary to help meet the urgent educational needs of the province.[86]

In consequence of the report of the law officers, and, perhaps, of this communication from Lieutenant-Governor Milnes, the king sent the following message to the House of Commons on July 11, 1803, and a similar one to the House of Lords the following day:

His Majesty acquaints the House of Commons, That in consideration of the eminent Services of the late Jeffery Lord Amherst during his command in America, and particularly in the reduction of the Province of Canada, His Majesty was induced, subsequent to the War during which those Services were rendered, to direct that a Grant should be made to his Lordship, his Heirs and Successors, of a certain tract of Land in that Province; but that in consequence of difficulties arising from local circumstances, His Majesty's intentions have not been carried into effect. His Majesty has ordered the Proceedings relative to this subject to be laid before this House, and His Majesty relies with confidence on the justice and liberality of His faithful Commons, to make such compensation to the Representatives of the late Lord Amherst, as, under the circumstances of the case, shall appear to them to be adequate and proper.[87]

Parliament, as a result, voted a life pension to William Lord Amherst, thus terminating the Amherst claims to the Jesuits' estates in Canada.[88]

CHAPTER FIVE

AN ANALYSIS OF THE JESUITS' ESTATES

THOUGH THE PROTRACTED Amherst efforts to get the Jesuits' estates failed, they had initiated an investigation that succeeded by 1790 in bringing to light sufficient evidence to make possible the following comprehensive analysis. As early as 1626 the Society of Jesus obtained from the Duc de Ventadour, the viceroy of New France, its first grant of lands, the concession of Notre Dame des Anges near Quebec. From that time on, the Order received grants in all parts of the colony at frequent intervals, until, before the close of the French period, it had become by far the largest landholder in the country. At the time of the British Conquest it owned not less than a dozen estates with a total area of almost a million *arpents* (French acres)—about one-eighth of all the granted lands. Moreover, the Jesuits' estates included hundreds of thousands of *arpents* of the very choicest lands of the St. Lawrence valley, the most fertile and the most favourably located for settlement.[1]

The following list will serve to give a comparison of the holdings of the Jesuits with those of other ecclesiastical bodies:

Bishop and Seminary of Quebec	693,324 *arpents*
Sulpicians	250,191
Ursulines of Quebec	164,616
Les Soeurs Grises	42,336
General Hospital at Quebec	28,497
Ursulines of Three Rivers	30,909
Hôtel Dieu at Quebec	14,112
Récollets	945
General Hospital at Montreal	404
Total	1,225,334
Jesuits[2]	880,705
	2,106,039

The church had thus acquired in perpetuity the ownership of no less than 2,106,039 *arpents* of land in the colony, while laymen had received much less than 6,000,000. Thus the church controlled nearly two-sevenths of the granted lands of New France, of which the Society of Jesus had a large share.[3] The following pages will be devoted to an enumeration of the various grants which were made to the Jesuits, particular attention being given to the motives and conditions of these grants, which continued to be questioned throughout the Jesuits' estates controversy.

I. LANDS HELD IN FIEF AND SEIGNIORY

(1) *Notre Dame des Anges, commonly called Charlebourg*. The seigniory of Notre Dame des Anges was approximately one league in front, partly on the St. Lawrence

River and partly on the St. Charles River, by four leagues in depth, running back toward the mountains (see Map I, p. 62). The original grant, as already observed, was made in 1626 by the Duc de Ventadour as viceroy of New France. For some unknown reason, the Jesuits entered into possession of only a half a league in breadth by two leagues in length on July 26 of the same year.[4]

In 1627 the Company of New France, more commonly called the Company of One Hundred Associates, was organized, and, in the spring of 1627 Cardinal Richelieu, on behalf of the king, handed over to the new Company all the territories claimed by France in North America.[5] By the royal edict establishing the Company, all previous gifts and grants were revoked and the whole made over to the Company. Consequently, on January 15, 1637, the Company of New France re-granted to the Jesuits the fief of Notre Dame des Anges with only minor changes in the original grant by the Duc de Ventadour. The Order now entered into possession of the full amount of the grant.[6]

By a deed of concession of January 17, 1652, Jean de Lauzon, governor of New France, acting for the Company of New France, re-granted to the Jesuits the same lands in full property—en franc aleu[7]—with all seigniorial and feudal rights, including the right of holding high, middle, and inferior courts of justice, along with the right of fishing on the rivers opposite the grant to the exclusion of all other persons, and the grant of the meadows covered and uncovered by the tides. By letters patent of May 12, 1678, Notre Dame des Anges, with other possessions of the Jesuits, was confirmed to "the Reverend Fathers of the Company of Jesus of New France" by the French king, with licence to hold it in mortmain.[8]

The original title of Notre Dame des Anges did not express in what quality the grant was made, but the motives were expressed as follows:

... For these causes and reasons and in order that every attention may be given to the propagation of the Christian faith and Religion, among the Savages who have no idea of the true God, and that they may be received and embraced by them and for this holy and laudable purpose, that the Reverend Fathers of the said Community may be always ready to contribute thereunto etc. by sending to that Country for the said purpose a good number of their Fathers to teach, instruct, and Catechise, and in order the better to enable them so to do.[9]

The Duc de Ventadour imposed no conditions or considerations upon the Jesuits; they were to have full enjoyment of the property.[10]

In its grant of January 15, 1637, the Company of New France took note of the original grant, of its revocation at the time of the establishment of the Company, and of the request of the Jesuits for a re-grant. The Company indicated that it was making the re-grant because of this request and because it was well informed of the assistance which the inhabitants of the country of New France received from the fathers of the Company of Jesus who exposed themselves daily to perils to bring the savage peoples to a knowledge of the true God and to the practice of a civil life. Notre Dame des Anges was held of the Company without being subject to any due or service, except an acknowledgment of their being so held. A list of the tenants, of the lands possessed by them, and of their stock and improvements was to be submitted at the end of every twenty years. The Jesuits were further obligated to celebrate one Mass on the first Tuesday in December of every year. Certain reservations were made concerning future road-building rights and the possible expansion of the town of Quebec, which might necessitate the withdrawal of part of the grant in exchange for other property elsewhere.[11]

Governor Jean de Lauzon's re-grant explicitly recognized the Jesuits' services to

C*

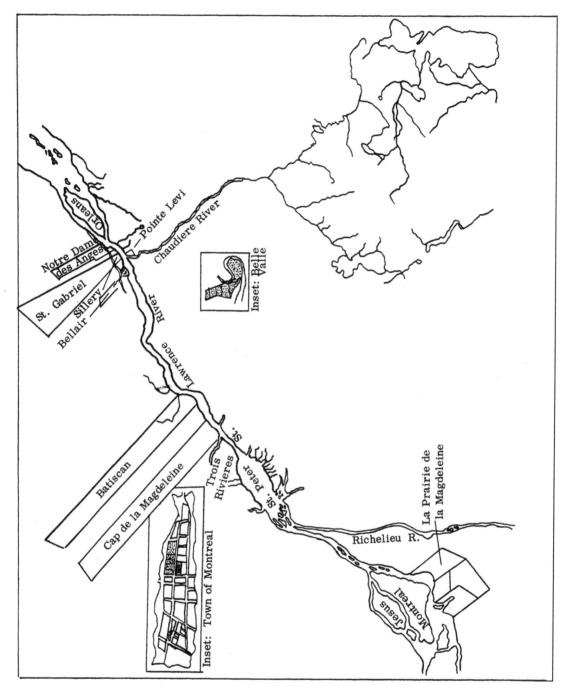

MAP I. "A Plan of the Province of Quebec Showing the Estates of the Late Order of the Jesuits." This map has been traced from an original, now in P.A.C., prepared in 1790 by Surveyor-General Samuel Holland.

both French and Indians and in the establishment of the colony. On May 12, 1678, Louis XIV amortized the fief and seigniory of Notre Dame des Anges, along with other grants made prior to that date. The letters patent indicate that this was done at the request of the Jesuits and that it was motivated by the Crown's desire to contribute, through them, to the establishment of the Catholic religion in Canada, and to share in their prayers for the king's prosperity and health and for the maintenance of the state. The confirmation of the right to hold in mortmain, free from all dues and services, was made on the condition that the lands (of which Notre Dame was only a part) should be settled and improved within four years from the date of the instrument, or in default thereof, that the grants should be void.[12]

A perusal of the motives and conditions of the grants of Notre Dame des Anges upholds the opinion of the provincial law officers, in their report of May 18, 1790, which was that

... The Motives or Causes inductive of the Grant, as well as the Special Terms in the recital of the last, and the express language of the whole shew, That the whole Society of Jesuits were the objects of the Grant. That it was given for services rendered; and that no trust was created, nor any uses proposed or limited, but those of the Institution of the Jesuits according to which alone they could accept thereof. ...[13]

The law officers concluded that the estate had therefore clearly fallen to the king, and might, as stated in their report, be lawfully granted by him.

(2) *St. Gabriel, commonly called the Two Lorettes.* The seigniory of St. Gabriel, commonly called Old and New Lorette, was supposedly a league and a half in front by ten in depth, located inland at a distance of a league and a half from the St. Lawrence River, and adjoining the rear of the seigniory of Sillery, which also belonged to the Jesuits (see Map I, p. 62). St. Gabriel was given originally to Sieur Robert Giffard by the Company of New France. Giffard received two leagues in front by ten in depth from the Company. He gave a half a league in front by ten in depth to the Nuns of the Hospital Hôtel Dieu of Quebec (Fief of St. Ignatius); the remainder, supposed to be one league and a half in front by ten leagues in depth, he gave to the Jesuits. It was later found to contain only one league in front, and since the lines separating it from the neighbouring fiefs were not parallel, it was found to be wider as it ran back. Its breadth at the depth of about two leagues and a quarter was one league and a half, and it continued to grow wider as it ran farther back. By an irrevocable deed, November 22, 1667, Robert Giffard and his wife gave the Jesuits the property in consideration of the great friendship between the Giffards and the Jesuits and because of good and agreeable services which the latter had rendered to the former. The deed imposed on the Jesuits the conditions of the grant made by the Company to Sieur Giffard, namely, fealty and homage at every change of possession, and other dues and services to which fiefs were subject by the Custom of Paris. Appeals from the seigniorial court were to be made directly to the *Parlement* or other sovereign courts to be established.[14] The provincial law officers, having surveyed the various title deeds, concluded that the seigniory of St. Gabriel appeared to be a pure gift to the Jesuits in New France, from motives of friendship and for services rendered, and seemed subject to no condition but those of the original grant to the donors. In their opinion, it might therefore certainly be given and granted by the British Crown.[15]

(3) *Sillery or Parish St. Foy.* The fief of Sillery, located on the north bank of the St. Lawrence River, was one league in front by approximately one league and a half in depth, and ran from the St. Lawrence to the fief of St. Gabriel, which bounded it

in the rear (see Map I, p. 62). Sillery was originally granted to baptized Indians under the supervision of the Jesuits, who had converted them to the Christian faith. The grant was made without derogating from prior grants of some parts of the estate to French inhabitants, which would still he held of the Christian captain of the Indians, as they were held before of the Company. It included all the seigniorial rights which the Company had possessed except the right of administering justice, which the Company reserved to be exercised by its officers at Quebec. The grant assured the exclusive right of fishing in the St. Lawrence along the front of their lands and the right to all the meadows, herbage, etc., along the shore, as well as to the land covered and uncovered by the tides. Public road rights alone were reserved. Sillery was to be held by the Indians *en franc aleu* without any due or service to the Company.[16]

By a grant of October 23, 1699, Sillery was given to the Jesuits on the basis of their petition, which stated that the savages had been obliged to abandon the fief because of the exhaustion of the soil and the supply of firewood. As a result of the petition, and in recognition of the great services which the Jesuits had rendered to the Indians at considerable cost to themselves, the seigniory was given to the Society ". . . with all the rights and privileges formerly conceded to the Savages, to hold the entire fief in true fief, depending only upon the King, with right of high, middle, and inferior justice, as they possess all the other lands which His Majesty had been pleased to accord them in this country. . . ."[17]

The law officers reported that Sillery appeared to have to have been granted *en franc aleu* to the Indians, with considerable privileges, and that it represented a more extended area than it had in 1790. In the grant to the Jesuits, the tenure was changed from a *franc aleu* to a fief, and therefore was subject to dues and services to which lands so held were liable, there being no clause of exemption, unless it might be understood from the words, "In the same manner as they possess the other lands granted to them by His Majesty in this country." This phrase, however, the law officers understood to refer to the conditions of the general title of establishment. The commissioners reported an ordinance issued by the Intendant, Jacques Raudot, in October, 1707, by which the *droit de haute justice* was suppressed and taken from the seigniory; there remained, therefore, only the right of middle and inferior justice. The law officers concluded that the motives for the grant were past services, and that there appeared to be no limitation of uses or conditions whatever imposed upon the Jesuits that could in any way prevent Sillery from being legally granted by the British Crown.[18]

(4) *Belair, commonly called Bonhomme Mountain.* The fief of Belair was one league and a half in front by approximately two leagues in depth. Located at the rear of the seigniory of Demaure or St. Augustin and running back towards the Jacques Cartier River (see Map I, p. 62), Belair was granted originally to William Bonhomme, subject to fealty and homage and the rights thereto annexed by the Custom of Paris. Such mines, ores, and minerals as might be found within the grant were to be reported to the Crown. The Crown reserved its rights to oak timber for shipbuilding and to construct necessary roads.[19]

The seigniory was purchased by the Jesuits in different parcels from some of the descendants of William Bonhomme and from others who had already purchased parts of it. By a deed of sale of August 28, 1710, the Jesuits purchased one-half of the seigniory from Nicholas, the eldest son of William Bonhomme, with all the seigniorial rights belonging to him as eldest son and heir. The deed of sale reserved six *arpents* in front by the whole depth of the seigniory, to be held as a *mesne* or *arrière* fief dependent upon the seigniory. By this purchase, the Jesuits received one-half of Belair, with the right of high, middle, and inferior justice, and all other rights and prerogatives enjoyed by the deceased William Bonhomme.

By a deed of sale of May 7, 1732, the Jesuits purchased one-half of the reserved *mesne* or *arrière* fief from Charles, the eldest son of Nicholas Bonhomme. This half (three *arpents* in front by the whole depth of the seigniory), with all its seigniorial rights, was to be enjoyed or disposed of as their own possession. The remainder of the *arrière* fief was purchased by the Jesuits as follows: one-fifth from Louise Bonhomme on May 24, 1732; two-fifths from Joseph Bonhomme on January 22, 1733; one-fifth from Francis Bisson (who had purchased it from Theresa Bonhomme) on May 31, 1738. The deeds conveyed the right to a full enjoyment of the properties by the Jesuits, with the right to dispose of them as they might wish.[20] It will be noticed that one-fifth of the remaining half of the *arrière* fief remains unaccounted for. No deed for this fifth was found by the commissioners in the archives of the Jesuits, but Casot, the manager of the temporal concerns of the Jesuits, assured them that one existed somewhere. The law officers concluded that it was immaterial to have it, since so long a quiet possession as the Jesuits had had of the fifth made title without deed.[21] With the absorption of the *arrière* fief, the Jesuits then had full possession of a half of Belair.

The other half of the fief was acquired by several purchases as follows: from Francis Stephen Cugnet by deed of sale of February 16, 1733; from Mary Josepha Baillie, daughter of Anne Bonhomme, by deed of sale of January 29, 1740; from six heirs, representing Catherine Bonhomme, daughter of William, by deed of May 7, 1740; and from John Petitclerc (who had purchased his portion from William Bonhomme) by deed of sale of February 1, 1743. The Jesuits received full and perpetual proprietary rights to these purchases with the freedom to enjoy or to dispose of the plots of land at their own pleasure.[22] The law officers concluded, concerning Belair, that as an acquisition by purchase there could be no doubt of the present right of the Crown to the seigniory, one-tenth of the *mesne* or *arrière* fief alone being unaccounted for. They noted that there did not appear to be any royal confirmation, or licence to hold in mortmain, for the acquisition; it stood, therefore, solely upon the edict for the establishment of the Jesuits of 1651. Letters patent of July of that year had (1) re-affirmed an annual grant of 5,000 *livres* to the Jesuits, (2) assured the Jesuits of exclusive fishing rights upon the lands purchased by them or granted to them, and (3) permitted them to make use of the present instrument to establish themselves in all the islands and in the mainland of New France and to possess lands and houses and other property for their subsistence upon the same footing as they did in the kingdom of France. Having been acquired prior to an edict of 1743, Belair was not affected by that law of restraint upon acquisitions by religious communities.[23]

(5) *Cap de la Magdeleine*. The seigniory of Cap de la Magdeleine was situated on the north side of the St. Lawrence and was two leagues in front (from the cape called Three Rivers, running down along the St. Lawrence to the seigniory of Champlain) by 20 leagues in depth (see Map I, p. 62). The Jesuits received it as an irrevocable gift from Jacques de la Ferté, abbot of St. Mary Magdeleine of Chateaudun and canon of the king's chapel in Paris, by deed of grant of March 20, 1651. It was accepted by Father Jerome Lalemant, superior of the colleges and houses of the Company of Jesus in New France, and Paul le Jeune, manager of temporal affairs of the missions of the Company in Canada, for the colleges and houses of the Society. The express

purpose of the gift was a desire to establish the Christian faith and to civilize and convert the savages, the donor taking into consideration the Jesuits' efforts on behalf of the Indians and seeking to provide them with further means of continuing their good work. The whole of the seigniory was to be possessed or disposed of as the Jesuits and their successors in New France thought proper for the benefit of the converted savages and in conformity to the rules of the Order.[24]

On February 9, 1676, at the request of Father Claude Dablon, Jacques Duchesneau, the intendant of New France, issued a deed of explanation and confirmation of the Jesuits' titles to Cap de la Magdeleine and Batiscan. This was considered necessary because the validity of the grant by the abbot was doubtful, both seigniories having been reunited to the king's domain. Duchesneau, subject to the king's pleasure, granted Cap de la Magdeleine and Batiscan to the Jesuits for the support of the College of Quebec, with fishing rights on the St. Lawrence River and around the islands and breakers lying along the front of the seigniories. The two properties were to be enjoyed by the college or its assigns as a fief, with every right of seigniory (including the right to hold high, middle, and inferior courts of justice, with appeals to the royal court of the town of Three Rivers until the king should otherwise order), and the Jesuits were allowed two years to obtain a licence to hold the seigniories in mortmain. This deed of explanation and confirmation was said to have been given by the Intendant because the property had been fully settled in front and a great way back by the care and at the expense of the college, and because of the great services which the Jesuits were rendering in the colony to both French and Indians. The grant was to be subject to fealty and homage to the king if not amortized within the two years given for that purpose.[25]

The provincial law officers questioned the validity of the Intendant's deed of explanation. In their opinion, the original deed of donation of 1651 clearly conveyed an estate under the same tenure as the donor himself held of the Company of New France, of which he was a member. The words "colleges and houses" therein mentioned were not only of themselves clearly descriptive of the body of Jesuits and their places of residence, but, from what went before as well as what followed in conclusion, there was no doubt that a free and unencumbered estate was meant to be transferred subject to no trust, use, or limitation but such as the Jesuits chose to apply under their own rules. The law officers questioned the authority of the Intendant to do what he had done, noting that in the amortization of the king of May 12, 1768, reference was made only to the original grant by de la Ferté. They concluded their analysis of the title deeds of this estate as follows:

. . . the explanation and reconcession containing the words, ["] To the Company of Jesus for the College of Quebec, ["] Seems but a Weak ground to Support a right in any Set of persons, to form a pretension to this Estate as an Endowment; For herein there are no uses mentioned, no trust created, and the words are more likely to import a conveyance to the College as the aggregate Body of Jesuits there established, which by their Institution is for the Whole Body and Subject to the controul of the General of the Order and the rules of the Institution, than to a foundation, which seems nowhere to be explained, but cursorily by an historian and which has neither charter, nor other Establishment to fix the Meaning of Such a Gift or Grant, as far as we are informed. We cannot therefore See any Solid reason to prevent this Estate from being given and Granted.[26]

(6) *Batiscan*. The seigniory of Batiscan was two leagues or thereabout in front upon the St. Lawrence by 20 leagues in depth, bounded on the north-east side by the seigniory of St. Mary, on the south-west side by the seigniory of Champlain, in front by the St.

Lawrence, and in the rear by lands not conceded (see Map I, p. 62). It was likewise granted to the Jesuits by Jacques de la Ferté by deed of donation of March 13, 1639, and was to be held as an absolute fief, with the right of holding high, middle, and inferior courts of justice. Batiscan might be fully possessed by the Jesuits, or transferred and applied at their discretion to the needs of the Indians or others who became Christians.

De la Ferté made the grant "of his good will and pleasure, for the love of God." It was subject to fealty and homage to the donor and his heirs, and the payment of a cross of silver of the value of sixty *sols* as an acknowledgment every twenty years, when the lands had been brought into cultivation. It has already been noted that Batiscan was included with Cap de la Magdeleine in Duchesneau's deed of explanation and confirmation of February 9, 1676, which, with reference to Batiscan, was subjected to the same criticisms by the provincial law officers in 1790. The original deed of grant of March 13, 1639, did not specify the depth of Batiscan, but the deed of explanation ascertained the depth of each of the two seigniories, Cap de la Magdeleine and Batiscan, to be 20 leagues.[27]

(7) *Island of St. Christopher.* This seigniory, containing about 80 *arpents*, was located in the middle of St. Maurice River, an eighth of a league from the mouth and the same distance from Cap de la Magdeleine. It also included the islands of Sauvaget and Claude David to the south, Boucher's Island to the north, and La Poterie to the east. The Island of St. Christopher was granted by Governor Jean de Lauzon on October 20, 1654, in recognition of the zeal and care of the missions of the Company of Jesus of New France and of the benefits to religion from their instruction and conversion of the savages. The island was given to the Jesuits subject to no charge or condition whatever, in *franche aumône*, to be held by them for ever, with power to concede to tenants who would be subject to *cens et rentes*.[28] The provincial law officers' report of 1790 concluded that St. Christopher appeared to be of very small value, the Jesuits having as yet received no benefit from it. It being held *en franche aumône*, nothing was due to the dominant seignior, as in other fiefs, upon mutation. It had been confirmed to the Jesuits by the king's letters patent of May 12, 1678, with licence to hold in mortmain.[29]

(8) *La Prairie de la Magdeleine.* This fief of two leagues in front by four in depth was on the St. Lawrence opposite Montreal (see Map I, p. 62). It was bounded on the north-east by the Barony of Longueuil and on the south-west by the seigniory of the Sault St. Louis. It also included several islands, Bocquet, Foquet, des Joncs, as well as the breakers and quarries along the two-league front. François de Lauzon, king's counsellor in the *parlement* of Bordeaux, deeded it on April 1, 1647, to the Jesuits at their request, in recognition of their assistance to the inhabitants of New France, and because of the donor's goodwill towards the members of the Order. The only conditions attached to the grant were that the Jesuits would send such persons as they might think proper to cultivate the lands, and that the donor should be a partaker of the benefit of their prayers and holy sacrifices.

On February 4, 1676, Duchesneau issued a deed of explanation and confirmation of the grant at the request of Father Claude Dablon, rector of the College of Quebec, supposedly because the grant of François de Lauzon was not explicit and the Jesuits feared they would be disturbed in the possession of the seigniory. Furthermore, it was stated by the Intendant that the seigniory had been settled entirely in front by the care and at the expense of the college, and that the remainder of the seigniory of

Sieur de Lauzon had been reunited to the king's domain, which raised some questions of exactly what had been granted to the Jesuits. The deed of explanation and confirmation was expressly in consideration of the great services which the Company of Jesus were rendering to the French and Indian inhabitants of the colony. This document was similar to that which Duchesneau issued for Cap de la Magdeleine and Batiscan on February 9 of the same year. As in the case of Batiscan, the college was not mentioned in the original deed nor did it include the islands above mentioned.[30]

Both the commissioners and the provincial law officers concluded that the grant was not made to the college but to the Order of the Company of Jesus. The law officers pointed out that no mention was made of Duchesneau's deed of confirmation and explanation in the king's letters patent of May 12, 1678, which amortized La Prairie. It should be observed that by the original grant, the lands, for want of a specification of their being held in fief and seigniory, would, under the original grant, be considered as held *en roture*. According to the Intendant's deed of explanation and confirmation, La Prairie was given to be enjoyed by the college or its beneficiaries in fief, with all rights of seigniory, including the right to high, middle, and inferior justice, with appeals to the royal justice in the town of Three Rivers. The commissioners reported a claim upon La Prairie by Pierre Panet for 20,000 *livres* by a type of mortgage called a *constitut*. The law officers were of the opinion that this claim, though it diminished the value of the estate, did not interfere with its conveyance. They concluded that the seigniory was granted for past services in order that the donor might be a partaker of the prayers and sacrifices of the Jesuits. No use or limitation was prescribed, and therefore it might be legally granted by the British Crown.[31]

(9) *Isle des Ruaux*. The seigniory of Isle des Ruaux was located in the St. Lawrence River, a little below the Island of Orleans, and it extended about half a league in length by eight *arpents* in breadth. The Company of New France gave Isle des Ruaux to the Jesuits by a deed of March 20, 1638, to be held by them and their successors in full property and seigniory. It was given in recognition of their services to the Indians and, specifically, to provide pasturage for the cattle which the Order needed for sustenance. The only condition imposed upon the Jesuits was that they should give acknowledgment of possession, together with a statement concerning the cultivation and improvement of the island, at the end of every twenty years. The Jesuits reported in their *aveu et dénombrement* of 1781 to General Haldimand that Isle des Ruaux was a dependency of the seigniory of Notre Dame des Anges. They had conceded it to the late Charles Guillimin, a member of the Superior Council of New France, for a rent of fifteen *livres* and a *cens* of two *deniers*. They reported, however, that the island had changed hands and that they did not know the present possessor because they had not been paid by him, nor, since the Conquest, had they received any *lods et ventes* at the various changes of ownership. The provincial law officers reported that the island was of very trifling value, having yielded nothing to the Jesuits for many years, that by their several *aveus* and *dénombrements* they had conceded it and made it dependent on the seigniory of Notre Dame des Anges, and that it was subject to nothing that could prevent its being legally granted by the British Crown.[32]

(10) *Pacherigny*. This diminutive seigniory was in the town of Three Rivers and consisted of four *perches* of land in front by eight in depth, and 20 square *toises* lying contiguous. It was bounded at the north-east side by St. Louis Street, on the south-west side by St. Anthony's Street, in front by the street that divided the fief from the enclosure or fortification of the town of Three Rivers, and in the rear by

Notre Dame Street. It was granted to the Jesuits by deed of concession of October 23, 1699, with the rights and privileges annexed to the seigniory of Sillery, both being included in the same deed. It had been previously held by an Indian captain, Charles Pacherigny, from about the middle of the seventeenth century.

Fief Pacherigny was given to the Jesuits because the Indian himself had held it under the tutelage of the Jesuits and they had remained in the enjoyment of the properties after his death. The grant recognized this fact, and the great spiritual and temporal assistance which the Society was rendering to the savages in their missions. It was given with the same title of fief and with the same rights and privileges as had been given in connection with Sillery, namely, to hold in true fief, depending only upon the king, with right of high, middle, and inferior justice.[33]

While Fief Pacherigny was granted in the same deed with Sillery, and upon the same terms, a royal confirmation of the grant by letter of May 6, 1702, mentioned only the grant of Sillery. In their *aveu et dénombrement* of 1781, however, the Jesuits stated that Pacherigny was also confirmed by that letter, perhaps because both Sillery and Pacherigny were included in the same original deed of grant. The provincial law officers concluded that whether or not it was confirmed by that letter, the letters patent of July, 1651, would have been sufficient to authorize their accepting the grant and enjoying the property upon its terms. The right of *haute justice* was taken from Fief Pacherigny by the same ordinance that took it from Sillery. In the opinion of the law officers, there was nothing to prevent Pacherigny from being granted by the Crown.[34]

(11) *Fief Near the Town of Three Rivers.* This fief consisted of 600 *arpents* near the town of Three Rivers and was granted by the Company of New France (in Paris) by deed of grant of February 15, 1634. This document explained the reasons for the grant as follows:

... the desire of firmly establishing the colony in New France causing us to look for those who can contribute thereto on their part, and remembering well the assistance which we have received in this worthy enterprise from the Reverend Fathers of the Company of Jesus, who still daily expose their persons to perils, in order to draw the peoples of the said New France to the knowledge of the true God, and the practice of a more civil life; for these causes and in order to give them a retreat near the habitations which we would establish in New France.[35]

According to the deed, the fief was to be enjoyed by the Jesuits for ever in full propriety and seigniory, subject to an *aveu et dénombrement* once only (that is, to be held in mortmain), upon the same terms as the king had granted the country of New France to the Company.

By deed of August 26, 1637, Father Paul le Jeune was put into real and actual possession of the 600 *arpents* in three separate parcels: one of 96 *arpents*; one of 500 *arpents*; and a final one of four *arpents* and eight *perches*. The commissioners reported that the measurement of the 500 *arpents* did not appear to have been exact, falling short of the quantity by about 25 *arpents*.[36]

There were two or three transfers and exchanges between the Jesuits and the inhabitants of Three Rivers involving the 600 (or rather, 575) *arpents* which had been conceded to the Jesuits, from which the Jesuits seem to have emerged with an equivalent amount of land. The amortization of May 12, 1678, is confusing, however, because the three articles pertaining to Three Rivers indicate a total of 600 plus *arpents*.[37] Article 22 of that instrument mentions 250 *arpents*; article 23 mentions 350; and then article 24 includes all the lands lying between these 350 *arpents* and a little river in the way leading up to St. Peter's lake, as having been given to them August 9, 1643.[38] Consequently, the commissioners' report mentioned this fief as consisting of 600 *arpents* and upwards. The provincial law officers noted the apparent confusion but did not succeed in clarifying it. The *aveu et dénombrement* which the Jesuits submitted in 1781 indicates that they regarded the fief as containing 575 *arpents*, although the language of this document is not very clear either. The law officers concluded that the whole of the lands involved in the grants in and near Three Rivers formed one seigniory and, having been given for services and without limitation as to uses, might lawfully be granted by the British Crown.[39]

II. LANDS HELD EN FRANC ALEU, EN ROTURE, AND EN ARRIERE FIEF

(1) *La Vacherie*. This freehold, *franc aleu roturier*, was located at the Quebec ferry where the boat passed over the River St. Charles and consisted of a point of land with one addition of 18 square *arpents* and another of 10 square *arpents*. These grants were included in the title deeds for the seigniory of Notre Dame des Anges and in the supplementary deeds of grant. By deed of gift of March 10, 1626, Henri de Lévy, Duc de Ventadour, granted the Jesuits a point of land, with the woods, meadows, etc., which was located opposite the Lairet River but on the other side of the St. Charles River, running up towards the Récollet Friary (later to become the General Hospital) on the one side and down towards the St. Lawrence on the other (see inset "Belle Valle" on Map I, p. 62).

This point of land was regranted by the Company of New France on January 15, 1637, and was described as located on the farther bank of the St. Charles River and as surrounded by this river on all sides except in one place where it was enclosed with a palisade. The Jesuits were granted this land on July 24, 1646, with an additional grant of 18 square *arpents* adjoining the point, which was to make up a deficiency of 12 *arpents* which they were to have had in Quebec by a deed of grant of March 18, 1637. By deed of January 17, 1652, Governor Jean de Lauzon granted the same lands to the Jesuits with the same descriptions contained in the earlier title deeds. On August 29, 1667, the Jesuits acquired an additional 10 *arpents* by an exchange with the Nuns of the Hospital of Quebec. At the time the commissioners were making their investigation of the estates, the three pieces of land were joined together and consisted of the farm called La Vacherie, held by David Lynd on lease from the Order, and the building lots on both sides of the road leading from Quebec to the General Hospital. The entire freehold included approximately 73 *arpents*.[40]

The first parcel of land was granted with the same motives as those stated for the seigniory of Notre Dame des Anges and, like that of the seigniory, was subject to no charge, due, or service. The second parcel was granted to make up a deficiency of a lot given in the town of Quebec for the college and was also free of any charge, duty, or service. The third, acquired by exchange and held in pure *roture*, was liable to *cens et rentes* and other seigniorial dues upon mutation. The law officers concluded that there did not appear to be any obstacle, either from the motives of the grants of the first two parcels or from the particular uses specified therein, to prevent a royal grant of La Vacherie. However, it would seem that since the grant of the 18 *arpents* had been made to replace a deficiency of a grant for building a college in the town of Quebec, these should be reserved for such a purpose. Yet the grant expressly gave this land free of any reservation as to uses.[41]

(2) *The freehold* franc aleu roturier *in the Parish of St. Nicholas* across the St.

Lawrence from Quebec and lying in the seigniory of Lauzon consisted of 28½ *arpents* in front by 40 in depth. The Jesuits received this freehold from the Seminary of Quebec by a deed of exchange of October 20, 1739.[42] The exchange grew out of a dispute between the Jesuits and the seminary over the possession of a lot one league in length on the Island of Jesus beside the Island of Montreal. By the deed of exchange, the Jesuits gave up all their claims to the Island of Jesus in exchange for about 28½ *arpents* in front by 40 in depth in the seigniory of Lauzon. The provincial law officers reported that as a freehold this estate owed nothing to the seignior of Lauzon or to the Crown. Having been acquired by exchange, it had no limitation as to uses and might therefore be granted by the British Crown.[43]

(3) *Pointe Lévi.* Pointe Lévi consisted of the following tracts of land, also situated in the seigniory of Lauzon: (a) four *arpents* in front along the St. Lawrence (two *arpents* on each side of a house formerly belonging to the Jesuits) by 20 *arpents* in depth to be held in pure and simple *roture*; (b) an adjoining tract of land in the same seigniory, consisting of 200 *arpents* (five *arpents* in front on the St. Lawrence by 40 *arpents* in depth), with fishing and hunting rights, to be held *en franche aumône* and pure *roture*; (c) another tract of land in the same seigniory, and adjoining that just described, consisting of six *arpents* in front along the St. Lawrence by 40 in depth, with all the rights of seigniory which the seignior of Lauzon himself enjoyed except the right of holding courts of justice; and (d) a tract of 11 *arpents* in front, adjoining the rear of the two preceding tracts, by 40 in depth, to be held *en roture* and subject to payment to the seignior of Lauzon of eleven *sols* of rent and eleven *deniers* of *cens* annually, with *lods et ventes* and other dues and services customarily rendered.[44]

Of these properties in the seigniory of Lauzon, tract (a) was granted to the Jesuits on August 1, 1648, by Governor Montmagny, the deed of grant stating simply that it was granted "by virtue of the power given to him by the Gentlemen of the Company of New France." It was to be held in pure *roture* on condition that the Jesuits would clear and cultivate the land and with the reservation of road rights by the Company. Tract (b) was granted by Jean de Lauzon on January 21, 1650, in consideration of the Jesuits' desire to give all the spiritual assistance possible to the inhabitants of the lands within the seigniory of Lauzon. The grant was given *en franche aumône* and *en roture*, with fishing and hunting rights and without any stipulation regarding the clearing of the land. Tract (c) was purchased on November 15, 1653, to be held as an *arrière* fief, with hunting and fishing rights (right to fish for salmon and eels). It was to be enjoyed in mortmain without any charge and to be disposed of by the Jesuits and their successors as they pleased. The Jesuits were given all rights except that of administering justice. Tract (d) was conceded to the Jesuits on January 20, 1676, by Claude de Bermen, Sieur de la Martinière, as guardian of the minor children of the now deceased Jean de Lauzon. The concession was given in token of the friendship between the Order and the Lauzons and in the hope that the settlement of the lands by the Jesuits would encourage other settlers. It was to be enjoyed by the Jesuits in mortmain, with the right of chase. They were, however, to permit the necessary roads to be built, to pay *cens et rentes* and also *lods et ventes*, and to send their grain to be ground at the seigniorial mill. By a deed of explanation of September 29, 1676, Bermen agreed that the meaning of the former deed relating to the obligation of grinding at the seigniorial mill should extend only to the grain to be consumed on the premises. On May 12, 1678, the four parcels of land were confirmed to the Jesuits with licence to hold them in mortmain.[45]

The provincial law officers' comment on the four parcels of land which made up Pointe Lévi was as follows:

The four parcels of land tho' adjoining are held by different tenures, the first and last are simple rotures and owe dues and Service to the Seignior as expressed in the Concessions, one of which however being directly from the Company appears to want further explanation. The Second is a grant in free Alms and Subject to no due or Service to the Seignior, and the third tho' called an arrière fief is certainly not so but either a Franc Aleu or Fief independent, there being no retention of fealty to the Seignior of Lawzon, nor any other mark of direct Seigneurie; His Majesty might therefore have received the Vassal so created as his own and have the benefit of the Mutation fine etc., or by discountenancing such dismemberment of the Fief under the Lands alien'd liable to feudal seizure. In this Case by the brevet of 1678, it may be Supposed a consent was given on the part of the Sovereign and therefore that the dismemberment is allowed but it may be proper to consider how far these Lands should now be made to hold of the Crown or Should be Granted as Franc aleu which ought to be explained in the Grant and conveyance of them.[46]

(4) *Tadoussac*. The Jesuits held six square *arpents* at Tadoussac on the north side of the St. Lawrence. Governor Jean de Lauzon conceded this tract of land to the Jesuits on July 1, 1656, for the purpose of building a chapel and other lodgings. The grant was made to be enjoyed by the Jesuits and their successors and beneficiaries in *franche aumône* without any charge and in perpetuity and full property. Tadoussac was also amortized on May 12, 1678. The provincial law officers advised that Tadoussac, being convenient for the use of the king's trading posts, should be retained in the hands of the government, though nothing in the title prevented it from being granted.[47]

(5) *Montreal*. The Jesuits bought several parcels of land in Montreal from Jean Vincent Philippe de Hautmesny and his wife on April 28, 1692. These parcels were as follows: (*a*) a remnant of land containing about eight *arpents* outside the enclosure of the town, which was part of 50 *arpents* acquired by Hautmesny from Gabriel Souard by deed of donation dated January 4, 1676; (*b*) eight *arpents*, apparently also acquired by Hautmesny from Souard, who was his uncle, consisting of one *arpent* in front on Notre Dame Street by eight in depth, adjoining on one side the first parcel and the lands belonging to the heirs of Sebastien Odiot, alias Laflèche, on the other; (*c*) one *arpent* of land purchased by Hautmesny from Souard, and by him from Urbain Brossard, by deed dated January 2, 1673; (*d*) 60 *arpents* purchased by Souard under a decree and by him sold to Hautmesny; (*e*) 112 *arpents* granted by the proprietors of the Island of Montreal to Souard and by him transferred to Hautmesny; and (*f*) one *arpent* sold to Hautmesny by Souard.

These several parcels of land (*a* to *f* inclusive) were sold to Father Claude Dablon, superior of the Jesuits in Quebec, and his assigns, to be enjoyed or disposed of as they pleased, subject to the payment of 58 *sols* rent per year to the seigniors of the Island of Montreal, and subject to other charges to which the parcels were liable by their respective grants. The Jesuits originally had to pay to the fabric of the parish of Montreal an annual ground rent of 50 *livres*, 19 *sols*, to which the parcels were subject, for the maintenance of a perpetual lamp. They were discharged from this obligation on September 20, 1692.

A large amount of the land acquired by the Jesuits in Montreal had been sold, after the cession of the country by France and before the establishment of British civil government, principally by a deed of sale to Charles Plessis Belair, dated May 5, 1764, by which three parcels were sold as follows: (*a*) a piece of land situated near the St. Lawrence suburb of Montreal consisting of one *arpent* in front by 30 in depth; (*b*) a lot above and contiguous to (*a*) containing two *arpents* in front by 30 or more in depth; and (*c*) another parcel of land containing four *arpents* in front by 28 in depth.[48]

The commissioners appointed to investigate the Jesuits' estates described these holdings in 1790 as follows: three *arpents*, 68⅓ *perches* enclosed by a wall and containing a church, chapel, house and out-offices; two house lots joining the west end of their enclosure; one house lot joining the north-east corner thereof and a vacant lot adjoining that lot; another area consisting partly of ground taken up by walls and fortifications, and partly by the Champ de Mars, or parade ground, lying between the walls and the Jesuits' enclosure; and the remainder outside the walls and fortifications of the town [49] (see inset "Town of Montreal" of Map I, p. 62).

The provincial law officers concluded that though the property was clearly indicated on a plan submitted by the commissioners, no description sufficient for a grant could be made without a further survey. The enclosed area containing the Jesuits' garden, houses, church, and chapel was sufficiently well described and bounded, but the lands outside the enclosure were not. As it was not likely that the Montreal properties would be granted to any one individual, there was less necessity in the opinion of the law officers to determine accurate boundaries at the moment. They pointed out that the lands were acquired by purchase and consequently clearly had fallen to the Crown. The parts which were sold in 1764, having been sold with the consent of the British commander-in-chief and military council of the day for a *bona fide* price, and the purchaser having had quiet possession since, he ought to be considered as entitled to them, although, in general, alienations by the Jesuits and other communities were not valid without certain formalities for the preservation of their property from the depredation of successive incumbents or administrators.[50]

(6) *Lands on the River Miamis.* By a deed of May 24, 1689, the French king confirmed a grant made on October 1, 1686, by Governor Denonville and the Intendant, Jean Bochart de Champigny, to Father Dablon and other missionaries of the Company of Jesus in New France. The grant consisted of 20 *arpents* in front and the same in depth on the south side of St. Joseph River (formerly called the Miamis). It was to be taken at whatever place the Jesuits should think most convenient, to be enjoyed by them and their successors and assigns for ever as their property and without the payment of any fine or indemnity for the same to the king or his successors. It was to be used for the purpose of constructing a chapel and other necessary buildings and for raising corn, roots, and other foodstuffs.[51]

The commissioners stated in their report that the Montreal commissioners, McGill, de St. Ours, and de Rouville, having been instructed by Chandler to inquire among the Indian traders concerning this tract of land, replied on March 9, 1789, that the Jesuits had had within the tract of land a French fort, a church, a dwelling-place and garden, which were then in a ruinous condition and probably occupied by traders, though not rented by the Jesuits or producing any income for their benefit. The law officers concluded, therefore, that the lands on the Miamis could be of little consequence, although equally fallen to the Crown and liable to be granted.[52]

(7) *Lands in the town of Quebec.* The Jesuits' holdings in the town of Quebec consisted of several parcels of ground acquired over a period of years beginning in 1637 (see Map II, p. 74). On March 18 of that year the Company of New France granted the Jesuits 12 *arpents* of land in the town of Quebec for the purpose of erecting a college and other appropriate building for the instruction of the children of the French

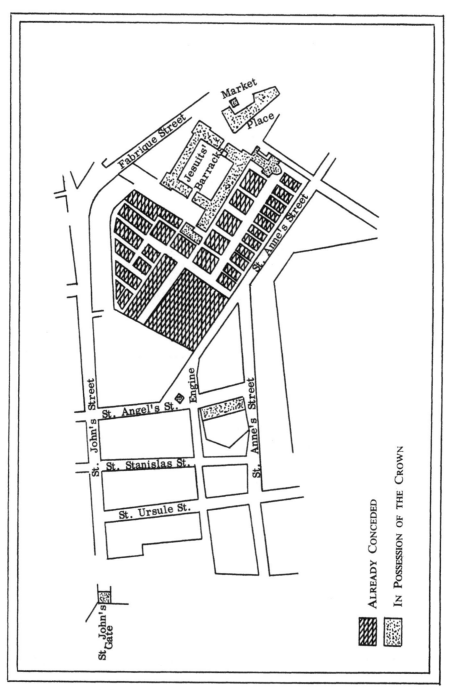

MAP II. "Plan of Property Belonging to the Late Order of Jesuits in the City of Quebec." This map has been traced from an original, now in P.A.C., prepared in 1803 by Joseph Bouchette.

inhabitants and those of the Indians, subject to the rendering of an *aveu et dénombrement* to the Company. It will be recalled from the discussion of La Vacherie that the Fathers were put into actual possession of only six *arpents* and 42 *perches* of the proposed grant and were compensated for the other six by a grant of 18 *arpents* outside the town, which became a part of La Vacherie. The Jesuits' possession of six *arpents* was confirmed with licence to hold in mortmain on May 12, 1678. This lot was by the original grant given for ever to the Jesuits and their successors to be held as their full property.[53]

On February 19, 1663, the Jesuits purchased two *arpents* of land from Guillaume Couillard and his wife. The two *arpents* were amortized on May 12, 1678, by the French king. An additional lot of two *arpents* was purchased from Marguerite Couillard, widow of Nicholas Macard, on September 3, 1664, a purchase that was also amortized by the same instrument of May 12, 1678.

In a grant of April 21, 1666, the Marquis de Tracy gave the Jesuits 40 feet in front by the same depth as their enclosure for the purpose of building a new church. This grant was amortized along with the others in 1678. An additional grant of 11 feet in front by the depth of their enclosure was made to the Jesuits by the bishop of Pétrée, on May 8, 1666, in order to give them sufficient space for the building of a more commodious church.

By deed of exchange of May 9, 1667, the Jesuits conveyed to Marie Hébert, widow of Guillaume Couillard, a farm in the seigniory of Notre Dame des Anges in exchange for eight *arpents* of land belonging to her in the City of Quebec. This quantity of land was also passed into mortmain in 1678. On May 14, 1668, the Company of Jesus purchased 58 *perches* of ground from Etienne Rageot, alias Lionnois, and his wife, which were located at a place called Quartier du Palais in the suburbs. This ground was sold to the Jesuits of the College of Quebec and their successors and assigns, to be enjoyed by them as they pleased subject to the payment of a ground rent that was later eliminated. Like the other properties, it was passed into mortmain by the French king in 1678.

Two other purchases were made by the fathers in Quebec. On June 8, 1680, Oliver Morel, Sieur de la Durantaye, and his wife sold them 104½ *toises* of land, to be enjoyed by them, their successors, and assigns as they pleased. To Father Dablon, superior of the college and missions of the Company of Jesus in Quebec, René Réaume of Charlebourg and Mary Chevreau, his wife, on October 1, 1691, sold all that remained to them of a plot of ground on Garden Street, adjacent to properties belonging to the Jesuits and Sieur Pinguet de Vaucour and the enclosure of the Ursuline Nuns. A part of the lot which Réaume had acquired from Sieur de la Durantaye was subject to eight *livres* ground rent at the time of purchase, but this was later eliminated by an arrangement between the Jesuits and de la Durantaye and his wife. In addition to the plot of ground, the Jesuits had purchased the right to certain ground rents which had hitherto been enjoyed by Réaume. The law officers concluded that since this piece of ground had been acquired by purchase, there could be no doubt that it fell to the Crown and might be granted.

By successive grants from the church wardens and trustees of the parish church of Quebec, the Jesuits received three additional parcels of land subject to specificed amounts of *cens et rentes*: 70 *perches* of land on June 10, 1661; 28 *perches* on January 27, 1663; and 11 *perches* in front by 96 feet in depth on May 12, 1666.[54]

RECAPITULATION OF THE ESTATES

I. LANDS HELD IN FIEF AND SEIGNIORY

Property	Year of Acquisition	How Acquired	Length-Depth Leagues		Total Arpents
1. Notre Dame des Anges	1626	Grant	1	4	(28,224)*
2. St. Gabriel	1667	Grant	1½	10	(119,720)
3. Sillery	1699	Grant	1	1½	(8,979)
4. Belair	1710–43	Purchase	1½	2	(14,112)
5. Cap de la Magdeleine	1651	Grant	2	20	(282,240)
6. Batiscan	1639	Grant	2	20	(282,240)
7. Island of St. Christopher	1654	Grant	—	—	80
8. La Prairie de la Magdeleine	1647	Grant	2	4	(56,448)
9. Isle des Ruaux	1638	Grant	½	8	
10. Pacherigny	1699	Grant	4	8	
(including 20 *toises* contiguous thereto)			(*perches*)	(*perches*)	(about 3)
11. Fief near Town of Three Rivers	1634	Grant	—	—	600 (575)

II. LANDS HELD EN FRANC ALEU, EN ROTURE, AND EN ARRIERE FIEF.

Property	Year of Acquisition	How Acquired	Length-Depth Lineal *Arpents*		Total *Arpents*
1. La Vacherie	(a) 1626	Grant	—	—	45
	(b) 1646	Grant	—	—	18
	(c) 1667	Exchange	—	—	10
					73
2. In Parish of St. Nicholas	1739	Exchange	28¼	40	1180
3. Pointe Lévi	(a) 1648	Grant	4	20	80
	(b) 1650	Grant	5	40	200
	(c) 1653	Purchase	6	40	240
	(d) 1676	Grant	11	40	440
					2140
4. Tadoussac	1656	Grant	—	—	6
5. Montreal	1692	Purchase	—	—	(a) 8
					(b) 8
					(c) 1
					(d) 60
					(e) 112
					(f) 1
					190†
6. Land on River Miamis	1686 & 1689	Grant	20	20	(400)
7. In the Town of Quebec	(a) 1637	Grant	—	—	6‡
	(b) 1663	Purchase	—	—	2
	(c) 1664	Purchase	—	—	2
	(d) 1666	Grant	40 feet by Depth of Enclosure		—
	(e) 1666	Grant	11 feet by Depth of Enclosure		—
	(f) 1667	Exchange	—	—	8
	(g) 1668	Purchase	—	—	58 (*perches*)
	(h) 1680	Purchase	—	—	104½ (*toises*)
	(i) 1691	Purchase	(not specified)		—
	(j) 1661	Grant	—	—	70 (*perches*)
	(k) 1663	Grant	—	—	28 (*perches*)
	(l) 1666	Grant	11 *perches* 96 feet		—

In summarizing the foregoing analysis of the Jesuits' estates, the following observations are most pertinent:

(1) The estates, totalling nearly 1,000,000 French acres, were acquired by means of *bona fide* deeds of grants, purchase, or exchange.

(2) A careful examination of the title deeds of the estates does not reveal any specified trust under which the Jesuits were to hold the properties. Their free use and disposal of the estates was limited only by their own constitution and certain feudal obligations attached to some pieces of land. In most instances, the grants had been made in recognition of services rendered in the past, rather than on condition of services to be rendered in the future.

(3) Only one of the grants (12 *arpents* in Quebec) appears to have been given originally and specifically for the purpose of providing a location for the College of Quebec. Cap de la Magdeleine, Batiscan, and La Prairie de la Magdeleine were said to have been given for the purpose of maintaining the college, but this appears only by later deeds of explanation, issued by an intendant, the propriety of which was seriously questioned by the provincial law officers. References to the College of Quebec lend themselves to confusion because the college was not exclusively an institution for teaching grammar, literature, philosophy, and sciences to youth, but it was also the general superior's residence and the administrative centre for all the different mission posts of New France, each one having its own accounts.

(4) If the British legal experts were correct in assuming that the Crown had a right to the estates, by conquest, confiscation, escheat, or whatever means, there was certainly nothing in the title deeds to hinder the Crown from disposing of them as it pleased.

---

* Figures in parentheses in parts I and II are taken from a "Statement Respecting the Jesuits' Estates," furnished by the Commissioner of Crown Lands in 1856; *J.L.A.P.C.*, 1856, XIV, 1, App.15.

† But according to the deed of sale of May 5, 1764, the Jesuits sold a total of about 202 *arpents* to Charles Plessis Belair. There is insufficient data available on their holdings in Montreal to clarify this discrepancy. It is possible that they had received more on April 28, 1692, by actual survey than by the deed of grant, or that they sold less by actual survey than by the deed of sale of May 5, 1764.

‡ Twelve granted, but only six taken in Quebec. Eighteen given in lieu of the other six in La Vacherie.

CHAPTER SIX

THE JESUITS' ESTATES IN PUBLIC AFFAIRS, 1800-32

AFTER THE BRITISH GOVERNMENT had assumed control of the Jesuits' estates in 1800, their management was entrusted to a commission composed originally of Chief Justice Osgoode, executive councillors François Baby and Thomas Dunn, Deputy Paymaster-General John Hale, and a Canadian barrister, Berthelot Dartigny.[1] For about the next quarter of a century this commission, its membership replenished from time to time as was necessary, continued to function as a public trustee. As it performed this duty efficiently, and had no concern with the disposition of the estates or the revenues from them, the activities of the commission need not be examined here.[2]

It will now be recalled that Lieutenant-Governor Milnes had repeatedly urged upon the home government the dire need for improved educational facilities in the province. The provincial legislature had sought to have the Crown relinquish its claim upon the forfeited estates of the Jesuits in favour of the legislature, which would devote the revenue from them to education. No reply came until the subject was pressed once again in 1801. On that occasion the Lieutenant-Governor, in his reply to the address, made the following announcement:

> With great satisfaction I have to inform you that His Majesty . . . has been graciously pleased to give directions for the establishing of a competent number of free schools for the instruction of their children in the first rudiments of useful learning and in the English tongue, and also as occasion may require for foundations of a more enlarged and comprehensive nature, and His Majesty has been further pleased to signify his royal intention that a suitable proportion of the lands of the Crown should be set apart and the revenue thereof applied to such purposes.[3]

On the strength of this promise, an Act was passed (41 Geo. III, c. 17) by the provincial legislature during the session of 1801 which provided for the creation of the Royal Institution for the Advancement of Learning.[4] The complicated administrative machinery of this Act need not be discussed here. It is important to notice, however, that the preamble reiterated the royal intention of endowing free schools and higher educational institutions with crown lands.[5] In the ensuing years when Canadians thought of the promise of crown lands, their minds quite naturally turned at once to the Jesuits' estates. The subsequent history of the Royal Institution will be considered in connection with later reports on the state of education in the province, which generally included the suggestion that the Jesuits' estates be turned over to the province to help relieve the distressing needs in education.

In the summer of 1805, prior to departing from Lower Canada, Milnes again wrote home urging the needs of higher education in the province. He called attention to Canadian sentiment against the diversion of the Jesuits' college from the educational functions which it had performed so well before the Conquest. Milnes noted that though he had been authorized to bring about the establishment of seminaries in Quebec and Montreal, it had been almost impossible to sell the Crown lands needed to acquire funds for the purpose, even at exceedingly low rates per acre. He concluded that there were no means, other than the Jesuits' estates, by which the establishment of the seminaries could be immediately effected.[6]

In the same letter, Milnes reminded the British government that the Assembly had more than once attempted to advance the provincial claims to the estates as having been granted originally for the express purpose of education. Since their effort of March 18, 1800, he reported, the Assembly had not taken any further action, although they had frequently made it a matter of discussion in the House. He concluded:

> It would be highly desirable to have this Source of discontent effectually removed so as no longer to be made a handle of by those Members of the House who are desirous to oppose the Measures of Government; and this is an additional Reason of no small importance for finally appropriating the Revenues of the Jesuits Estates, which were they allotted to so beneficial a Purpose, there is no reason to doubt would effectually set aside all the Claims which otherwise might be brought forward.[7]

It is unfortunate that the advice of Milnes went unheeded. The subject of the disposition of the revenues of the estates did, in fact, furnish "a handle" on more than one occasion before the matter was finally laid to an uneasy rest in 1832. His plea on behalf of the educational needs of the provinces was supported by a report of the Executive Council which he enclosed in his letter. The Council, like Milnes, complained of having to send Canadian youths to the United States for their education, where they might learn to condemn the religion and to hate the government of their native country.[8]

Milnes left Canada in 1805. The next significant development in the involved history of the Jesuits' estates question is connected with the mission of Herman W. Ryland, Governor James Craig's confidential secretary, to the Imperial government. Born and educated in England, Ryland first entered public life in 1781, and during that year went to New York as assistant deputy paymaster-general of British forces in North America. When those forces evacuated New York, he returned to England with the Commander-in-Chief, Sir Guy Carleton, who, as Lord Dorchester, brought him out to Lower Canada in 1793 to serve as his confidential secretary. In this capacity Ryland continued to serve successive governors of Lower Canada for a period of twenty years, resigning under the administration of Sir George Prevost. He also held the confidential and important office of clerk of the Executive Council until his death on July 20, 1838. As secretary, Ryland had the best possible opportunity of making himself thoroughly acquainted with public affairs and with the principal men in Lower Canada.[9]

In his sympathies and antipathies, prepossessions, and prejudices, Ryland was an Englishman to the core, and, like his friend and chief, Governor Craig, he was not inclined to conciliate the prejudices of a people whose language, religion, laws, usages and customs were foreign to those of his own country. He was anxious to anglicize the French-Canadian people by compulsory and distasteful means.[10] In addition to his other official capacities, Ryland was appointed as one of the commissioners for the management of the Jesuits' estates on April 24, 1807, and he succeeded Henry Caldwell as treasurer for the estates when Caldwell died in 1810.[11]

On May 1, 1810, Governor Craig, who had already run into difficulties with the Assembly,[12] sent Secretary of State Lord Liverpool a lengthy dispatch that was extremely hostile to the French inhabitants of Lower Canada.[13] In order that Liverpool might have a more complete account than it was possible to convey in a letter, Craig confided the delivery of his dispatch to Ryland who proceeded to England where he was to remain for a period of months to complete a threefold mission: (1) to obtain an alteration or suspension of the constitution; (2) to make the government financially independent of the Assembly by appropriating the revenues of the estates of the Sulpicians and the Jesuits; and (3) to persuade the government to assume the patronage hitherto exercised by the Roman Catholic bishop of Quebec over the benefices in his diocese.[14]

Governor Craig directed Ryland to press the subject of the Jesuits' estates upon the British government. The great object, said Craig, was to get a grant of the property to act as a suitable fund for the education of the English part of the colony. He proposed to invest the accumulated income (amounting to about £9,000) in British stocks in order to make it a productive fund.[15] Ryland was well chosen for this particular mission. As early as May, 1808, he had suggested that in order to proceed with the assimilation of the colony in its religion, laws, and manners with the parent state, it would be advisable to establish a corporation for the advancement of learning and to seek a favourable decision from the Crown concerning the estates of the Jesuits and the Sulpicians.[16]

Liverpool declined to bring the affairs of Lower Canada before Parliament, but he promised to consider the matters covered in Craig's dispatch during the course of the winter.[17] In February, 1811, Ryland drew up a statement of the matters to be discussed, calling attention to the fact that the Assembly, in its session of 1810, had proposed and carried a resolution which would provide the necessary sums for the civil expense of the provincial government. The resolution was followed by separate addresses to the king and to the British Parliament declaring the intention of the Assembly. Ryland concluded that the Assembly's real purpose was to reduce the salaries of public officials and to exercise unlimited control over the executive.[18]

It was this particular development in Lower Canada which made the Governor anxious to get a decision on the estates of the Jesuits and the Sulpicians. Ryland stated the matter clearly:

... This extensive and very valuable property (the right to which is indisputably vested in the Crown,) would, under able management, not only afford ample means for the purposes of public education, but the surplus monies arising therefrom, if added to the casual and territorial revenues of the Crown, and to the permanent duties already established by Acts of the Legislature, would, there is reason to believe, soon render the Provincial funds, that are at the disposal of the Crown, adequate to the payment of the ordinary expenses of the Civil Government, and preclude the necessity of having recourse either to the House of Assembly, or to the Military Chest (as hitherto has been customary,) to make good the yearly deficiencies.[19]

In the course of conversations with Robert Peel, under-secretary of state, Ryland urged that the total revenues of the Sulpicians' and Jesuits' estates, even after allowing a certain sum to the self-established seminary at Montreal, would be more than sufficient to make good the ordinary deficiencies of the provincial revenues and might be applied to that or any other purpose at the Crown's discretion. Peel expressed a wish that the accumulated funds from the Jesuits' estates be appropriated to build a barracks at Quebec.[20] To this suggestion Ryland replied that

... a very sanguine hope is entertained throughout the Province, and more particularly by the English part of the community, that a portion, at least, of the revenues arising from these estates will eventually be appropriated to the advancement of learning, and to the establishment of public schools in Lower Canada; and I am persuaded that a considerable sensation of regret would be occasioned among all classes by the entire alienation of those funds from the above purposes. . . .[21]

He then referred to a plan of the Protestant Bishop of Quebec, Jacob Mountain, calling for the establishment of a public grammar school at Quebec, for which the revenues of the Jesuits' estates were the only available fund.

Ryland's contemplated disposal of the estates is succinctly stated in a communication to Peel of February 1, 1812:

I feel confident that the revenues of the Jesuits' estates may be speedily and very considerably augmented, and I think it evident that Government may derive great advantage, in point of power and influence, from keeping this a separate and distinct fund, to be appropriated to such purposes, whether civil or military, as His Majesty may from time to time see fit to direct. . . .[22]

In a word, Ryland thought it desirable to acquire the means of making the executive branch of the provincial government financially independent of the Assembly. While Ryland was in England, Governor Craig was replaced by Sir George Prevost who continued him in the mission on which he had been dispatched by Craig. On February 6, 1812, he reported to Prevost an interview with Peel, the substance of which was almost identical with the contents of his letter to Peel of February 1.[23]

Toward the end of February Ryland was very disturbed when John Caldwell called his attention to an order from the Lords of the Treasury directing him (Caldwell) to pay into the military chest at Quebec the Jesuits' estates funds which had accumulated during the treasurership of his deceased father, Henry Caldwell. Ryland immediately expressed to Peel a fear of great dissatisfaction and irritation in the province if the funds were henceforth appropriated entirely for military purposes. Ryland emphasized that the unsalaried commissioners who were managing the estates had been encouraged to improve them in the hope that the revenues would eventually be appropriated for the general benefit of the province. If the revenues were used solely to defray Imperial military costs, as seemed to be implied by the order to Caldwell, Ryland anticipated a very contrary effect upon the commissioners and more trouble from the factious.[24]

Ryland's anxieties were relieved by a decision of the British government not to make any appropriation of the accumulated Jesuits' estates funds until Lord Liverpool had consulted Governor Prevost. Liverpool, nevertheless, thought it proper that Caldwell should render an account of the sums received by his father and that he should deposit them in the military chest.[25] The outcome of Ryland's rather prolonged mission is revealed in a letter which he wrote to Earl Spencer on May 10, 1813:

I flattered myself . . . that I might have materially assisted in bringing these important measures into execution. After much exertion, success at one moment seemed about to crown my efforts. A despatch comprehending the several objects was drafted . . . in the very terms that I myself had suggested; but the Secretary of State thought it necessary to submit this despatch to the Lord Chancellor, and "the Lord Chancellor had doubts;" and there the whole business has ever since remained, to the infinite detriment of His Majesty's interests.[26]

Actually, two of the objects of Ryland's mission (to make the government financially independent by appropriating towards its support the revenues of the estates of the Sulpicians and the Jesuits, and to induce the government to assume the patronage hitherto exercised by the Roman Catholic bishop of Quebec over benefices in his diocese) appear to have been entertained and after some hesitation determined upon by the Cabinet. However, Lord Chancellor Eldon entertained certain scruples on the subject and Ryland's mission consequently proved a complete failure.[27]

In the spring of 1812 the Legislative Council decided to make an attempt to secure the Jesuits' estates revenues for provincial education, possibly as a result of an awareness of that part of Ryland's mission dealing with the disposition of the estates and of the decision to deposit the accumulated funds in the military chest. A petition to the Prince Regent was adopted which called attention to the deplorable state of education in the province. The petition stressed the great increase of population in the province, the inability of most of the inhabitants to pay the cost of educating their children in private seminaries, the inadequacy of the funds of the few educational institutions of a public nature which existed in the province, the original destination of the estates for education, and the pre-Conquest application of the rents and revenues of the estates to that important and worth-while purpose. The Prince Regent was asked to take the educational needs of the province into consideration and to allow the accumulated and future Jesuits' estates revenues to be appropriated to the relief of those needs. The Legislative Council sought the concurrence of the Assembly with this petition, but the Assembly does not appear to have acted upon it.[28]

The next proposal to use the Jesuits' estates for education in the province came not from the province but from the home government. On December 30, 1815, the Secretary of State for War and the Colonies, Lord Bathurst, notified the recently appointed Administrator of Lower Canada, Sir Gordon Drummond, that in recognition of the exertions of the province in the War of 1812 the Crown intended to endow one or more colleges. Because of its central location, Montreal had been selected as the site for the first such establishment. Drummond was given directions for the selection of an exact site, and he was told to inform the trustees of a legacy of £10,000 from the late James McGill, to be used in the establishment of a college, that it was the intention of the British government to begin such an undertaking. Drummond was therefore to seek from the trustees the application of the legacy for the erection of the college building. The Secretary of State also suggested the possiblitity of using Jesuits' estates income to endow a college and he indicated that as soon as complete information on the estates was received, the government would promptly make final arrangements for an establishment which would afford proper provincial facilities for higher education.[29]

Before the Imperial government communicated further with the provincial government concerning the proposed college, the Assembly once more directed its attention to the subject of the Jesuits' estates. On February 3, 1816, a special committee of five members was appointed to inquire into the state of the Jesuits' property, with instruction to draft an address to the Prince Regent asking for the restitution of the property for the purposes of education in the province.[30] There was hardly time for the ordered report, however, because Sir Gordon Drummond prorogued the session on February 26 as a result of the Assembly's action to impeach chief justices Monk and Sewell.[31]

On May 10, 1816, Bathurst instructed the Administrator of the province[32] to transfer all the Jesuits' estates to the trustees of the Royal Institution for the Advancement of Learning in order that they might possess the means for establishing and maintaining necessary educational institutions. In making the transfer, however, the Administrator was to retain for future disposal the accumulated funds of preceding years, a detailed account of which he was to send home as soon as possible.[33]

Bathurst sent these orders before he had received word that Drummond had prorogued and called for an immediate dissolution of the Assembly over the question of the impeachment of the two chief justices. On May 31, having got this disturbing news, Bathurst wrote the new Governor-in-Chief, Sir John Coape Sherbrooke, suspending the orders of May 10, and directing the new Governor to retain at the disposal of his government all funds belonging to the Crown, whatever their source, because the new Assembly might refuse to vote money for carrying on the public services. Referring specifically to the Jesuits' estates, the Secretary of State said:

... the necessity of providing for the other necessary expences of the Province in the event of the Legislature declining that duty, compels His Royal Highness to retain at his disposal the Funds which he was under other circumstances prepared altogether to abandon and which he is not the less desirous of appropriating annually to the purposes of education whenever the Legislature shall previously provide for the current expences of the Year.[34]

In spite of difficulties experienced with the Assembly of Lower Canada, the home government persevered in its proposal to give financial assistance to the building of a college at Montreal. As the Roman Catholic Bishop of Quebec raised objections to employing Jesuits' estates funds for non-sectarian education, Sherbrooke suggested the application of a sum from other provincial revenues, equal to the annual produce of the Jesuits' estates, for the maintenance of the college in order to overcome the Bishop's objections. Bathurst agreed to submit this suggestion to the Prince Regent upon receipt of a draft proposal from the province.[35]

James McGill, a public-spirited merchant of Montreal who died in 1813, willed 46 acres of land with buildings on the outskirts of Montreal and a sum of £10,000 to found a college in a provincial university. His will directed that the property be given to the Royal Institution on condition that within ten years of his death it would erect on his estate a university or college. It was further stipulated that the college or one of the colleges in the university should be named McGill College.[36]

Bathurst informed the recently appointed Governor, the Duke of Richmond, in March, 1819, that the home government had had no change of opinion as to the usefulness of establishing a provincial college and he urged the need for immediate action because of the time-limit imposed by McGill's legacy. The Duke was instructed to adopt the necessary measures for erecting the college building upon the land bequeathed for that purpose with as little delay as possible. To expedite matters, he was authorized to defray the initial expenses from the funds which were in the hands of the receiver of the Jesuits' estates.[37]

Several obstacles lay in the way of the founding of McGill College, however. McGill had left his property called Burnside to the Royal Institution for the Advancement of Learning. Actual possession of the property was delayed because McGill's stepson, Desrivières, contested the will and refused to convey the legacy.[38] The chief obstacle to the founding of the college was the lack of financial resources. Dalhousie, as governor-in-chief from 1820 to 1828, was opposed to any appropriation of funds for education from the Jesuits' estates and he refused to pay even the salary of the secretary of the Royal Institution from the revenues of the estates.[39] The situation for the Royal Institution became so serious, particularly because of the litigation by Desrivières, that in March, 1823, it petitioned the Lieutenant-Governor, Sir F. N. Burton, for aid. A memorial, drawn up and signed by Bishop Mountain as principal, drew attention to the Institution's destitute condition and pleaded for relief from the

Jesuits' estates.[40] Over a period of years £780 of the funds from the estates was actually spent to contest the claims of Desrivières.[41]

In 1823, Charles James Stewart, who eventually succeeded Bishop Mountain, was sent to England to resist the claim of the Church of Scotland to a share in the Clergy Reserves. He used the opportunity to urge upon the Under-Secretary of State, Wilmot Horton, the needs of the Royal Institution, as well as the danger of forfeiting the McGill bequest unless financial help were immediately forthcoming. He advanced Bishop Mountain's argument that the order of May 10, 1816, transferring the Jesuits' estates to the Royal Institution, ought to be renewed. It had been suspended in that year only because of the temporary financial embarrassments of the provincial government, and the Bishop maintained that it had not been found necessary since to appropriate any sum from the Jesuits' estates to relieve such difficulties.[42] In conversation with Horton on January 1, 1824, Stewart was told that the Lords of the Treasury had been strongly advised to advance £5,000 on the credit of McGill's legacy. This advance was never made, although small sums were from time to time doled out from the Jesuits' estates revenues to keep the Royal Institution alive.[43]

The decade from 1820 to 1830 was marked by repeated efforts of the Assembly to gain control of the revenues of the Jesuits' estates. It voted an address to the governor on March 15, 1823, asking for the communication of such instructions or dispatches as might have been received from the home government relating to the estates and to the use of the revenues for education in the province.[44] Governor Dalhousie, having referred to proceedings upon the subject recorded in the Assembly Journal of 1800, replied that he did not think that he could comply with the request of this address without obtaining special permission to do so. Thereupon, the House voted 16 to 4 to refer this answer to the committee of privileges.[45]

Two days after the address to Governor Dalhousie fuel was added to the fires of popular discontent by the report of a special committee which had been examining that part of the Governor's speech, given at the opening of the 1820 session of the legislature, which related to the waste lands of the Crown. The committee had interviewed Ryland, now chairman of the board of commissioners for the management of the Jesuits' estates, in order to get particular information on the estates. To a number of very specific questions regarding the application of the income from the estates, the amount of that income, and the status of the Jesuits' college in Quebec, Ryland had replied that, as the estates were in possession of the Crown and under the immediate direction of the home government, he did not feel authorized to give any information without the express permission of the government's representative.[46] The report of the special committee conveying Ryland's refusal to answer its questions was referred by the House to the committee of privileges on March 17 but, as in 1816, there was scarcely time for it to be considered because of the prorogation of the legislature on March 22, 1823.[47]

Between March 22 and November 23 when the Assembly reconvened, another matter excited the attention of the province. By 1823 the financial embarrassment of the Receiver-General, John Caldwell, had become a matter of painful notoriety. Caldwell had speculated in the construction of mills, in the manufacture of lumber, and in the purchase of seigniories—undertakings that had not been productive. In 1822, and again in 1823, Dalhousie had drawn £30,000 from the military chest to provide for the immediate needs of the civil government. The House, when called upon to make good this advance, argued that it could not consider what it regarded as a private loan to Caldwell on the part of the Governor. It was contended that there should be £100,000, or so, of the public funds in the Treasury. The Assembly accordingly ignored the request to make good the advance to Caldwell.[48]

On August 14, 1823, control of the revenue was taken from Caldwell and placed under two persons, a member of the Executive Council and a member of the Assembly, without whose authorization he could neither receive nor pay money. On November 23 he was suspended from his duties. The defalcation in the provincial chest amounted to £96,117 13s. 4d., according to Caldwell's own statement. He had, on entering office in 1811, assumed responsibility for £39,874 10s. 10d., charged to his father and predecessor in office, Henry Caldwell. That amount, though never in reality paid over to John Caldwell, accounted for so much of the deficit.[49] Of particular relevance to the history of the Jesuits' estates is the fact that the £39,874 10s. 10d. obligation which John Caldwell had assumed from his father included about £8,000 belonging to the Jesuits' estates fund, which the latter had accumulated as treasurer of the estates. Judging from the accounts of Ryland, Caldwell's successor as treasurer, the accumulated funds from the estates were not paid into the military chest, as ordered in February, 1812, and one might venture to assume that this was simply because Henry Caldwell had used them for other purposes of a personal nature.[50] The House took the view that, as the Receiver-General was an official of the British Treasury, it was the duty of the home government to make good the total amount of Caldwell's defalcation.[51]

The non-committal character of the responses of the Governor and of Ryland on the question of the Jesuits' estates undoubtedly helped to determine the nature of a report,[52] submitted on February 25, 1824, of a special committee named to inquire into the actual state of education in the province. The report painted a dismal picture. According to information gathered from Father Parent, superior of the Seminary of Quebec, one-fourth of the population had a passable reading knowledge; one-tenth knew only how to sign their names. It was his opinion that the situation would have been worse if the curés had not made great efforts to educate their parishioners. The operation of the Act creating the Royal Institution was not regarded as beneficial, the schoolmasters having been chosen without consultation with those best qualified to judge. The lack of financial means of a large number of parents, the difficulty of procuring schoolmasters of irreproachable morals, and the want of good elementary schools in the country were listed as causes which had retarded progress. Parent, of course, mentioned the deleterious effects of the closing of the College of Quebec and the withdrawal of the funds of the Jesuits' estates.[53]

According to Joseph L. Mills, secretary of the Royal Institution, the chief obstacle to educational progress was the opposition of the Catholic clergy. Opposition was uniform and systematic: the Roman Catholic bishop of Quebec refused to become a member of the Institution, and the priests refused to serve as visitors in these schools. This opposition was natural, for by Mills's own admission the personnel of the Royal Institution had always been predominantly English and Protestant. Indeed, its prime object was to denationalize French Canada. It is not surprising, therefore, that other documents submitted to the committee likewise bore witness to clerical opposition to the establishment of schools under the Royal Institution.[54]

The crux of the matter was that the ruling English minority had devised an English mould into which they were trying to force the French youth and had blocked a counter-attempt of the Assembly to set up a public educational system that would

D

meet the needs and fit the character of the huge French majority of the population.[55] But the committee discreetly avoided this obvious conclusion and shrewdly concentrated on the diversion of the profits of the Jesuits' estates from the primary purposes for which they had been given.[56]

A major part of the report of February 25 and its substantiating documents dealt with the Jesuits' estates, the committee having gained access to several pertinent documents from the heirs of J. A. Panet (one of the commissioners of 1787).[57] The committee reviewed the history of the proceedings concerning the estates up to the date of their inquiry. They concluded their report with the conviction that this information would furnish to the people of the province a new proof of the benevolence of the British government, and they asked why the Governor had deemed it necessary to keep the documents secret. The committee also advised the House to renew its efforts by asking the king to direct that the buildings, lands, and revenues hitherto belonging to the Jesuits be used for the advancement of education.[58]

About a year later, on February 4, 1825, the Assembly appointed a committee of seven members with full powers to report on the best means of obtaining the application of the Jesuits' estates "to their original destination." The committee was composed of Amable Berthelot, Joseph L. Borgia, Louis Lagueux, John Neilson, Joseph B. Vallières, Denis B. Viger, and Jean T. Taschereau, all French except Neilson who had espoused the French cause.[59] It was also instructed to assess the results of the Act of 1801 which had provided for the establishment of the Royal Institution.[60]

The committee reported on February 18 that it could not acquire any better information on the subject than was in the report of the special committee of 1824 on the state of education in the province. From that report and from information of its own members, the committee of 1825 concluded that the Act of 1801 had done little for education, though the operation of the Act had already cost the province nearly £28,000. In the opinion of the committee the inefficacy of the status arose

... from the distrust inspired into Roman Catholics, as well as into other classes of His Majesty's Subjects in this Province, by the appointment of the Trustees of the Royal Institution . . . and of the appointments made by the same Institution. Those Trustees in fact, at the beginning of the year [1824] . . . consisted of Twelve Anglican Protestants, and four Roman Catholics only. Among the Commissioners and Visitors appointed by that Institution, [numbering 132] . . . there were only Thirty-two Roman Catholics, nearly all the rest being Anglicans. Among the Twenty-five School-Masters appointed by that Institution, there were only Five or Six Roman Catholic Masters, while the rest were almost all Anglicans; and the number of Pupils Eleven hundred or thereabouts, in the charge of those Twenty-five Masters, may be supposed to include hardly one-fourth their number of Roman Catholics.[61]

The report also pointed out that the administration and professors of McGill College who were appointed by the Institution were exclusively Anglican, although Anglicans constituted only one-fourth of all the Protestants in the province, while Roman Catholics formed seven-eighths, at least, of the whole population.

The committee concluded that the effects of the Act of 1801 had not answered the intentions of the legislature and that an address ought to be presented to the king, asking him to order that the Jesuits' estates be placed at the disposal of the provincial legislature to be applied, according to their initial purpose, for education.[62]

The committee submitted a draft of such an address, which directed attention to the fact that the province was deprived of the facilities of the Jesuits' college because of its retention by the Imperial government as a barracks. The proposed address then repeated the familiar arguments first clearly advanced in the petitions of 1787 and 1793, that the college and its estates had never belonged to the Jesuits as their property but were held by them in trust for the education of the youth of the province; that the suppression of the Jesuits could not extinguish provincial rights to those estates; and that in the several countries of Europe, the Jesuits' colleges had continued to exist notwithstanding the expulsion of the Order, that event not having conveyed to the government more rights in the estates than the Jesuits themselves had possessed.[63]

After reminding the king that the Protestant and English complexion of the Royal Institution had caused much uneasiness among a great part of the French inhabitants of the province, the prospected address concluded with a plea that the college and its estates "be restored to their original destination," and that, to achieve this end, they should be placed at the disposal of the provincial legislature. A committee of the whole House concurred in the report and the proposed address. At the request of the House Sir Francis Burton, administrator in the absence of Dalhousie, agreed to forward the address to the home government,[64] which he did on March 25.[65]

The House pursued the matter on January 25, 1826, with an address to the Governor, asking whether he had received any answer from the Imperial ministers, and that he relay any such communication to the House.[66] Dalhousie replied on January 30 that he had not yet received an answer.[67] On March 23 the Assembly requested the Governor to suspend the sale and alienation of the Jesuits' property located in and near the City of Quebec until a reply was received concerning the claim of the public of the province. Two days later, Dalhousie replied that he was convinced that the Imperial government had no intention of acceding to the provincial claims to the estates and therefore must decline to comply with their request.[68]

The first known reaction of the Colonial Office to the address of the Assembly appears in a private communication from Wilmot Horton of August 29 asking Governor Dalhousie to offer his opinion on the Jesuits' estates before the home government received a public dispatch on the subject. He was reminded that

It would appear to be very desirable that all practicable means should be taken of increasing the Revenue of these Estates, and that such Revenue should be strictly appropriated according to the intention of those who bequeathed them, for the purposes of Education—These funds would appear to be capable of furnishing in part the means for the Establishment of the University now in progress [McGill]. It would indeed be desirable that they should be all wholly directed in that manner considering the immense importance it is that the Youth of Canada should be educated within His Majesty's Dominions, but unfortunately Lord Bathurst has already experienced how impossible it is to induce the Roman Catholics to unite with the Protestants in the Establishment of an University common to all, and as the University now in progress must therefore be Protestant, it would be unfit that the Jesuit Funds should have an exclusively Protestant direction.[69]

Replying on November 10, Dalhousie insisted that the Jesuits' estates, having fallen to the Crown by the conquest of Canada and as a result of the extinction of the Order, had always been considered Crown property and the revenues had been applied exclusively to the Protestant Church and to Protestant education.[70] The Governor thought it would be inexpedient to alter that destination now, particularly under existing circumstances in the province.[71]

The Assembly again returned to the charge in February, 1827, calling for a reading of the entry in the *Journal* of the House containing the Governor's answer to the address of the House of March 15, 1823. Following the reading, an address to the Governor was adopted, asking him whether he had obtained permission to communicate to the House such instructions or dispatches as he had received relating to the Jesuits' estates. Dalhousie told the House that the Secretary of State had inquired about the revenues of the Jesuits' estates but he, the Governor, had no permission to share these dispatches with the legislature nor had he yet received any communication from the home government regarding the Assembly's address of 1825.[72]

While wading through the details of these repeated efforts of the Assembly to get control of the Jesuits' estates, it should be kept in mind that they were only one aspect of the attempt by the House during the crucial first four decades of the nineteenth century to seize the "purse strings" in order to control the executive branch of the government. As Milnes had predicted, the question of the disposal of the Jesuits' revenues was being used as "a handle" by members of the House who desired to block the measures of the government.

The session of the Assembly which began on January 23, 1827, ended on March 7 as a result of a deadlock with the executive. The House adopted by an overwhelming majority on March 6 a series of resolutions relating to financial affairs which precipitated a prorogation on the following day. Three of the resolutions clearly reveal the issue at stake:

1. That this House continues to adhere to the Resolutions and Addresses passed by this House relating to the subject of the Expenses of the Civil Government, as expressed in its journals.

2. That the manner and form of auditing the Public Accounts, and of accounting for the due Application of the Public Revenues, is insufficient to secure a just, correct and responsible Application of the Public Monies, and that there is still no adequate security against the misapplication of the Funds deposited by Law in the hands of His Majesty's Receiver General of the Province.

3. That the House does not acknowledge or in any way sanction any Payments made out of the Public Revenue of the Province which have not been authorised by an Act of the Legislature, or advanced on an Address of the House.[73]

In other words, the House refused implicitly to grant supply for the current year except upon its own terms, which included the right to consider and to fix the salaries of all officials in the province.

In his speech of prorogation censuring the House, Dalhousie stated his view of the matter in these terms:

In my Administration of this Government, I have seen Seven Years pass away without any conclusive adjustment of the Public Accounts; thus accumulating a mass for future Investigation, which must lead to confusion and misunderstanding. In the same Years I have seen the Measures of Government, directly applicable to the wants of the Province thrown aside without attention and without any reason assigned. I have seen the Forms of Parliament utterly disregarded; and in this Session a positive assumption of Executive Authority, instead of that of Legislative, which last is, alone your share in the Constitution of the State. . . . It only remains for me now, compelled by existing circumstances, to prorogue this Parliament, whatever may be the inconvenience resulting to the Province by such a measure.[74]

Christie and Kingsford, the two English-speaking historians who have dealt with this period in detail, are in general agreement upon the French-Canadian reaction to Dalhousie's stand. Christie, a contemporary, writes:

It is impossible adequately to describe the seditious agitation in all quarters of Lower Canada, that followed the prorogation, and the absurd tales, improbable, palpable untruths resorted to by the agitators to excite the *habitants*, (for whom, in their credulity and implicit faith in their leaders, nothing could be too gross,) and beget a feeling of hatred against the government and towards the governor personally. . . .[75]

In July, the provincial Parliament was dissolved and a general election followed immediately, "but the government was no better accommodated, nor more likely to fare better with the new assembly than it had with the previous body."[76]

The new House proved to be of very short duration. When it met on November 20, 1827, Louis Joseph Papineau, the outstanding hero of his people and adversary of Dalhousie, was re-elected speaker by a large majority (41 to 5). After the prorogation of March 7, Papineau with seven other members of the Assembly had issued a manifesto on public matters in which they strongly censured the Governor personally; and, on other occasions, particularly in an address to his constituency after his re-election, Papineau expressed his disrespect of the Governor so pointedly that it was next to impossible that Dalhousie could overlook the affront. When the French leader went up to be received by the Governor, he was informed by the speaker of the Legislative Council that the Governor did not approve the choice of the Assembly. The members of the Assembly were therefore instructed to retire and choose another speaker, whom they should present to the Governor for approval on the following Friday (November 23) at two o'clock.

On the following day the House adopted by a large majority (39 to 4) five resolutions, of which the last stated "that this house doth persist in its choice, and that the said Louis Joseph Papineau, esquire, ought to be and is its speaker." In addition to these resolutions, an address reported to be in imitation of one to Charles II on a similar occasion was proposed and voted to the Governor. Dalhousie refused to receive either the address or message relating to an address until the House had chosen its speaker. As there was not the least prospect of a compromise, or any arrangement that would permit a session for the dispatch of public business, Dalhousie issued a proclamation on November 23 proroguing the Parliament.[77]

In the weeks which followed, petitions on behalf of both the Assembly and the Governor were drawn up.[78] Of particular interest is one addressed to the king of December, 1827. The following paragraph appears in the midst of complaints about alleged financial abuse and mismanagement by the executive:

Your Majesty's faithful subjects in these provinces have already forwarded humble representations to your Majesty's government on the subject of the college and estates heretofore in the possession of the late order of jesuits in this province, and while we deplore the unfavourable result of our past endeavours, we nevertheless continue to entertain the most perfect confidence, that so soon as the truth shall be fully known to your Majesty, justice will be rendered unto us; and we humbly represent that as the said order was never the proprietor of the said college and estates, but merely the depositary thereof, for the education of the youth of Canada, the extinction of that order could not confer on the sovereign any other rights on that property than were possessed by the said order; and your Majesty succeeded to the possession of those estates, subject to their being applied to the education of the youth of this province, conformably to their primitive destination; and it is with the most profound grief that we find ourselves still deprived of the benefits which were formerly derived from the actual application of that property to these objects under the direction of the Jesuits, while education is languishing amongst us for want of those resources.[79]

John Neilson of Quebec and D. B. Viger and Austin Cuvillier of Montreal were delegated to carry the petitions to England. They left on their mission, via New York, in February, 1828.[80]

William Huskisson, the colonial secretary, brought the subject of the petitions of grievances from Canada before the House of Commons on May 2, 1828, and moved for a select committee to inquire into the civil government of the province. Huskisson himself did not favour the strong pretensions of the Assembly but they found a champion in Sir James Mackintosh, who had been entrusted with the presentation of their petitions.[81] The select committee examined nineteen witnesses, after which they made their report to the House of Commons on July 22. Regarding the control of finances, a question which had been a major source of dissension in Lower Canada, the committee reported:

> Although from the opinion given by the law officers of the crown, your committee must conclude that the legal right of appropriating the revenues arising from the act of 1774, is vested in the crown, they are prepared to say that the real interests of the province would be best promoted by placing the receipt and expenditure of the whole public revenue under the superintendance and controul of the house of assembly.
>
> On the other hand, your committee, while recommending such a concession on the part of the crown, are strongly impressed with the advantages of rendering the governor, the members of the executive council, and the judges independent of the annual votes of the house of assembly, for their respective salaries.[82]

As to the estates which formerly belonged to the Jesuits, the committee lamented that they did not have more complete information, but it appeared to them desirable that the proceeds should be applied to general education.[83] This report never became the subject of debate in the House of Commons. It was tabled on the last day of the session of 1827–8 and it remained unconsidered during the following session. According to Kingsford, it was stated on creditable authority that the report was carried in the select committee by one vote only, the knowledge of which fact might have exercised some restraint on the majority when they brought the subject before Parliament. The retirement of William Huskisson from the position of colonial secretary may likewise help to explain why Parliament took no action on the report.[84]

In December, 1827, Dalhousie applied for a leave of absence to take his place in the House of Lords and thereby to justify his conduct. He was informed, however, that it was the intention of the government to appoint him commander-in-chief in India on the arrival in England of Lord Combermere who had held that post. On September 8, 1828, Dalhousie gave over both the command of the forces and the civil government to Sir James Kempt.[85] Christie reports that Kempt

> ... was resolved to spare no pains to appease the agitators; and, accordingly, it soon was apparent to all, that while courting the leading demagogues of the day, with an assiduity approaching to obsequiousness, he studiously affected to keep aloof from those who were known, or believed to have been in the confidence of his predecessor, or favourably disposed towards him; a false and fawning policy that availed him nothing in the end, rightly appreciated as it was, from the outset, by those even whom it was intended to flatter.[86]

A later historian has written: "If the Canadian issue could be settled by the application of rational principles, Sir James Kempt was pre-eminently the man whom Canada needed."[87] The latter view would seem to be borne out by the sincere efforts of Kempt in the troubled situation.

Efforts were made by Kempt to discourage the editors of the *Quebec Gazette* and the *Quebec Mercury* (both designated as "official" by Christie) from exploiting politically exciting topics of discussion. One of his earliest acts was the public notification to all persons responsible for the expenditure of public money to close their accounts to September 10, 1828, and to report the balances in their possession. Many of the accounts had remained open for years, and the proceeding was deservedly popular.[88]

The meeting of the Assembly got off to a mild start on November 21, Kempt seeing fit to accept Papineau as speaker. The government's position on financial matters was not made known for a week. Then on November 28 a message from Kempt to the Assembly stated that until the Acts of 1774 and 1791 were repealed the revenues stemming from them should be applied to the salaries of the officer administering the government and of the judiciary, and that the House should provide for the further exigencies. All other balances in the hands of the receiver-general were to be dependent upon the vote of the legislature. This announcement drew from the Assembly, on December 6, a series of sixteen resolutions, the second of which "observed with great concern" that it might "be inferred from the expression of that part of the said Message which relates to the appropriation of the revenue, that the pretension put forth at the commencement of the late Administration to the disposal of a large portion of the Revenue of this Province" might be persisted in.[89]

Again a reference to the Jesuits' estates "cropped up" in the midst of other grievances, as appears in the sixteenth resolution. The question of the "application of the late Property of the Jesuits to the purposes of general Education" was raised "as most desirable to be adjusted and most essential to the future peace, welfare and good government of the Province." The Assembly also drew up a special address to the Governor for the restoration of the Jesuits' estates to the original design. This address asked that the estates be placed at the disposal of the legislature for the purposes of encouraging education in the province and that further sales of the property might be prevented. Although Kempt promised to transmit this resolution to the Imperial government without delay, he did not do it until a year later (March 8, 1830).[90]

The 1831 session of the legislature was opened on January 27 by Lord Aylmer who had assumed the government of the province, first as administrator and then as governor-in-chief.[91] By the end of February he had aroused the ire of the Assembly by refusing to comply with their request for copies of any dispatch or instruction from the Imperial government concerning the financial affairs of the province. On February 28, a number of addresses were voted to the Governor, two of them pertaining to the Jesuits' estates. One requested a detailed financial statement of the accounts of the estates to date. The other called for a detailed statement of the intended future application of the income from the estates.

In answer to the first of the addresses, Aylmer said that the information sought had hitherto been withheld in conformity with instructions from the home government. Until he had precise instructions on the subject, he could not feel justified in furnishing the desired information. To the second of the two addresses, he replied that he could not take upon himself to say what might be the future intentions of the home government with regard to the appropriation of the revenues, which were considered as the property of the Crown. He could only state generally that it was the intention of the home government to apply them to the public interests of the province, and he had reason to believe that the following items would be made chargeable upon the revenues: (1) the advancement of education; (2) the payment of the clergy of the established church; (3) £1,000 *per annum* to the Roman Catholic bishop of Quebec; (4) an annual allowance of £600 to Presbyterian ministers.[92]

From March 8 a committee of the whole House sat for several days considering the state of the province, and then adopted a series of resolutions submitted by John Neilson for petitions to the king, Lords, and Commons. The petition to the king did not differ materially from the sixteen resolutions of December 6, 1828. First among the items submitted for royal consideration was that pertaining to the Jesuits' estates; it complained

That notwithstanding the progress that has been made in the education of the people of this province, under the encouragement afforded by the recent acts of the legislature, the effect of the impediments opposed to its general dissemination by the diversion of the revenues of the jesuits' estates, originally destined for this purpose, the withholding of promised grants of land for schools, in 1801, and the rejection in the legislative council of various bills in favour of education, are still severely felt throughout the province, and materially retard its prosperity.[93]

Governor Aylmer agreed to transmit the petition without delay but, in what Christie characterizes as an "eccentric" answer, he belaboured the members of the Assembly to determine from them if it contained *all* that they had to complain of to date.[94]

Kingsford, who had access to F. M. U. M. Bibaud's account of the debate on Neilson's resolutions, remarked that "the language used was unrestrained and aggressive in the extreme, assailing the imperial system, the colonial connection, the executive government of the province, the composition of the legislative council, indeed, the whole administrative system."[95] Speaking in defence of the resolution concerning the Jesuits' estates and education, Austin Cuvillier affirmed that the provincial government was opposed to the diffusion of intelligence.

... it reproached the people with being ignorant, at the same time refused the means of education. The French government, with royal munificence, had met the increasing wants of the people with endowments that had been advantageously employed for the education of youth. They had been witnesses of the happy results for the country. What ought to be felt at seeing that building, [the Jesuit College of Quebec] where formerly knowledge was with such success imparted, applied to-day to the use of a thousand soldiers? Has not every sentiment of humanity been cast aside to add insult to injury? ...[96]

Papineau was not to be outdone by Cuvillier on the subject of the estates. Kingsford, relying on Bibaud's account, reports Papineau's remarks as follows:

... In his view, those ... remarks [of Cuvillier] should appeal to the sensibility that should rend the heart of every husband and father, when he reflects upon the perversity of a small number of men that despoiled them of the possessions destined to their use, and wasted the revenues which ought to be devoted to a noble and useful purpose, in order to pay salaries to themselves, the enemies of the country, who added insult to injury. The British government desired that the jesuit estates should be applied to their primitive purpose. They were the victims of the cupidity of the public *employés*, and were deprived of the incalculable advantages to enrich a dastardly faction (*lâche faction*). England, informed of these abuses, has not as yet ordered the punishment of these leeches. If by bayonets they were impeded from entry to their colleges, they must send their children to a free country to receive instruction. The same iniquitous system adopted in Canada had hastened the period when the old colonies ceased to form a part of the British empire. Let them revert to this period. ... [Papineau hinted at the possibility that oppression and tyranny on the part of the executive might lead to rebellion, in which the rebels would enjoy the support of the United States.] The mother country can effect the continuance of our connection with her, by her liberality and justice, not in expending millions upon fortifications which we do not ask, when she has meanness, in order not to incur the modest and necessary expenses for barracks, to refuse to restore to them their colleges.[97]

Such language was an earnest of stronger to follow in the period of the 1830s, after the disposition of the revenues from the Jesuits' estates had been placed in the hands of the Assembly. The legislature was prorogued by Aylmer on March 31.[98]

The petition of the Assembly to the Crown was answered by the Colonial Secretary, Lord Goderich, in a dispatch to Aylmer of July 7, 1831. Goderich reported that the home government did not deny that the Jesuits' estates were appropriated to the education of the people upon the dissolution of that Order, and he readily admitted that the revenue from that property should be regarded as inviolably and exclusively applicable to that object. It was to be regretted that any part of those funds were ever applied to any other purpose. It was Goderich's impression, however, that the rents of the estates had, during the last few years, been devoted exclusively to education. He referred Aylmer to a dispatch of December 24, 1830, which indicated that the British government had decided upon a strict adherence to that principle several months before the present address was adopted.[99]

Goderich advised Aylmer that the only practical question which remained for consideration was whether the application of the Jesuits' estates funds for education should be directed by the Crown or by the provincial legislature. The Governor was informed that "The King cheerfully, and without reserve confides that duty to the Legislature in the full persuasion that they will make such a selection amongst the different plans for this purpose which may be presented to their notice, as may most effectually advance the interests of Religion, and sound Learning amongst his Subjects."[100] It could not be doubted, this dispatch went on to say, that the Assembly would see the justice of continuing to maintain those scholastic establishments to which the funds had hitherto been applied. Goderich understood that certain buildings on the Jesuits' estates which were formerly used for collegiate purposes had since been employed as a barracks for the king's troops. He thought it would obviously be highly inconvenient to attempt any immediate change in this respect and he was convinced that the Assembly would regret any measure which might diminish the comforts or endanger the health of the king's forces. He indicated, however, that if the Assembly would provide adequate barracks, the Crown would acquiesce in the appropriation of the college buildings to the same purposes as those to which the general funds of the Jesuits' estates were about to be restored.

In the same dispatch Goderich expressed the fear that ill-founded expectations might have been harboured as to the value and productiveness of the Jesuits' estates. He thought that in this, as in most other cases, concealment had led to exaggeration. Had the Assembly's request for an account of the proceeds of the estates been granted, much apprehension would probably have been dispelled. Disavowing any wish for concealment, the Colonial Secretary instructed the Governor to provide detailed accounts for the Assembly at the beginning of its next session and to supply the House with any further explanatory statements which they might require regarding the estates.[101]

Goderich's dispatch was given to the Assembly shortly after the legislature was opened on November 15, 1831, and the passages dealing with the Jesuits' estates and education were referred to a standing committee on education and schools.[102] On December 3, the Assembly asked the Governor for such documents as had been prepared concerning the Jesuits' estates since they came into the possession of the Crown, a request with which Aylmer complied on December 21.[103]

As the objects for which the revenue from the estates was spent were so frequently open to question in the period from 1800 to 1831, the following table has been prepared from the "General Statement of the Expenditures and Receipts," one of the documents submitted by the Governor.[104]

D*

EXPENDITURES FROM THE JESUITS' ESTATES INCOME
1800–31

	£	s.	d.	
Management:				
Visitor and Inspector	2,495	2	4	
Treasurer (Commissioner after 1827)	3,406	14	2	
Clerks (after 1827)	500	0	0	
Agents (1824 only)	52	8	6	
Advocates	866	6	3	
Contingencies	1,331	11	1	
Total	8,652	2	4	
Education:				
Royal Institution (after 1821)	619	12	6	[942 12 6]
Royal Grammar Schools:				
Quebec (after 1817)	4,737	10	3	
Montreal (after 1817)	4,008	8	9	[4,008 4 0]
Kingston (after 1817)	2,682	0	8	
Total	12,389	7	6	[12,370 7 5]
Prosecution of Claim for McGill College	780	0	0	
Protestant Churches				
Quebec: Episcopal	7,093	2	11	
St. Andrew's	300	0	0	
Aubigny	100	0	0	
Sorel	300	0	0	
Chambly	200	0	0	
Trois Rivières	200	0	0	
Montreal	1,000	0	0	
Nicolet	100	0	0	
Hull	500	0	0	
Total	9,793	2	11	
Repairs and Improvements				
Beauport Farm	953	5	10	
Mills, etc.	3,779	3	2	
Total	4,732	9	0	
Object Unknown:				
1813	461	11	3a	
1814	1,518	8	6	
1815	2,081	1	3	
1816	2,060	15	10	
Total	6,321	16	10	[6,121 16 10]
Rents and Capitals Due:				
1821	923	6	7	
1822	90	0	0	
1823	180	0	0	
1824	180	0	0	
1825	176	6	0	
Total	1,549	12	7	
Services Unknown:				
1801	64	18	9b	
1802	100	0	0	
1819	1,054	12	2½c	
Total	1,719	10	11½	[1,219 10 11½]

EXPENDITURES (contd.)

	£	s.	d.
Pensions:			
1827	50	0	0d
1828	200	0	0
1829	322	2	0
1830	125	0	0
1831	125	0	0
Total	822	2	0
Chaplain:			
1829	760	18	10e
1830	222	4	4
Total	984	3	2 [983 3 2]
General Total of Expenditures	47,744	7	3½
	[47,024	7	2½]

a The items under this heading were paid to the commissary-general, but were later refunded by him.
b This sum was paid to S. Sewell. c This sum was paid to the Honourable J. Sewell, "to reimburse him so much in going to England in 1814, and returning in 1816." d The items for pensions were an allowance to H. W. Ryland and George Ryland of half the salary which they had received, the first as treasurer and the second as clerk to the Jesuits' Estates, and of a pension granted to Misses de Salaberry.[105] e The items for "Chaplain" were paid to the Reverend E. Sewell, as Minister of the Chapel of the Holy Trinity at Quebec.

	£	s.	d.
Revenue as shown by Table A and Tables 4 and 5[106]	49,583	14	3
Expenditures as shown by Table A	47,744	7	3½
Balance	1,839	6	11¼
Sum paid to commissary-general, and refunded	6,321	16	10
Balance which should have been on hand in 1831	8,161	3	9½

By way of comment on the foregoing tabulation, it should first be observed that there were several errors in calculation in the more comprehensive table of information placed before the Assembly. As these errors may have been due to the omission of certain items, the totals of those who prepared the account are given above, with what appear to be the correct totals in brackets alongside the apparently incorrect ones. Most of the items are self-explanatory, while two or three of them call for special notice. No additional information has been found regarding the use to which the £64 18s. 9d., allotted to S. Sewell in 1801, was put. The payment of £1,054 12s. 2½d. to Jonathan Sewell was made by order of Lord Bathurst to Sir John C. Sherbrooke, dated April 14, 1817. The Chief Justice had gone to England to clear himself of charges brought against him by the Assembly. As he was cleared, Bathurst considered him to be fairly entitled to remuneration for his expenses and ordered that they be paid out of the produce of the Jesuits' estates.[107] Of all the items of expenditure in the period from 1800 to 1832, the reimbursement of Sewell was undoubtedly the most revolting to the House of Assembly.

The payment of pensions to H. W. Ryland and his son George was occasioned by the fact that in 1826 Dalhousie undertook a general overhauling of the system of managing the Jesuits' estates to reduce costs. John Stewart, as sole commissioner, replaced the board of commissioners which had operated since 1801, and Ryland

and son lost their respective positions as treasurer and clerk for the management of the estates, which led to a very bitter quarrel between Dalhousie and H. W. Ryland. Ryland later was allowed a pension consisting of half his old salary.[108] After the control of the Jesuits' estates funds passed to the House of Assembly, Ryland petitioned the Imperial government for the continuance of his half-salary pension of £75, but was informed that unless he could satisfy the Assembly that he ought not to be deprived of the allowance, there was nothing that the Imperial government could do.[109] Ryland, having served on both the Executive Council and the Legislative Council, had not the smallest chance of securing a pension from the Assembly.

It will be observed that a total sum of £984 3s. 2d. was paid to the Chief Justice's son, Reverend E. Sewell, as minister of the Chapel of the Holy Trinity at Quebec, with arrears from November 27, 1825. This payment had its origin in a situation which greatly displeased the House of Assembly. It appears that Chief Justice Jonathan Sewell erected the Chapel of the Holy Trinity, or Chapel of Ease, at Quebec at a cost of £3,500 under an express understanding that his son was to receive a salary of £200 from the Jesuits' estates.[110] This was subject to the condition that if the rent of the pews exceeded the allowance of £200, the amount of that allowance was to be reduced by the amount of the surplus. Bathurst later sanctioned the continuance of the salary of £200 from the Jesuits' estates funds until the rent of the pews should exceed £400, in view of the fact that the Chief Justice had also purchased the site for the Chapel.[111] In 1828 the Anglican bishop of Quebec asked to have the salary form an item of the general expenses of the ecclesiastical establishment of the province since the funds of the Jesuits' estates had proved insufficient to defray it. The colonial secretary, George Murray, suggested instead that the charge of £200 for the salary of the master of the grammar school at Kingston be transferred to the province of Upper Canada, which would permit that sum, hitherto paid from the Jesuits' estates funds, to be used to pay Sewell's salary.[112]

An examination of the record of expenditures suggests that there was ample cause for Roman Catholic discontent over the uses to which the revenues of the Jesuits' estates were put. While a large sum (£12,389 7s. 6d.) was spent for the purposes of education, the Roman Catholics, although they had deliberately boycotted the institutions upon which it was spent, would insist the sum was spent for Protestant interests. Certainly there could be no satisfaction with the expenditure of nearly £9,800 for the maintenance of Protestant churches. Finally, it must be recognized that the expenditures which had benefited certain members of the executive branch of the government angered the members of the Assembly as a result of the hostilities which existed between it and the executive.

The House of Assembly, acting upon Lord Goderich's dispatch of July 7, 1831, introduced a bill on February 11, 1832, to appropriate the Jesuits' estates funds to education exclusively. The bill was passed by the House on February 15 and by the Legislative Council on February 21. Royal assent was given to the Act on February 25.[113] The appropriation bill, 2 Will. IV, c. 61, provided

... that from and after the passing of this Act, all monies arising out of the Estates of the late Order of Jesuits which now are in or may hereafter come into the hands of the Receiver General of this Province, shall be placed in a separate Chest in the vaults wherein the public monies of the Province are kept, and shall be applied to the purposes of education exclusively, in the manner provided by this Act, or by any Act or Acts which may hereafter be passed by the Provincial Legislature in that behalf, and not otherwise.[114]

With the passage of 2 Will. IV, c. 61, another phase of the history of the Jesuits' estates problem came to a close. The Assembly had finally achieved its goal of gaining control of the appropriation of the revenues of these estates for the purposes of provincial education. It should be observed, however, that there still remained a fly in the ointment. According to Lord Goderich's dispatch, the old Jesuits' college and the properties appertaining immediately thereto would remain in the hands of the Crown until the province made some provision for barracks for the troops stationed in Quebec.[115] The standing committee on education and schools, to whom that part of Goderich's dispatch had been referred, reported on February 7, 1832:

Among the parts of the property of the Estates which is [sic] occupied for public purposes, . . . is the College latterly known as "the Jesuits' Barracks." There are few of the permanent Inhabitants of Canada who can view this Building without painful sensations. Founded so early as 1636, by an Order of men who crossed the Ocean to inhabit unknown Lands among Savage Inhabitants, to do good to their fellow men, and were frequently rewarded with sufferings and death amidst cruel torture, this Building rose by their labour and care, and by pious donations, to be the most extensive Seminary of Learning at the time in North America. Many of the Fathers of the present generation received a liberal education at this College, and all flattered themselves that it was destined to spread and perpetuate for ever that blessing throughout the Country. It now stands a melancholy monument of a change of Government, which in so many other respects has been beneficial.

The committee could not entertain a doubt but that it would be finally restored to its original use without conditions, "which would absorb the revenue of the Estates for many years to come, and render a signal act of Justice incomplete."[116]

CHAPTER SEVEN

PROVINCIAL CONTROL, 1832-9

THE ASSEMBLY, having gained control of the Jesuits' estates revenues, found other matters relating to the estates to engage its attention in the period leading up to the Rebellion of 1837. One of the first of these matters was the recovery of the old Jesuits' college. On December 7, 1832, the House asked Governor Aylmer for any communication that he might have had from the British government relating to the continued occupation of the college buildings as a barracks and for any information as to when that occupation might cease. The Governor replied on December 10 that he had not had any communication on the matter except the dispatch of Lord Goderich of July 7, 1831, which was already known to the Assembly.[1] To a similar address of January, 1834, the Governor made a similar reply, with the addition that he considered Goderich's dispatch to be conclusive. This reply was referred to a special committee for examination and report.[2]

The special committee, in its first report on February 3, 1834, referred to the 1828 report of the committee of the House of Commons which had concluded that it was desirable that the proceeds from the Jesuits' estates should be applied to the purposes of general education, without any exception. The special committee also cited Goderich's dispatch of July 7, 1831, as convincing proof that it was the British government's intention that the college building be under the control of the provincial legislature in order that the income for its use as a barracks might be applied, along with the rest of the Jesuits' estates funds, for the purposes of education.[3]

The special committee concluded that the condition attached to the offer to restore the college (that is, for the province to provide other barracks) would detract from the act of justice by which the British government had relinquished control of the revenues of the estates. The provincial legislature, they reported, "by accepting that condition would sanction the application of the Funds which His Majesty's Government had recognized as inviolably and exclusively appropriated to the great object of promoting Education . . . to a purpose totally foreign to the said object." The committee recommended an address to the king,

. . . praying Him to . . . complete the work of justice already begun in favour of Education in this Country, by the unconditional restitution of the College, and the ground adjoining it, which forms part of the property of the late Order of Jesuits, to the Provincial Legislature.[4]

The Assembly concurred in this report,[5] but it does not appear from the *Journals* that such an address to the king was actually drafted and forwarded. There was, however, a complaint in the celebrated Ninety-two Resolutions, which were passed during this stormy session, of "the unjust retention of the college at Quebec, which forms part of the estates of the late Order of Jesuits, and which from a college has been trans-formed into a barrack for soldiers."[6]

The spirit of 1834 persisted and, on November 4, 1835, the House once again addressed the Governor, asking for such further information as he might have rece d from the home government concerning the prolonged occupation of the college by Imperial troops.[7] Lord Gosford, who had replaced Aylmer as governor-in-chief, and also had the role of high commissioner,[8] replied on November 13 that he had been directed to inform the House that the home government was anxious that the college buildings be restored as promptly as possible to their original use, and that this measure should not be delayed a day after other and adequate provision should have been made for the accommodation of the troops. Gosford reminded the Assembly that a proposal made at the opening of the session, to place all the sources of local revenue under the control of the representatives of the people, would deprive the Crown of the means of providing for the lodging of the troops. As soon, therefore, as suitable barracks were provided, the board of ordnance would immediately issue the necessary instructions for evacuating the college.[9] Four days later, the Governor's message was referred to a standing committee on the Jesuits estates, with an order to ascertain the actual value of the college, the annual revenue which might be derived from it, and the average annual revenue which might have been derived from it for the years during which the military authorities occupied it.[10] The committee, which had been appointed on October 30, 1835, was composed of Edouard Bernard, Louis T. Besserer, Joseph N. Cardinal, L. G. de Tonnancour, Joseph René Kimber, Alexis Mousseau, and Pierre Elzéard Taschereau.[11]

The committee reported on January 19, 1836, that the value of the college as it was laid out for barracks would scarcely exceed £5,000, including all the buildings attached to it, and that the ground on which the buildings stood was estimated worth £35,000, the interest of which, at six per cent, would amount to £2,100 *per annum*. Assuming that this sum was the average annual revenue of the Jesuits' college since its entire occupation by the military authorities in 1800, it would follow, reported the committee, that the province would be entitled to claim from the Imperial government the sum of £73,500 for thirty-five years' rent of the property from 1800 to 1835. The committee suggested that improved use of the property would increase the annual revenue to a sum of £3,500, if the British government restored it to the province.[12]

After considering the Governor's message of November 13, 1835, the committee regretted to find

... that the same condition is always attached to the restoration of the Jesuits' College to the purposes for which it was originally intended, the more so as His Majesty's Government in consideration of their having enjoyed up to the present time free of expense, a property to which they were aware did not belong to them, ought to erect new Barracks for the Troops out of the money which they ought to have paid to the Province as rent, and thereby give full effect to Lord Goderich's Despatch of the 7th July 1831, which cheerfully and unreservedly entrusts to the Legislature the appropriation of all monies arising from the Estates of the late Order of Jesuits, for the purposes of Education.[13]

The committee was certain that the Imperial government could easily secure another site for barracks at a comparatively small cost. Such being the case the committee was convinced that the college ought to be restored unconditionally.[14] In the mounting tensions that led to the Rebellion of 1837, the issue of the restoration of the college appears to have become obscured by other concerns, though it again made its appearance in Lord Durham's *Report.*

A different tack was taken to the question of the final disposition of the Jesuits' college by at least one other group besides those who pressed for its restoration to the province in the Assembly. The adoption of the Ninety-two Resolutions had been opposed by John Neilson and a constitutional party. The division on the Resolutions widened the breach between Papineau and Neilson and led to the formation of two hostile camps, each suspicious of the other. Patriotic associations were formed by Papineau and his lieutenants in Montreal, Three Rivers, and Quebec, and committees of correspondence were constituted to ensure common action. On their side, the British inhabitants of Quebec and Montreal formed constitutional associations pledged to maintain the authority of the Crown and respect for the constitution.[15] Among the items submitted to the Constitutional Association of Montreal for its consideration on November 28, 1835, was one relating to the disposition of the college at Quebec. After commenting upon the establishment of several French colleges which derived their support principally from the public revenue, a committee report continued:

The numerous French Colleges, supported chiefly by grants from the Public Funds, warrant the Association in demanding, as an act of justice, proportionate grants for the instruction of youth of British and Irish origin; and further, they conceive that the Jesuits' Estate and College at Quebec should be dedicated to the establishment of an institution for the higher branches of science and learning, open to all classes, and divested of all sectarian religious test, in either its professors or its students.[16]

One may conclude from all this that it was unfortunate that the British government did not give up the college and its immediate environs when it relinquished control over the other parts of the Jesuits' estates. It must be observed, however, that the Assembly had other concerns relating to the estates with which to occupy itself. It seems almost certain that the House would not have been perfectly satisfied even if the college had been surrendered to provincial control.

An issue which agitated the Assembly concurrently with the disposition of the college of Quebec was the lease of the St. Maurice forges and the establishment of a reserve in the Jesuit property of Cap de la Magdeleine to provide wood for the charcoal needed by the forges.

One of the most interesting industries connected with the old régime in Canada was that of the iron forges near Three Rivers in the fief of St. Maurice. The forges were continued in operation by the British after their conquest of Canada. Haldimand thought that they should be carried on by the government, and they were accordingly continued on a semi-military and feudal basis by the enforcement of *corvée* or statute labour. In 1764 the men working at the forges received the same regular rations as were furnished to the troops. In 1765 Haldimand was removed to New York, and the forges were closed. In June, 1767, Carleton granted to C. Pelissier a lease of the mines and forges with the accompanying buildings and equipment. Pelissier set them in operation once more, and they continued to produce bar iron, stoves, pots and, later, potash kettles.[17]

In 1829 Matthew Bell, long-time lessee of the forges of St. Maurice,[18] began negotiations with the provincial government for the renewal of his lease for a period of ten or fifteen years. His lease, held under the Crown, required a rental of £500 *per annum*, a sum which had been determined in 1806.[19] On April 9, 1831, Aylmer transmitted to the British government an address from the Assembly, the object of which was to obtain the settlement of lands belonging to the Jesuits' estates. Aylmer indicated that it would affect the interest of Bell, whose lease of the forges of St.

Maurice was about to expire. The Governor suggested that the consideration of the Assembly's address be deferred until the Imperial government should have made a final decision regarding the disposal of the estates. Meanwhile, he had taken it upon himself to extend Bell's occupation of the forges for one year more, dating from April 1, 1832.[20]

The connection between the lease of the forges of St. Maurice and the settlement of lands in the Jesuits' estates becomes clear upon an examination of the third report of the special committee of the Assembly, mentioned above, of February 8, 1834. According to this report, Bell had used the greater part of the unconceded cultivable lands of Cap de la Magdeleine to secure wood for the forges, without charge, and under a mere permission given by the Duke of Richmond in 1819. The committee also stated that in 1831 the commissioner of the Jesuits' estates, John Stewart, had the area surveyed and designated as the "Reserve for the Forges of St. Maurice."[21] It was almost certain that the House of Assembly would become greatly excited about the renewal of the lease of the forges, especially about the setting aside of a reserve in one of the Jesuits' properties. It was all the more certain because Matthew Bell was a member of the Legislative Council and John Stewart a member of both the Legislative and the Executive Council.[22]

In a letter of March 12, 1832, Bell again sought a renewal of the lease of the forges for ten or fifteen years. He assured the Governor that he would faithfully perform all the duties of a good tenant, carry on the works to the fullest extent as long as wood and ore could be procured within the limits, "protect the work people, and make the young take care of the old," as he had done since he acquired the works. He reminded the Governor of the experience which he had gained in the management of the forges "for upwards of forty years," and of the employment opportunities afforded by the forges under capable management. Bell then suggested the expediency of annexing a portion of the Seigniory of Cap de la Magdeleine to the property of the forges to insure the needed supplies of wood and ore.[23] Aylmer forwarded this letter to the home government with a strong recommendation in favour of Bell and against opening the lease to general public competition. He asked that Bell's lease be renewed for ten years from March, 1834, the date to which he had now extended it.[24]

Goderich approved of Aylmer's renewal of the lease for one year and agreed that it would not be expedient to lease a property like the forges, requiring an outlay of considerable capital, merely to the highest bidder. He suggested, however, that it might be reasonable to expect some additional rent from Bell in consideration of the renewal of the lease without public competition. The increasing population and the wants of the colony, said the Secretary of State, would seem to warrant an expectation that the rent of £500 *per annum*, fixed in 1806 under less favourable circumstances, could be increased without diminishing the reasonable profits of the lessee.[25]

Bell rejected the suggestion of an increase, maintaining that £500 was as much as could possibly be afforded. While persisting in his offer to take a lease for ten to fifteen years at the old rent and upon the conditions of 1806, he nevertheless offered to relinquish the forges if any man with sufficient capital would take the works and secure to him the value of the stock and raw materials belonging to it.[26] Thereupon, Aylmer recommended to Goderich the expediency of renewing Bell's lease for ten or fifteen years at £500 per year on the ground that in a new country like Canada few persons could be found possessing the necessary capital to engage in so large a concern as the forges of St. Maurice.[27] E. G. Stanley (later Lord Derby), the new

Colonial Secretary, replied on May 25, 1833, that he could see no objection to a renewal of the lease for a period of ten years at the old rent.[28]

The final arrangement of the lease, and the reserve in Cap de la Magdeleine to supplement it, was made in 1834. On February 5 a committee of the Executive Council, acting upon a letter from Bell, recommended that a lease of 25,940 *arpents* of land in Cap de la Magdeleine be granted to him for a period coinciding with his lease of the forges, at an annual rent of £75. The Governor approved,[29] and a lease of the 25,940 *arpents* was accordingly drawn up on April 24.[30] The lease of the forges of St. Maurice was executed on November 25 of the same year, to run from January 1, 1834, to January 1, 1844. The rent was still to be £500 *per annum*, but £75 of this was to be paid to the commissioner for the management of the Jesuits' estates.[31] Such, then, were the principal negotiations leading up to the granting of the forges and the reserve lands to Matthew Bell, a member of the Legislative Council. The reaction of the House of Assembly to all this business must now be sketched.

On February 21, 1831, the Assembly addressed the Governor, seeking the adoption of measures for the granting and settlement of land within a tract in the vicinity of Three Rivers which was comprised in the lease of the St. Maurice forges. The address asked that precautions be taken that the renewal of the lease of the forges should not in any manner be an obstacle to the granting of lands within the tract specified. The Governor replied on February 25 that the matter would have to be referred to higher authority, and he promised to transmit the address of the Assembly, without delay, to the British government.[32] Other addresses relating to the subject of the renewal of the lease of the forges were made by the House in the fall of 1831 and 1832. An address of December 22, 1832, asked for a copy of the instrument by which the lease was being renewed, a request with which the Governor refused to comply.[33]

On January 14, 1834, the Assembly again addressed the Governor, asking him to acquaint the House with further information he might have received from the British government since 1832 concerning the extension of the lease of the forges and the lands formerly included in it. To this address, the Governor replied on the following day that he had been authorized by the British government to extend the lease of the forges to Matthew Bell for a period of ten years.[34] On the same day, two petitions were introduced into the House, both from persons seeking grants of land in the Seigniory of Cap de la Magdeleine in the area which was being contemplated as a reserve for the forges of St. Maurice. The petitioners from Three Rivers reported that they had recently applied to the commissioner for the Jesuits' estates for grants but had been told that the latter had no order to concede lands in that area because they were reserved for the use of the St. Maurice forges. The petitioners therefore urged the House to reform the management of the Jesuits' estates. They thought it would be expedient to abolish the office of chief commissioner of the estates for the whole province and to appoint an accountable agent in each district. Such an agent, they thought, having a better knowledge of local circumstances, could serve the government and the public more efficiently and at less expense. This petition, along with a similar one from certain inhabitants of the Parish of St. Grégoire and Bécancour, was referred to a special committee which was also to consider the Governor's answer.[35]

On January 18 the House pressed to find out whether the Governor had actually extended the lease of Bell, as he had been authorized to do by the home government, and to secure a copy of the lease if he had. The Governor replied on January 21 that the instrument by which the extension of the lease was to be effected was being completed by the proper official. However, in conformity with his decision on a similar address of the House of December 22, 1832, he must again decline to furnish the House with a copy of the lease.[36] This answer was likewise referred to the special committee.

This committee reported on February 8, 1834, that the settlement of the reserved area of Cap de la Magdeleine should not be impeded by an exclusive use of that area by the lessee of the forges of St. Maurice.[37] Examining the situation in the light of Goderich's dispatch of July 7, 1831, the committee concluded that if they might interpret the dispatch in a manner most favourable to the advancement of education, it was the province of the Assembly not only to provide for the equitable distribution of the Jesuits' estates funds, but also, jointly with the other branches of the legislature, to take care that the unconceded portions of the estates should be conceded and made available "in the manner most efficacious and best adapted to increase the revenue." They expressed surprise at the Governor's plan to dispose of a considerable portion of Cap de la Magdeleine without the concurrence of the House of Assembly, which alone possessed the right to originate such measures.[38]

The committee concluded that to effect the king's intentions in favour of education as expressed in Goderich's dispatch, all applications tending toward the speedy settlement of the unconceded lands of the Jesuits' estates on the usual terms ought to be favourably received and every facility be given to the applicants by the commissioner for the management of the estates. The committee advised an address to the Governor asking him not to include in Bell's lease the reserve in Cap de la Magdeleine and to co-operate with the legislature in granting the request of more than five hundred petitioners who were anxious to settle on this tract of land.[39]

Toward the close of the 1835 session of the legislature, a standing committee on the Jesuits' estates was appointed, consisting of Dr. Joseph René Kimber, Louis R. Blanchard, L. Michel Viger, Edouard Bernard, Jacques Dorion, J. Moise Raymond, and Pierre Garreau.[40] A new standing committee was named at the opening of the 1835-6 legislative session, on which Kimber and Bernard continued to serve, as did Louis T. Besserer, Joseph N. Cardinal, L. G. de Tonnancour, Alexis Mousseau, and Pierre E. Taschereau.[41] The French complexion of these committees is self-evident.

On November 4, 1835, the Assembly again sought from the Governor such further information as he might have received from the British government regarding the lands comprised in the former lease of the forges of St. Maurice. The Assembly also asked for a copy of the instrument under which Bell held the reserve for the forges, as well as that by which his lease of the forges was renewed, and Lord Gosford, who had replaced Aylmer on August 24, 1835, replied that he would gladly comply with this request.[42] In answer to the request regarding further instructions from the British government, Gosford indicated that the only information that he had received was that the lease of the forges of St. Maurice was now to be considered as irrevocable. The British government, however, regretted that this property was not disposed of by public auction to the highest bidder and had directed that in the future the leasing of Crown property by private contract was to be avoided.[43]

The House's reaction to Gosford's reply was an address on December 7 requesting a copy of the correspondence between the former Governor, Aylmer, and the Colonial Office relative to the renewal of the lease of the forges in favour of Bell,[44] a request with which Gosford indicated a willingness to comply. In a word, under the new administration of Gosford, the House was now permitted to examine all the materials that Aylmer had previously withheld.[45] While the evidence compiled by the standing committee on the Jesuits' estates furnished ample material to prolong the discontent of the Assembly with the lease of the forges and the reserve,[46] the best assurance the Assembly could get from the Governor was that whatever arrangements might be made respecting the territorial revenue, there would be no leasing of any Crown property by private contract.[47]

In summary it may be said that the Assembly was justified in its resentment over the granting of the reserve in one of the Jesuits' estates to the lessee of the forges of St. Maurice. It appears, however, that, at least among the more radical element of the Assembly, the resentment was prompted as much by the fact that special favour was being shown to a member of the Legislative Council as by the fact that it was Jesuits' estates property which was being bestowed. This is evident from two references in the Ninety-two Resolutions passed by the Assembly in 1834. It has been pointed out that for the sake of convenience the Ninety-two Resolutions might have been divided into two groups—laudation of the French-Canadian people, the House of Assembly, the constitution of the United States, Daniel O'Connell and Joseph Hume, and condemnation of the Secretary of State for the Colonies, of the colonial Governor, of the Legislative Council, and of the judges and officers of the administration.[48] In the thirty-fourth resolution, a derogatory reference was made to "Matthew Bell, a grantee of the Crown, who has been unduly and illegally favoured by the Executive, in the lease of the forges of St. Maurice, in the grant of large tracts of waste lands, and in the lease of large tracts of land formerly belonging to the order of Jesuits."[49] The eighty-fourth resolution complained of

the renewal of the lease of a considerable portion of the [Jesuits'] estates, by the provincial executive, in favour of a member of the Legislative Council, since those estates were returned to the Legislature, and in opposition to the prayer of this House, and to the known wishes of a great number of His Majesty's subjects to obtain lands there, and to settle them; and the refusal of the said executive to communicate the said lease, and other information on the subject, to this House.[50]

Benjamin Sulte, in his treatise on the forges, seems to have hit the nail squarely on the head when he wrote:

L'agitation contre les Forges paraît n'avoir eu d'autre base que la passion politique. Bell était 'bureaucrate,' c'est-à-dire du parti des fonctionnaires nommés par la couronne et qui jouissaient de privilèges contre lesquels les députés canadiens à la Chambre d'assemblée luttaient avec persistance.[51]

One other important matter concerning the Jesuits' estates in the 1830s remains to be considered briefly—the administration of the estates by John Stewart, who had been appointed sole commissioner in 1826 by Dalhousie in lieu of a board of commissioners. By a general overhauling of the administrative machinery, Dalhousie had hoped to curtail expenditures in the management of the estates.[52] Stewart was, however, bitterly criticized by the Assembly for his failure to facilitate the settlement of the unconceded lands in the estates, for the accumulation of large arrears in the payment of the dues pertaining to the estates, for the laxity of his agents in the performance of their duties, and particularly for the granting of the reserve in Cap de la Magdeleine to Matthew Bell. "Minutes of Evidence" from the *Journals* of the House abound with evidence of the haphazard manner in which the agents performed their duties. Said one member of the House, "God knows what account they render."[53]

A special committee, with René J. Kimber as chairman, reported on February 8, 1834, that there was a real need for a change in the administration of the estates.

The committee, however, was not at that time prepared to make recommendations because of a lack of adequate information on the estates.[54] Two years later, on February 20, 1836, a bill was finally passed by the House for the proper management of the Jesuits' estates.[55] The bill, however, failed to become law because disputes between the two Houses so entirely engrossed attention after it was sent up to the Legislative Council as to prevent its passage, amendment, or rejection.[56]

An abundance of testimony came before the various investigating committees appointed from time to time by the Assembly which indicated a gross laxity on the part of the local agents charged with the management of the estates. It would appear, however, that the animus of the House was stimulated as much by resentment stemming from the several positions which Stewart held in the province as from the faulty management of the estates. This is evident in the thirty-fourth of the Ninety-two Resolutions of 1834, wherein a reference is made to "John Stewart, an Executive Councillor, commissioner of the Jesuits' estates, and the incumbent of other lucrative offices," and to his being placed by his pecuniary and personal interests under the influence of the Executive.[57] One of the witnesses in the investigation of 1835–6 called attention to the fact that, in addition to being commissioner for the Jesuits' estates, Stewart was a Legislative Councillor, an Executive Councillor, and that he held some place in the Trinity House. This witness (Joseph Rémi Vallières de St. Réal), a resident of Three Rivers, also mentioned that John Stewart and Matthew Bell had formerly been partners in trade under the firm of Bell and Stewart.[58] Nothing was made of this by the investigating committee. One is left with the impression that had the estates been managed badly under the charge of the House, there would not have been nearly so much excitement about it. A special committee appointed in 1836 to inquire whether there was any improper accumulation of public offices in any one person reported:

That the cumulation of the offices of Executive Councillor, being a Member of the Court of Appeals, of Commissioner of the Jesuit's [sic] Estates, and of Master of the Trinity House at Quebec, in the same person, is contrary to the public good, and incompatible with the due and efficient performance of the duties of the said offices; and that each of the said offices ought to be held by a separate person.[59]

John Stewart was, of course, the person concerned.

The standing committee on the Jesuits' estates had prepared a six-page report on the mal-administration of Stewart, but the shortness of the sessions of both 1836 and 1837 was such that they had no opportunity to present it.[60] The report was drawn up by René Kimber, the chairman of the committee. Several years later (1843) he wrote a blistering indictment of Stewart in a "Mémoire," whose chapter headings suggest the nature of its contents: (I) Fausseté, prévarication, favoritisme; (II) Ignorance, négligence; and (III) Incapacité.[61]

The story of the "Troublous Times" in Lower Canada between 1836 and 1839 has been too often told to need re-telling here. On August 26, 1837, Gosford prorogued the legislature, and, as events turned out, it never re-assembled.[62] In November the first shots of the Rebellion in Lower Canada were fired. On January 16, 1838, a bill was introduced in the Imperial Parliament which, after amendment and re-casting, was passed on February 10 as "An Act to make temporary provision for the government of Lower Canada."[63] The constitution of 1791 was suspended from the date of the proclamation of the Act to November 1, 1840. Power was given to the Crown to constitute a special council by authorizing the governor to summon special councillors.

Laws passed by this council were limited in operation to November 1, 1842, unless they should be continued by competent authority. The special council could impose no new taxes and make no constitutional changes. The governor could introduce a law, and five councillors must be present to give it legal force. The Act was sent to the Administrator, Sir John Colborne, who was instructed to summon a special council for temporary needs, leaving the new governor free to form his own. Colborne's Council, which met on April 18 and was prorogued on May 5, 1838, consisted of twenty-one members, of whom eleven were French Canadians.[64]

Lord Durham, who arrived in Canada on May 29, 1838, and assumed the duties of governor-in-chief, came with exceedingly wide powers which can be summed up in the words of the Colonial Secretary, Lord Glenelg. He was given a general super-intendence over all British North America, and he was to consider any proposals which might be "conducive to the permanent establishment of an improved system of government in Her Majesty's North American possessions."[65] The fruits of Durham's short stay in Canada are so well known that there is no need to examine them in any detail here.

Lord Durham's *Report* is justly celebrated for its recommendation of responsible government for the provinces of British North America. The *Report*, moreover, presented a thorough analysis of the ills that had beset the provinces since the beginning of British rule. What, then, had it to say about the problem which is the subject of this study, the problem of the disposal of the Jesuits' estates? There is only one short paragraph in the report itself which refers to the estates. It comes at the very end of Durham's account of education in Lower Canada.

I am grieved to be obliged to remark, that the British Government has, since its possession of this Province, done, or even attempted, nothing for the promotion of general education. Indeed the only matter in which it has appeared in connexion with the subject, is one by no means creditable to it. For it has applied the Jesuits' estates, part of the property destined for purposes of education, to supply a species of fund for secret service; and for a number of years it has maintained an obstinate struggle with the Assembly in order to continue this misappropriation.[66]

The brevity of Durham's comments on the Jesuits' estates is probably due to the fact that his report was published before all the supplementary reports which form the appendices had been received.[67] For a more complete commentary on the use (or mis-use) of the Jesuits' estates revenues, one must turn to two of these documents: the report of the commissioner of inquiry into the state of education in Lower Canada (Arthur Buller), and the report of the secretary to the Education Commission (Christopher Dunkin).

In reviewing the history of education in the province, Buller paid tribute to the work of the Catholic Church under the French régime, noting the devotion of the "ample estates and active benevolence of the Jesuits to the education of the people." It was impossible, said Buller, to pay too high a tribute to the merits of this most exemplary church. The Jesuits' estates, however, he observed, soon ceased to be available for the purposes for which they had been granted.

. . . The British Government, on the dissolution of that order, entered into possession; and, not content with diverting their proceeds from their original destination, unfortunately adopted the mode of appropriation the most obnoxious possible to that part of the population for whose benefit they were first granted, and who were the most clamorous for their restitution.[68]

In discussing the uses to which the Jesuits' estates funds had been put, Buller relied upon the statement of revenue and expenditure (1800–31) that had been submitted to the Assembly in the session of 1831–2. It appeared to him that the funds had been applied predominantly to the uses of the Protestant Church, and, in his opinion,

> . . . The English Government might maintain that in these appropriations it merely exercised the right which it undeniably possessed of doing what it liked with its own; but it cannot be matter of surprise that the Catholics of Canada should have felt discontented, when they saw the great Catholic legacy of their forefathers thus converted into a fund for the establishment of a rival church.[69]

Buller thoroughly investigated the matter of the disposal of two sums of money which had been recovered by the sale of property belonging to John Caldwell and awarded by provincial judicial authorities to the Jesuits' estates funds.[70] One amounted to £7,154 15s. 4½d., the other, £1,280 3s. 4d.[71] It had been Sir James Kempt's opinion that the larger sum belonged in equity to the province rather than to the Jesuits' estates. He had therefore directed the receiver-general to take both sums into his custody, but not to apply them to the account of the Jesuits' estates until he might receive instructions from the Imperial government.[72] Such instructions were given by Goderich to Aylmer in the celebrated dispatch of July 7, 1831. The sum of £7,154 15s. 4½d. was to be placed at the disposal of the legislature for general purposes; the smaller sum was also to be placed at the disposal of the legislature but was to be considered applicable to the purposes of education exclusively.[73] Buller criticized the government's diversion of the larger sum to the general fund of the province instead of earmarking it for education.[74]

Buller also criticized the provincial government for its failure to adhere to that part of 2 Will. IV, c. 41, which required that Jesuits' estates revenues that came into the hands of the receiver-general should be placed in a separate fund. Buller found that these funds had been invariably mixed with the other public revenue, a separate account being kept only to show their amount. By that account it appeared that the balance on October 10, 1838, had accumulated to £13,436 4s. 6¼d. Buller concluded that if the £7,154 15s. 4½d. currency, or £6,439 5s. 10½d. sterling, were added to the accumulated balance (as it unquestionably ought, in his opinion), the whole fund applicable to education in respect to the Jesuits' estates would amount to £19,875 10s. 4d.[75]

In considering the condition which had been attached to the surrender of the Jesuits' barracks (the college) in Goderich's dispatch of July 7, 1831, Buller feared it was not capable of fulfilment. He had communicated with the military authorities on the subject, who informed him that the Crown possessed no land sufficient for their site within the walls where the barracks must be. It would be bad economy for the province to recover the lost property by purchasing land already built upon, pulling down the buildings, and then erecting new barracks. There was also the cost of tearing down the old college buildings and replacing them with more profitable structures. The most equitable arrangement, Buller said, would be for the Crown to pay the proper market price for what it had so long withheld.[76]

After giving a rather bleak review of the history of education in the province,[77] Buller concluded that there must be a permanent provision of £35,000 a year for education. As he saw it, the only means at present available were the yearly revenues of the Jesuits' estates and the £20,000 belonging to the same fund. The £20,000, if well invested, might produce £1,200 a year; and the estates under good management might soon yield an available income of £3,000 a year. Still, £30,000 a year remained to be permanently secured. The only sources to which to look for this, thought Buller, were probably (1) a compensation from the home government for the Jesuits' barracks, which rightly belonged to the education fund as much as any other part of the estates, and (2) the Clergy Reserves.[78]

Dunkin, in his report, outlined the history of the Jesuits' estates as an educational endowment in Lower Canada.[79] He, too, called attention to the fact that, contrary to 2 Will. IV, c. 41, the Jesuits' estates funds were not kept in a separate chest. Furthermore, he declared that the decision to transfer the £7,154 15s. 4$\frac{1}{2}$d. to the general fund of the province ought to be reversed, and that sum ought once again to be credited to the educational fund.[80]

Dunkin emphasized the fact that the appropriations by the Act of 1832 had been for one year only, so that the revenues of the estates had been accumulating in the hands of the receiver-general since October 1, 1832. The allowance to the two grammar schools at Quebec and Montreal had ceased at that date. The expenses of the commissioner's office had continued to be paid as before. The payments were not, however, drawn by warrant in due form upon the receiver-general, but by the commissioner himself out of the monies received by him before paying over the balance to the receiver-general. This was allowed by the terms of his commission, which empowered him to pay out of the receipts of the estates all necessary expenses of collection. Dunkin remarked that though this mode of procedure received the sanction of the executive government, there could be no doubt that the majority of the Assembly intended, as one consequence of the non-renewal of their appropriations from this fund, to have reduced the commissioner to the position of the other public officers during the period of the stoppage of the supplies, and, if possible, to have forced him to resign his office.[81]

Here the whole problem of the Jesuits' estates rested until the resumption of government under the union of 1841. After a long and sometimes acrimonious struggle, the bulk of the revenue from the estates had been placed at the disposal of the House of Assembly for the purposes of education. But certain "thorns in the flesh" remained. The British government refused to relinquish the Jesuits' college buildings until the province should provide an alternative barracks for the troops. The Assembly objected to the system of administering the estates before they had come under its control. Finally, there would develop, as soon as the question of specific appropriation of the funds to educational purposes was re-opened, a cleavage of interests between Protestants and Catholics, with Catholics objecting to their being used for non-sectarian education or for institutions in which there was a predominance of Protestant control.

CHAPTER EIGHT

PROVINCIAL CONTROL, 1841–67

ON JULY 23, 1840, "An Act to re-unite the Provinces of Upper and Lower Canada, and for the government of Canada" was passed by the British Parliament. The bill established the Province of Canada, with a legislative council named for life and an elected assembly composed of forty-two members each from Lower and Upper Canada. A property qualification of £500 was established. English was to be the only language of record for the legislature, but the existing laws of the two provinces were to be preserved. The revenues of the Crown were renounced to the new province in exchange for a civil list of £45,000, covering the salaries of the governor and judges, and of £30,000, covering the salaries of the principal civil servants. The governor preserved the right of veto and the right to reserve legislation for the royal sanction, while the Queen could disavow any bill within a period of two years.

There was much in the Union Act to make the inhabitants of Lower Canada extremely dissatisfied, and to some extent this dissatisfaction was reflected in all the considerations given the Jesuits' estates question during the first decade of union. By giving the same representation to the 650,000 people of Lower Canada as to the 450,000 of Upper Canada, the bill violated Durham's recommendation in favour of representation by population. By merging the revenues of the two provinces and their public debts, it compelled Lower Canada to share the enormous debt of the upper province. This debt had been accumulated largely in connection with the St. Lawrence canals which would be of mutual value in the future, but which were presently of benefit mainly to Upper Canada. The article establishing English as the sole official language was deeply resented by the French Canadians. "It was the first official measure directed against an essential element of their survival, and the first step in Durham's proposed programme of Anglicization."[1] The Act was brought into force by a proclamation issued February 5, 1841, and, in the following June, the first Parliament of United Canada met at Kingston.[2]

The Parliament was not long in session before the matter of the Jesuits' estates was brought to the attention of its members. On August 17, 1841, the Legislative Assembly asked the Governor, Lord Sydenham, for a statement of the revenue from the Jesuits' estates that had accumulated in the receiver-general's chest since February 25, 1832, and the amount presently at the disposal of the legislature for the "purposes of education exclusively."[3] On August 25, the inspector-general of accounts presented the account shown overleaf.

The inspector-general's return was referred to a select committee already appointed to work out provision for the establishment and maintenance of common schools throughout the province of Canada.[4]

After having received this information, on August 26 the Legislative Assembly asked

STATEMENT OF MONEYS RECEIVED FROM JESUITS' ESTATES[5]

	Year	Amount Received
		£ s. d.
*Balance	1831	1,870 10 8½
Amount received in	1832	2,695 14 9½
	1833	1,600 6 6½
	1834	1,654 11 6½
	1835	1,767 5 8½
	1836	2,139 2 9
	1837	2,207 17 11
	1838	1,911 4 8½
	1839	1,563 5 5½
	1840	1,497 18 8¾
Total Currency		20,831 6 4½
Less amount of payments made in 1832 on appropriations by 2 Will. IV, c. 41		917 11 11
Balance		19,913 14 5½
Sterling		17,922 7

* In receiver-general's hands on October 10, 1831.

the Governor for a detailed statement of the expenditures from the Jesuits' estates funds for the past five years and for a statement of the authority for these expenditures.[6] In answer to this request, the inspector-general reported on September 1 that no expenditures had been made within the last five years "of monies which came into the Receiver General's hands, as rents, issues and profits, of the Estates appertaining to the late Order of Jesuits."[7] It is clear from the tone of the inquiries which were being directed to the Governor that there were a substantial number of the members of the Legislative Assembly of United Canada who had been members of the Assembly of Lower Canada and who were anxious to determine if there had been any unauthorized expenditures from the estates funds. As will soon appear, these members were also zealous to maintain these funds for the use of what had been the province of Lower Canada, now known officially as Canada East.

In the second session of the legislature, on September 17, 1842, a rather inclusive petition was received from the Reverend T. Cooke, S. B. Hart, and other inhabitants of the district of Three Rivers,

... praying for amendments to the Municipal District Ordinance; for the repeal of the Judicature, Winter Vehicles, and Rural Police, Ordinances; also, for the application of the Jesuits' Estates to the purposes of Education, in Canada East; for the concession of the lands of the Crown, in the rear of the town of Three Rivers; and protesting against the Union Act.[8]

The petition was referred to a special committee, composed of René Kimber, Joseph E. Turcotte, George Moffat, John Neilson, Amable Berthelot, Francis Hincks, and Denis B. Viger.[9] On September 21 the committee was given the further assignment of inquiring into Lord Durham's report on the management and the value of the Jesuits' estates, and also into the several documents relating to the estates which were contained in the *Journals* and appendices of the late House of Assembly of Lower Canada. The committee was also asked to consider a petition of certain *censitaires* in the seigniories formerly belonging to the Jesuits within the town and district of Three Rivers which complained of the accumulation of arrears of *cens et rentes* and *lods et ventes* and prayed for relief.[10]

The first report of the special committee resulted in an address to the Governor reviving the question of the lands in the vicinity of the lease of the forges of St. Maurice. The Assembly requested that the Governor consider the benefits which might be derived by the province, as well as by the town and the neighbourhood of Three Rivers, from opening the unoccupied lands on the River St. Maurice, or in the rear of the town, to actual settlement and from preventing large tracts in that vicinity from being held without completion of the settlement duties. The Governor was also asked to consider the ruinous effects which the present agricultural population of the Jesuits' estates in that neighbourhood would suffer from prosecutions for arrears which had long been permitted to accumulate, and to suspend such prosecutions until after the close of the next session of the legislature.[11] On October 6 the Governor informed the Assembly that the advantages to be gained from opening the unoccupied lands in the vicinity of Three Rivers would be carefully considered before the termination of the lease of the St. Maurice forges reserve and that he had given instructions to the law officers of the Crown to suspend, for a time, any prosecutions for the arrears which had accumulated.[12] With the exception of a single petition, there was no further consideration of the estates question until it was prominently raised in 1846.

On December 11, 1844, a petition from the mayor, aldermen, and citizens of Quebec was presented, calling for measures to enable them to purchase a certain part of the Jesuits' estates in Quebec City not occupied by the military government. The petitioners wanted the property for the improvement of the city.[13] The submission of this petition might well have re-opened the bitter question of the continued use of the Jesuits' college building as a barracks, but it does not appear to have done so. The petition was referred to a select committee but the *Journals* do not reveal the final disposition of the specific question it contained.

The petitions that have been enumerated, though significant for the moment as an indication of the malaise that surrounded the question of the disposition of the Jesuits' estates, are perhaps of very little ultimate importance compared to an event that took place concurrently with them. The decade of the eighteen-forties marked the return of the Society of Jesus to Canada, and their return was to complicate immeasurably the problem of finding a satisfactory solution to the estates question.

The Order had been revived by the papacy in the early nineteenth century. The bishop of Montreal, Mgr Ignace Bourget, was primarily responsible for their return to Canada. Mgr Bourget was alarmed by renewed proselytizing efforts of Protestant missionaries and felt that the best corrective would be the establishment of a Catholic university in Canada. The idea of charging the Jesuits with the establishment of such a university undoubtedly came because of their historical successes in combating heresy and because they had already established two universities in the United States. A college was founded in 1829 at St. Louis, Missouri, which, three years later, received the power of granting university degrees, and Fordham College in New York obtained the same privilege in 1845.[14]

Efforts at weaning Catholics from their faith would have been cause for alarm under any circumstances, but such efforts were especially alarming in the eighteen-forties because many French Canadians had the conviction, and with much justification, that a concerted effort was being made to de-Catholicize and to de-nationalize them. There appears to have been an especially vigorous campaign to bring about the conversion of the Catholic population during the early part of the first decade of union. Bibles were distributed by the thousands in order to diffuse among the Catholic population the idea of free investigation of religious beliefs for themselves. A missionary society was formed to carry on the work of evangelizing the French Canadians. Efforts were made to use French-speaking Protestants to win the French from their traditional faith. Protestants from Switzerland settled among the French Canadians, distributing Bibles and tracts, visiting the countryside, erecting free schools, preaching publicly in the villages, even up to the doors of the Catholic churches, and also challenging Catholic missionaries to public debates.[15]

In 1839 Father Pierre Chazelle, director of a Jesuit college in Kentucky, was invited to preach the first sacerdotal retreat at Montreal. Here the plans for a Jesuit college or university at Montreal were first mooted. In 1841, both Chazelle and Mgr Bourget were in Rome and urged the plans upon the authorities there. As a result, a group of Jesuits destined for Madagascar were sent to Canada instead. Chazelle was officially named superior of the mission on April 22, 1842, and the small contingent arrived at Montreal on May 31.[16] The question of the Jesuits' estates very early made its appearance in the discussions that led to the return of the Order to Canada. On April 25, 1841, Mgr Bourget wrote:

. . . Si jamais ces bons Pères mettent les pieds dans ce pays il faudra bien que le Gouvernement régorge leurs biens qu'il n'a pu posséder que comme dépôt en attendant qu'il plût à la Divine Providence de les rendre à la Religion. . . .[17]

Mgr Bourget and the Jesuit fathers experienced grave difficulties in determining upon a suitable location and in acquiring the necessary property for the proposed college.[18] Financial problems undoubtedly led to an attempt to secure the return of the Jesuits' estates to the hierarchy of the Catholic Church, with Mgr Bourget committed to the use of the revenues of the estates to further his beloved project of a Catholic university under Jesuit leadership. In the preliminary discussions among the hierarchy, some difficulty was encountered when an attempt was made to solicit the support of the higher clergy of Upper Canada. Mgr Michael Power, bishop of Toronto, was particularly reluctant to endorse any move to give the hierarchy of Lower Canada exclusive possession and use of the estates, and there was apparently a clear understanding that the clergy of Upper Canada would share in the estates should they be regained by the church.[19]

Having reached a determination to try to secure the return of the Jesuits' estates to the church, Mgr Bourget felt that before making any official attempt at this, it would be very useful to secure a judicial opinion on the question of the rights of the Catholic Church to the estates. This was one of the missions with which his Grand Vicar, Canon Hyacinthe Hudon, was charged when, in December, 1843, he went to Europe. P. Clément Boulanger, provincial of the Order in France, confided the task to P. de Ravignan, who in turn introduced Canon Hudon to the Count de Vatimesnil, former minister of public instruction under Charles X and a distinguished jurist, who willingly undertook the task of composing a document that would serve the purpose.[20]

While Hudon was in France on this mission, several important developments took place at home. The ministry of Lafontaine and Baldwin, which had apparently been sympathetic towards the idea of a university, came to an end when the two resigned in protest against Governor Metcalfe who had refused to consult them regarding nominations to certain public posts. The Draper–Viger ministry did not have the same disposition toward establishing a university, at least not along the lines proposed by Mgr Bourget. Mgr Power of Toronto continued to express his displeasure at what he thought was an attempt to secure the estates for Lower Canada, arguing that they had been nearly all given for Indian missions and that therefore he had as much right to them as the bishops of Lower Canada. P. Félix Martin had replaced P. Chazelle as superior of the Jesuits at Montreal and had undertaken, in concert with Mgr Bourget, steps for the establishment of a college.[21]

Hudon returned to Canada on October 30, 1844, and almost immediately thereafter, the document that had been provided by the Count de Vatimesnil was printed in English and French with the intention of giving it as wide a circulation as possible and of having it accompany a petition of the bishops for the return of the estates. On December 17, P. Martin reported to his provincial that the bishops were actively engaged in preliminary endeavours among members of the legislature. A petition of the bishops of the entire province had been drawn up and was to appear in the legislature in a few days. Martin anticipated that the division of the estates would cause friction among the bishops, but he reported that the intention of Bourget was to return them to the Company of Jesus. Ten days later, P. Martin announced to P. Roothan that if the petition succeeded, Mgr Bourget would attempt to establish a university over which the Jesuits would be given entire control. In addition to a college for the study of languages and suitable courses in commerce and industry, the Bishop proposed to offer public courses, given by the Jesuits or under their direction, in other areas in which one would be able to take degrees.[22] On January 15, 1845, P. Martin wrote that a certain number of the deputies of the two chambers had already manifested favourable opinions. It was still impossible to know the opinion of the majority in the ministry, though several members had already pronounced in favour of the petition.[23]

During the year, the Vatimesnil document was printed and circulated in both languages. It was published anonymously under the title, *Memoir upon the Estates which the Jesuits Possessed in Canada, and the Objects to which these Estates Should be at Present Applied.* Following a very sketchy history of the grants to the Jesuits[24] and a longer treatment of the status of the properties under British rule,[25] the author pointed out that it had been definitely settled that the estates should be used for education. Then he raised the question of whether all the money should go to the maintenance of Catholic colleges or schools, or a portion for Protestant schools. This, he said, could be decided only by the Canadian legislature. In his own mind, however, considerations of "justice, equity, and the general interest" united in favour of using them all for the support of Catholic institutions.[26] His strongest argument was that if a benefice or a society were suppressed, the property possessed by that establishment did not become the property of the state as vacant property without an owner; it remained in the patrimony of the Catholic Church.[27]

Pursuing a line of reasoning which omitted all reference to the very adverse legal opinions of the latter part of the eighteenth century, the writer of the memoir satisfied himself that the estates belonged to the Catholic Church, that they could not be applied to any other objects but such as should be useful to that church, and that as it was at present proposed to devote the revenues to education, the estates ought to be appropriated exclusively to the endowment of Catholic colleges or schools.[28] The only alternative that he would allow was the support of Catholic missions for the conversion of the Indians to the Catholic faith. The memoir concluded: "With respect to the capitulations and the treaties, and the legislative enactments that succeeded them, all will interpret them, as we doubt not, in the most liberal sense, and in that spirit which presides over all deliberations of the British mind: *render unto every man that which is his*."[29]

Prepared in January, 1845, the petition of the bishops was not, however, presented to the legislature until the following year.[30] Meanwhile, the Vatimesnil memoir was circulated and other measures were taken to secure a favourable response from the legislators. Mgr Bourget made a separate appeal to the members of the Cabinet which, without any reference to the Jesuits, urged that the revenues of the Jesuits' estates be restored to the Catholic Church to be used for purposes of Catholic education alone. He committed the bishops to provide for the needs of the existing Catholic colleges out of the revenues, to relieve the government from the annual payment it made to the missionaries of the Indian villages, to provide for the instruction of the Indians and to encourage them toward a settled agricultural existence, and finally, to provide for the maintenance of the proposed college in Montreal.[31]

The petition, dated January, 1845, and signed by the Archbishop of Quebec, the bishops of Kingston, Montreal, and Toronto, and their respective coadjutors, was presented to the Assembly in May, 1846. It asked that the Jesuits' estates might be placed under Catholic control for educational and other purposes, according to the original intention of the donors. Accompanying the petition was a project of education. Re-affirming the rights of the Catholic faith in Canada and stressing the need for education related to that faith, the project called for the establishment of a university in which the religious authorities would have a wide control over the choice of teachers, the curriculum, and regulatory measures.[32] A separate petition by certain members of the Lower Canada hierarchy alone was also drawn up; it indicated an awareness of the intentions of the legislature to regulate the estates question, sought to uphold the rights of the episcopate, and requested that the estates be used for the purpose or purposes for which they were originally destined.[33]

On May 14, Solicitor-General Henry Sherwood laid the petition on the table of the Legislative Assembly. Each of the members of the two Houses had already received a copy of Vatimesnil's memoir, and, for purposes of creating a favourable public opinion, *Les Mélanges Religieux* reproduced it in instalments.[34]

On May 28 a resolution was introduced from a committee of the whole on supply, proposing

> . . . that the Revenue and Interests arising from the Estates and funded Property of the late Order of Jesuits, and now at the disposal of the Legislature for Educational purposes in Lower Canada, shall be devoted to the purposes of Education in that part of the Province of Canada, heretofore called Lower Canada; and that for the year one thousand eight hundred and forty-six, the said Fund shall be divided according to [an] annexed schedule.[35]

When the question was put and the resolution and schedule were read in the Assembly, A. N. Morin moved in amendment, and was seconded by James Leslie, that all the words after the word "Jesuits" in the resolution be struck out and the following substituted:

> . . . now held in trust for Educational purposes, according to an Act of the Provincial Legislature of Lower Canada, ought to be vested in the Catholic Church of Lower Canada for the said Educational purposes, under such regulations as may be hereafter adopted, as being the best means to conform to the nature and original destination of the said Estates.

Morin's amendment was defeated by a vote of 29 to 18, as was another introduced by Louis Lafontaine and seconded by Pierre J. O. Chauveau which stated that all the words after the words "Lower Canada," where they occurred the second time, be struck out. The resolution and schedule as introduced were then passed by a vote of 37 to 10.[36]

Lafontaine, Morin, Pierre Chauveau, Lewis T. Drummond and others from Lower Canada presented vigorous arguments against the resolution, though Lafontaine voted for it after the defeat of his amendment. Chauveau accused the government, under pretext of doing justice to Catholics, of despoiling Lower Canada of a revenue of seven or eight thousand *louis* in order to throw that amount into the consolidated funds. He argued that the schedule that accompanied the resolution included the allocations which were regularly regarded as part of the consolidated funds of the province for Lower Canada. But these allocations were now to be provided from the Jesuits' estates revenues, whereas allocations of a similar nature for Upper Canada were still to be drawn from the consolidated funds. Chauveau argued therefore that Lower Canada was being deprived of that much of the consolidated funds.[37] The following words of Chauveau were probably representative of the strong feelings of the Lower Canadian deputies who voted against the government's proposal for economic reasons:

Pour tout homme qui comprend que deux et deux font quatre, n'est-il pas clair que le résultat de cette opération est le même que si l'on prenait les biens des Jésuites et si on les jetait dans le fonds consolidé, et à quoi servent-ils alors si ce n'est à payer ces allocations pour l'éducation dans le Haut-Canada? Dans tous les cas on sait ce que veut dire le fonds consolidé. Le fonds consolidé, c'est la dette du Haut-Canada, c'est le canal Welland, ce sont les améliorations publiques dans le Haut-Canada. . . . Je demande en quoi l'éducation dans le Bas-Canada se trouve plus avancée. Je demande s'il y a un sou de plus donné à l'éducation, soit des catholiques, soit des protestants, dans le Bas-Canada. . . .[38]

The Vatimesnil document was heavily relied upon to substantiate the ecclesiastical arguments against the measure. Drummond reminded the House that though the Jesuits had been suppressed, the order of the Pope specified that their estates must be used in support of the Catholic Church and according to the intention of the original donors. He questioned the legality of the right of the English Crown to assume possession of the estates after the suppression of the Jesuits in Canada.[39]

Representative French-Canadian newspapers were unanimous in their denunciation of the measure that was passed, *Le Canadien* expressing its inability to conceive how French-Canadian ministers had been able to consent to such an act of spoliation and to sanction it by remaining in office.[40] These newspapers, however, tended to assume markedly partisan positions as to which French Canadians were most to blame for the passage of the Act. *La Minerve* expressed sharp indignation at Denis B. Viger and Denis B. Papineau, a brother of Louis Joseph, for voting against Morin's amendment, accusing them of acting on grounds of political expediency.[41] Viger had made a lengthy speech in support of the government's proposal, which was singled out for special condemnation.[42] *La Revue Canadienne*, Lafontaine's organ, included F. J. P. Taschereau in its condemnation of Viger and Papineau. It accused Viger of having made recriminations against Catholicism, of having associated the Catholic Church with intolerance and injustice, and it went so far as to say: "Le génie du mal qui l'a poussé, mercredi dernier, à dire des paroles sacrilèges et blasphématoires contre la religion de ses compatriotes ne saurait le soustraire au juste châtiment qui l'attend dans ce monde et dans l'autre."[43] *Le Canadien* chided the *Revue* for usurping the role of God in condemning Viger, and tended to shift the burden of condemnation upon

Lafontaine and Morin for not having opposed the Act of 1832 that had initially appropriated the revenues for education in Lower Canada. It went on to argue that, after Union, Lafontaine and Morin had both been ministers in the strongest government Canada had ever had. Why had they not used their strong position to rectify the Act of 1832, to which they had given their ready assent; Viger, Papineau, and Taschereau were absolved of this responsibility because they were not in the Assembly that year.[44] Other French-Canadian newspapers seemingly followed the pattern of *Le Canadien* and *La Minerve* by devoting their editorial comment to condemnation of either Lafontaine and Morin on the one hand, or Viger and Papineau on the other, all the while agreeing that the measure was contrary to the religious and economic interests of the Lower Canadians.[45]

Having failed in the legislature, the Archbishop of Quebec, the Bishop of Montreal, and their respective coadjutors now vainly sought to have the Governor, Earl Cathcart, disallow the proposed Act on the grounds that it affected the interests of the Catholic subjects of Her Majesty in the province in so grave a manner.[46] An Act for the appropriation of the revenues from the Jesuits' estates for 1846 received the royal assent on June 9.[47] The Act, 9 Vict., c. 59, clearly stipulated that the Jesuits' estates funds should be applicable for educational purposes in what was formerly the province of Lower Canada, and for no other purpose.[48]

In 1847, despite the failure of the previous year's effort to have the revenues of the estates designated for Catholic purposes only, another petition was presented to the Legislative Assembly by Reverend J. Demers and other members of the Catholic clergy of the dioceses of Quebec and Montreal. These clergymen stated their belief that the Act of Appropriation of 1846 was to apply for one year only, and they asked the legislature to take the necessary steps immediately to appropriate the Jesuits' estates for the objects for which they were originally intended.[49] Governor Elgin, in answer to the petition, pointed out that the legislature had formerly appropriated the revenues of the Jesuits' estates to educational purposes, and that these revenues could not be diverted therefrom into the hands of the Catholic clergy without the previous sanction both of the Crown and the legislature. Lord Elgin made it quite clear that it was his opinion that this was an objective which it was neither expedient nor desirable to attain.[50]

During the same session, an Act (10 and 11 Vict., c. 111) was passed to facilitate commutation of the tenure of lands held *en roture* in the Crown domains into free and common soccage. The Jesuits' estates were specifically embraced by the terms of the Act, and provision was made for the extinction of all seigniorial rights upon payment of commutation, or for a declaration of option that these rights form the capital of a *rente constituée* (redeemable quit-rent), and for the execution of the release deed. Commutation funds arising from the Jesuits' estates were to be kept separate from other funds, and a regular annual report was to be made to the legislature.[51]

Elections were held in December, 1847, after a manifesto issued in the previous month by the Quebec Constitutional Committee of Reform and Progress, headed by René E. Caron, had violently attacked the three-year-old government.[52] The Committee had been formed during the preceding summer and had announced that its goals were to look out for the political interests of the country and to promote the material interests of the district of Quebec in particular. The manifesto, published in *La Minerve* on November 15, denounced the government for favouring the economic interests of Upper Canada at the expense of Lower Canada. In the midst of a statement of financial grievances was a comment regarding the Jesuits' estates revenues that harked back to the debate of 1846:

Les revenus des biens appartenant au ci-devant ordre des Jésuites ont été appropriés de manière à mécontenter toute la population du Bas-Canada et principalement la population catholique, et ont servi à payer des dépenses qui avaient été jusques-là défrayées à même le fonds consolidé, ce qui équivaut à un partage de ces revenus entre les deux sections de la province.[53]

Publication, in 1847, of *A Note, in Addition to that of 1845, on the Jesuits' Estates*, served to keep alive the hope that the Jesuits' estates would be returned to the Catholic Church. In this additional note, Vatimesnil reviewed the history of the properties of the Jesuits in several countries after their suppression in 1773, emphasizing the continued use of these properties for the purpose of education. He concluded with the observation that it seemed "as if an especial providence had watched over those estates, to preserve them in order that they might one day return to their primitive object, namely, the propagation of the catholic faith and catholic education."[54]

Several petitions concerning the Jesuits' estates were introduced into the Legislative Assembly in 1848 but received no special action because the disposition of the Jesuits' estates funds was considered as settled by the Act of Appropriation of 1846. On March 1 the Assembly received an interesting petition from the missionary, Reverend Joseph Maurault, and the chiefs and warriors of the Abenakis village of St. François du Lac St. Pierre, asking for a grant of money out of the Jesuits' estates revenues for the reconstruction of a schoolhouse in the village. Another petition was introduced at the same time from Joseph Metsalabolet and other Abenakis and Malécites of the Indian village of Bécancour, praying for a grant of money from the estates revenues for the support of a missionary among them.[55] Two separate petitions were presented to the Assembly on March 13 by numerous Catholic clergymen and inhabitants, both petitions seeking the allocation of funds from the Jesuits' estates for the support of the recently founded Catholic college of Regiopolis at Kingston.[56]

In addition to the several petitions, a memorial was addressed to the Governor by the president and officers of the Association of Canadian Settlement in the Townships that related to commutation procedures in the estates. It suggested that the government should speedily grant the unconceded lands in the Jesuits' estates at fixed rates of moderate rents, and free those lands from the burden of *lods et ventes* in case of commutation. Lord Elgin, in his reply to Bishop Bourget, the president of the Association, stated that he looked upon the Jesuits' estates as devoted to a special purpose in Lower Canada; to recommend to Parliament the removal of the burden of *lods et ventes*, he felt, would be practically to recommend destruction of the fund which those lands were intended to create. He concurred with the Association's recommendations for the speedy concession of the lands in the seigniories, at moderate rents, and with the easiest and least burdensome terms for commutation of the dues to the Crown. In a word, the Governor promised that the government would do everything in its power to facilitate settlement of the seigniories for the public good, but that it would not do anything that might jeopardize the income that had been designated for education in Lower Canada.[57]

The widespread circulation of the *Memoir* of 1845, the additional *Note* of 1847, and the several petitions to secure the Jesuits' estates for the Catholic Church provoked a major Protestant work, the object of which was to prevent this from happening.

E

Reverend A. Rankin, a Congregational clergyman, after considerable research into the history of the Jesuits' estates, wrote a series of fourteen letters which were published in the *Sherbrooke Gazette*. According to an introductory note in the work which later resulted from this publication, the letters attracted much attention, and in several quarters it was felt that they should assume a more permanent form for reference and should be circulated extensively throughout the country. In 1850, the fourteen letters were brought together and published as so many chapters of a book.[58]

In the letters, or chapters, Rankin did a very commendable job of bringing together documentary materials which threw some light on the whole question of the Jesuits' estates. He made, however, a grave error in the third letter when he assumed that the British *government* was in control of the revenues of the estates from 1763 to 1800; as a matter of fact, the intention of the government to confiscate the properties was not indicated officially before the instructions issued to Carleton in 1775, and the estates were not formally brought under the control of the government until after the death of Father Casot in 1800. This error led Rankin to remark, despite the tolerance accorded the Jesuits by the British government, that "the exact amount and the disposal of the revenues, during that period, are a blank, which no living man can fill. It was, doubtless, regarded as common plunder, which the Government had a right to dispose of, or use as convenience, or cupidity, might suggest."[59]

Rankin's Protestant bias was as evident in his selection and use of materials as was Vatimesnil's Catholic bias in the *Memoir* of 1845 and the *Note* of 1847. While Vatimesnil had relied heavily upon the Capitulations of Montreal and Quebec and the Treaty of Paris to justify the conclusion that the British government had promised to respect the proprietary rights of the Jesuits, Rankin cited at length those legal opinions of the post-Conquest period which had taken a very adverse view of the Jesuits' claims.[60] Rankin's seventh letter clearly indicates that the writing of it had been provoked in part by the *Memoir* of 1845, which he concluded was written either by a Catholic bishop or by some other high ecclesiastic. In seeking to demolish the arguments of the *Memoir*, Rankin brushed aside the provisions of the Capitulations and the Treaty of Paris and dwelt upon the clause of the Quebec Act, 1774, which had excepted the religious orders from the guarantee of proprietary rights. In answer to the Catholic argument that by canonical usage the property of a suppressed order would revert to the Catholic Church as a whole, Rankin pointed out that canonical usage could not be binding upon a Protestant government.[61]

Concerning Catholic efforts to regain control of the estates, Rankin commented:

. . . the desires, positions, designs, plans and efforts of the Roman Catholics, with respect to these Estates, are clearly manifest to the country. Their plans are, doubtless, matured to make a united effort to secure this extensive and valuable property, at no distant day. To the knowledge of the writer, covertly, but to some extent, certainly, Catholics have given their suffrages with direct reference to the acquisition of it. They are laying [*sic*] in wait for it, with all the arts and schemes of Jesuitical cunning and craftiness. . . .[62]

He depicted any possible Catholic success as being an injustice against western as well as eastern Canada—against the Protestant population of United Canada. The financial argument used by the French Canadians was given a different twist:

. . . if the Jesuits' Estates are taken from education and given to the Romanists, then the common Revenue, the Revenue of both Provinces must be taxed to make up the deficiency occasioned by such an unrighteous procedure. Moreover, give the Jesuits' Estates to the Papal Church, and they would, doubtless, soon be so appropriated as to leave their old and new Institutions in a situation to render it plausible for them to call on Government for aid, as they have hitherto done. It is with men, Corporations as with rich men—the desire to acquire increases in geometrical ratio, or in proportion to acquisitions made.[63]

Rankin alluded to a rumour, given currency by certain of the Montreal press, that Lord Elgin was negotiating with the Catholic bishops to give the estates to them. He was pleased that the Governor had telegraphed from Toronto to Montreal a direct and unequivocal denial of any participation in "such a nefarious and unrighteous transaction." But, Rankin warned,

. . . If the Governor or his constitutional advisers should, *for any purpose or design* conceive the idea of such an immoral procedure themselves, or countenance and approve it in others, they would betray a degree of unfaithfulness and of treachery to the interests and rights of the majority of the Colonists, which would prove them to be unworthy of the confidence of the country and which would be condemned and denounced by the civilized world.[64]

Rankin called attention to the accumulation of funds from the estates in the eighteen-forties and to the failure of the government to make regular appropriations. He bluntly asked: "Have we here the development of a covert, secret design to preserve these Estates until a Parliament can be elected to give them to the Jesuits?"[65]

The final letter of Rankin's polemic was a clarion call to all Canadian Protestants to unite against Catholic aggression. The language was an earnest of stronger to come when, in 1888, the Jesuits' estates question was finally settled to the satisfaction of most Roman Catholics and to the violent dissatisfaction of many Protestants. Rankin wrote, for example,

. . . If they [the Protestants] yield an iota here, the Catholics will soon, most naturally, attempt greater encroachments and infringement of rights. If they give the Romanists the advantage over them, which they will obtain by the accomplishment of their purpose, in this instance, the result may be as the letting forth of the mighty waters. And if the Protestant population cannot defend and protect their rights, in this matter—if their wishes and prayers are to be disregarded and outraged . . . are they not already vassals of Papal domination? Connected as they are, in the Colony, with the Church of Rome, whose history is that of injustice, intrigue, and oppression . . . they cannot neglect to do their duty in this case, and not put in jeopardy their richest civil and religious privileges, and their dearest worldly interests![66]

The foregoing is a small sample of about a dozen pages of similar material, the whole of which was designed to thoroughly rouse Protestants of the entire province.[67] Such writing, had its purpose been realized, could have aroused the kind of bitter religious animosity throughout the province in 1850 that finally did prevail in 1888–9. Fortunately, however, the Canadian legislature had already taken something of a bi-partisan stand regarding the appropriation of the funds of the estates in 1846.

In the session of 1852–3, the Legislative Assembly passed a bill to appropriate the unexpended balances out of the school fund for Canada East, and certain other sums out of the Jesuits' estates fund, for educational purposes in that part of the country.[68] Such a bill of appropriation served to take the edge off Rankin's suggestion that the funds were being allowed to accumulate as part of "an ulterior reference to some purpose, foreign from education," "a covert design to preserve these Estates until a Parliament can be elected to give them to the Jesuits."[69]

An article in *L'Ordre Social* gives a very interesting Catholic reaction to Rankin's work. Despite grave errors, wrote the editor, the work contains important data on the pillage of the Jesuits' estates from 1800 to 1832. He extracted tables from Rankin's study to show that from 1763 to 1832 the estates had been shamelessly plundered by the Protestants of Upper as well as Lower Canada, and he concluded that "c'est sans doute sur une prescription résultant de ce pillage constant et sans interruption, que M. Rankin se fond à réclamer les biens des Jésuites comme propriété protestante."[70]

Though the hierarchy of the Catholic Church had failed in its efforts to secure the Jesuits' estates, the small band of Jesuits, encouraged and assisted by Mgr Bourget, had successfully launched the Collège Sainte-Marie in 1848–9. The affiliation of a law school with the Montreal college increased the pressures to secure the incorporation of the latter in order to meet certain standards set by the Bar Association of Lower Canada. This step was contemplated with a great deal of misgiving by the Jesuits because, in 1845, the Oblates had sought legal recognition as a community, and had failed in the Legislative Council because they were not British subjects. This rebuff of the Oblates had prompted the Jesuits to seek naturalization in the same year, and P. Félix Martin, their Superior in Montreal, alone succeeded in securing this privilege in 1846.[71]

On August 27, 1852, a bill to incorporate Collège Sainte-Marie was introduced by John Young, commissioner of public works and deputy from Montreal. Three days later it underwent the first reading without discussion. On October 13, there was a motion for a second reading which received the strong opposition of George Brown, editor of the *Globe*. Brown had been very greatly influenced by a contemporary anti-Papal, anti-Catholic movement in England that was an outgrowth of the Anglican drift toward Rome, represented by the Oxford Movement, and of a papal rescript dividing England into dioceses for the government of the Catholic Church that led, in turn, to Lord John Russell's Ecclesiastical Titles Bill. Separation of church and state became a goal for Brown and his followers, and Clergy Reserves, sectarian schools, and the use of public funds for sectarian purposes were assailed.[72] When Brown understood that Collège Sainte-Marie was to be incorporated under the direction of the Jesuits, he launched into a fiery speech, enlarging upon all that had been held against the Jesuits in the past.[73]

Recognizing that the kind of sentiment expressed by Brown might spell the doom of the move to incorporate Collège Sainte-Marie, Lewis T. Drummond introduced a measure for a general regulation of the incorporation of all educational and charitable institutions. The intention of the government in presenting this general measure was to obviate the rancorous discussions that arose in the chamber when the incorporation of a specific religious association was asked for. Drummond therefore asked his colleague in the ministry, John Young, to delay the report on the incorporation of Collège Sainte-Marie until after the more general measure, which might suffice for that purpose as well, had been considered. Young agreed and the second reading was postponed. Drummond, as well as Louis-Joseph Papineau, used the occasion to try to assure Brown that his worst fears were groundless.[74]

On November 3, because the general bill had not yet been voted upon, Young called for the second reading of the bill he had introduced, in order to have it considered before the session ended. Before there was time for the discussion to become heated, a vote was called for, and the Assembly voted 30 to 10 in favour of the incorporation of Collège Sainte-Marie. Among those who opposed it were George Brown and three ministers from Upper Canada, Francis Hincks, Malcolm Cameron, and John Rolph.

Two days later Young proposed the third reading of the bill, and Hincks, Cameron, and Rolph, having been taken to task by *Le Journal de Québec*, used this opportunity to clarify their position regarding it. The bill was passed by the Assembly by a vote of 54 to 7 on November 5, by the Council on November 9, and it received the royal sanction on November 10. George Brown's name was among the seven who opposed it in the Assembly, but Hincks, Cameron, and Rolph now voted with the majority.[75]

In view of the tendency of Protestant agitators, in 1888 and 1889, to assume that the grant of any kind of official recognition of the Jesuits in Canada had come only with the Quebec provincial Act of Incorporation of the Order in 1887 and the Jesuits' Estates Act of 1888, the Act of Incorporation of their college is significant. In the midst of the agitation after the Jesuits' Estates Act, Sir John A. Macdonald very slyly called attention to the nature of the vote that had carried it by remarking that of the 54 who voted for the Act, 29 were Protestants, while 25 were Roman Catholics. Not a single Protestant from Lower Canada voted against it.[76]

In 1856 the question of the apportionment of the funds arising from the Jesuits' estates was again temporarily laid to rest by the passage of an Act in the Legislative Assembly. This Act (19 Vict., c. 54) provided for the creation of two funds: the Lower Canada Superior Education Investment Fund, and the Lower Canada Superior Education Income Fund. The revenues from the Jesuits' estates were combined with certain other funds to be used exclusively for superior education on a non-partisan basis, and this condition was spelled out in some detail in the Act.[77] After the passage of 19 Vict., c. 54, neither the question of the possession of the Jeuits' estates nor that of the uses of the revenues from them were again raised in the Parliament of United Canada. All that one finds in the *Journals* are the annual financial reports on the estates, indicating the number of concessions, commutations of tenure, and the amount of revenue from all sources. In retrospect, one must feel that it was singularly unfortunate that the arrangement whereby the estates were to be used for superior education on a non-partisan basis could not have constituted the final solution to what had been a thorny problem for well nigh a century. Unhappily for the province, and for the Dominion of which it later became a part, this was not to be. Rougher terrain had to be traversed, with even graver and more far-reaching consequences than hitherto, before the matter of the Jesuits' estates could be finally laid to rest.

CHAPTER NINE

THE JESUITS' ESTATES AND THE
UNIVERSITY QUESTION

THERE WAS HOPE after Confederation that the constitution of a province which was essentially French Canadian and Catholic would permit the settlement of the old and vexatious question of the Jesuits' estates. The Jesuits expected that a Catholic government would, if not restore the estates, at least indemnify the Order for the loss of them. They hoped that with the assistance of their friend and patron Mgr Bourget they might be able to use any monetary compensation for the support of their educational institutions and thus realize the function for which the estates themselves had originally been granted.

During the period from 1870 to 1890 a considerable amount of in-fighting in the ranks of the clergy developed which was to have a decisive bearing upon any proposal to settle the question of the estates. Altercations between church and state in Europe, together with Pope Pius IX's *Syllabus of Errors* (1864) and the Vatican Council's assertion of the dogma of papal infallibility (1870), helped to foster an extreme ultramontane position among certain of the Quebec clergy.[1] Robert Rumilly's volumes give a detailed, though perhaps one-sided, account of these growing conflicts and of the rivalries between the ultramontane faction and the more liberal (with reference to ideas on church–state relations) faction of the Catholic Church. Leadership for the ultramontanes was given by Bishop Bourget of Montreal and the even more zealous Bishop Laflèche of Trois-Rivières. The Jesuits, historically staunch supporters of a strong papal position in the relationship between church and state, naturally allied themselves with the ultramontanes. Roman Catholics, who took a somewhat more liberal view of the crucial question of the relative roles of the church and the state in society, adhered to the leadership of Archbishop (later Cardinal) Taschereau of Quebec. It has been remarked of French-Canadian ultramontanism that "some French Canadians became more French than the French and more Catholic than the Pope."[2]

In addition to differences of opinion on the church–state question, other factors tended to militate against a completely harmonious relationship between Bishop Bourget of Montreal and Archbishop Taschereau of Quebec. Ideological and personality differences were exacerbated by frictions of a non-religious kind that developed between the two ecclesiastical centres over which the bishops presided. From the standpoint of economic (and consequently, population) development, Montreal tended to leave Quebec in the shadows during the second half of the nineteenth century. A bone of contention that in a great measure reflected the ideological differences between the ultramontanes and their opponents, and which also prolonged the controversy over compensation for the estates, was that of whether one university should have sole responsibility for the education of Catholics in the province. Of all the matters that bore some relationship to the problem of the Jesuits' estates in the three decades before the final settlement of 1888, that of the university became most inextricably linked to the problem of achieving that settlement.

On February 1, 1853, the Archbishop of Quebec announced that the Seminary of Quebec had been given university status as Laval University, and during March its new programme was defined. Bishop Bourget at this juncture was openly enthusiastic concerning the inauguration of Laval University and about the possibility of other colleges becoming affiliated with it. P. Félix Martin, rector of Collège Sainte-Marie, objected to the length and the number of examinations included in the programme, while other colleges had somewhat stronger reservations. From 1853 to 1859, Laval made new overtures to these colleges, offering certain concessions that were generally insufficient. The question of how to reconcile the independence of the separate colleges with the special prerogatives that Laval claimed, especially that of being governed by a council that was composed essentially of its own partisans, was one that persisted.[3]

Laval continued to expand, adding a faculty of medicine in 1853 and a faculty of law in 1854. Construction of buildings was begun in 1854. The university was confronted at once by the problem of securing adequate funds. The student response to the university was not as great as had been expected and there were annual deficits. For a number of reasons students did not leave other colleges and flock to the university. Distance and costs seem to have been major factors in the lukewarm response.

Bishop Bourget, who dreamed of a Catholic university that would be a mainstay in the cultivation and preservation of orthodoxy and morals, was disappointed by the apparent failure of Laval to meet the need. There was a school of law and a school of medicine and surgery in Montreal that were both essentially Catholic, the former being connected with Collège Sainte-Marie. However, the School of Medicine enjoyed an inferior position vis-à-vis that associated with the Protestant McGill University. University affiliation for both of these professional schools would offer a more secure position for their students, degree-granting privileges being among the obvious advantages.

During the summer of 1858 Bourget made another effort to bring about an affiliation of the Catholic institutions of the province with Laval, though the superior of the Jesuits' Missions had expressed his disapproval of having Collège Sainte-Marie included. The conditions posed by the remainder of the colleges were such that Bourget despaired of success in getting them accepted by Laval.

Because of the seeming impossibility of any modus vivendi between the colleges and Laval, Bourget, beginning in 1859, contemplated more seriously the establishment of a Catholic university in Montreal independent of Laval. Laval soon became aware of this idea and did its utmost to discourage it, contending that the province could not adequately support two universities.

Bourget, taking note of the attitude of Laval authorities, waited patiently until 1862, meanwhile becoming more and more disturbed about the needs of Catholic students, which he felt were not being met. During this period of waiting, however, he began to sound out the Jesuits at Collège Sainte-Marie concerning the possibility of its becoming the nucleus of a Catholic university in Montreal. Toward the end of 1860 he interviewed PP. Tellier and Vignon, who considered with him the potential problems as well as the advantages of such an arrangement. Their outlook was on the whole optimistic.[4]

On March 22, 1862, Bourget decided to consult the Holy See regarding the establishment of an independent Catholic university in Montreal. He arrived in Rome several weeks before a delegation from Laval also made its appearance. In Rome, Bourget was presuaded by the Cardinal Prefect of the Propaganda, Barnabo, to renounce his project, which he did, hoping that better terms of affiliation might now be secured from Laval.[5] Bourget's hopes were doomed to disappointment. The colleges were asked to try again for affiliation, but Sainte-Thérèse was the only one to affiliate, despite Laval's refusal to modify its regulations. Bourget also pressed the professors of the School of Medicine to try again (it had attempted unsuccessfully to affiliate with Laval in 1860), which they did in vain. Once again the Bishop decided to appeal to Rome. On February 5, 1863, he forwarded to Cardinal Barnabo a memoir that he had received from two college rectors and a doctor, urging the necessity of a university in Montreal.[6]

Cardinal Barnabo decided to consult with the entire Canadian episcopate. Baillargeon, as administrator of the See of Quebec, was charged with gathering the opinions of the members of the hierarchy. Nearly all of these were indecisive. Mgr Lynch of Toronto suggested that a branch of Laval be opened in Montreal. Only the Bishop of Kingston, Mgr Horan, formerly associated with Laval, declared himself to be opposed to Bourget's project. Horan felt that two Catholic universities were not desirable because the existing one would be destroyed, thus throwing higher education into the hands of the Protestants. He accused the proponents of a university in Montreal of "miserable jealousy." On the contrary, Mgr Taché, bishop of Saint-Boniface, ranged himself squarely on the side of Bourget. Because of the inconclusive nature of the clergy's response, Baillargeon was very slow in transmitting a report to Rome, despite the urgings of Cardinal Barnabo.[7]

Finally, in September, 1864, Baillargeon convoked an assembly of the episcopate at Three Rivers to consider what opinion he should express to the Holy See on the renewed efforts of Mgr Bourget to obtain permission to found a university. The assembly was held on October 18 and 19, at which time no common resolution was reached. Bourget concluded from the deliberations that the bishops had come around to his point of view; Baillargeon insisted that such a conclusion was illusory.[8]

On November 14, Bourget departed once again for Rome, and he was followed a week later by Taschereau. Upon his arrival in Rome, Bourget was surprised to hear from the Prefect of the Propaganda that Baillargeon had written saying that the bishops of the province had asked permission for Mgr Horan, a known opponent of Bourget's project, to go to Rome with a report on the university question and that permission had been granted. Bourget was much taken aback and he wrote all the bishops, who denied involvement in such a request. The arguments advanced by the partisans of Laval and of Montreal were similar to those of 1862. Laval argued that the establishment of a university in Montreal would bring about its ruin. Bourget dwelt upon the inability of his diocese to get students to go to Laval and also upon the threat of McGill's influence upon Catholic young people. When all the arguments had been heard, the Congregation of the Propaganda announced its decision on March 28, 1865. It pronounced against Bourget, chiefly on the grounds that a university at Montreal was not presently expedient and that it would ruin Laval. Bourget accepted the decision, though he could only foresee troublesome results. He did get Barnabo to agree that he might renew his efforts at a later date, should the results that he foresaw indeed come to pass.[9]

From 1865 to 1872 difficulties increased for the students of law and medicine in Montreal. The defiant attitude of the two schools toward Laval University remained the same, though their desire to be relieved of their inferior position resulted in the troubles anticipated by Bourget. In 1866 the School of Medicine became affiliated with Victoria University of Cobourg, Ontario. Despite the protestation by the president of the school, that it intended to maintain its Catholic doctrine, Bourget did not welcome the news of this arrangement.

Moreover, in 1866, under the auspices of the *Institut Canadien*, Joseph Doutre began to give courses in law. When the School of Law of Collège Sainte-Marie ceased to function the following year, some of its students enrolled in the *Institut*. Without privileges at first because of its lack of affiliation with a college or a university, this school became affiliated with Victoria University, then with McGill University, where it constituted the French section of the Faculty of Law. To the great dismay of Bourget, there were also rumours to the effect that the School of Medicine would seek to attach itself to the *Institut*.

The odium that became attached to the *Institut* in the eyes of conservative Catholics, as well as the seeming loss of the schools of medicine and law to the Catholic cause, brought about a renewal of the pressures for a Catholic university in Montreal. The dean of the medical school directed an impassioned plea to Bourget for the establishment of a university with which it might affiliate. As to the law students, the Bishop continued to found his hopes upon Collège Sainte-Marie.[10]

In the spring of 1869 there was some thought given to requesting degree-granting privileges for Collège Sainte-Marie from the government of Quebec. In the discussions that took place concerning this possibility, Bourget was of the opinion that these privileges would not constitute any infringement upon the rights of Laval. He recognized, however, that such a request would be displeasing to the partisans of that institution. It would be better, he thought, very quietly to seek action from the Dominion Parliament. For some unknown reason nothing came of these discussions. Nor were discussions relating to the re-opening of the Law School of Collège Sainte-Marie any more fruitful, particularly because of the sad financial condition of the college. In fact, toward the end of 1870, it appeared that the college might be forced to close its doors.

In September, 1870, the rector of Laval asked Bourget if he would support the establishment of a branch of the university in Montreal. Bourget agreed to support such a move, and in October the university made a formal proposal to establish a division of its faculties of law and medicine in the city, to enjoy the same prerogatives as the division in Quebec. Details included a provision that the religious welfare of the students would be left to the bishop of Montreal. In mid-October Bourget went to Quebec and entered into conversations with the Rector, Taschereau. As the project was unfolded, Bourget remained non-committal, probably because he felt that the move was too late (the School of Medicine had already affiliated with a Protestant university), and because certain conditions as to professors appeared to be inadmissible. Furthermore, his own position as bishop in the scheme of organization appeared to be that of an outsider.[11]

The following year passed without any new manœuvres concerning a Catholic university in Montreal. The eyes of its partisans were directed toward the continued

E*

progress of the *Institut*. There was a growing feeling that French Catholic lawyers were influenced either by McGill or by the *Institut*, and there were expressions of alarm because of the alleged influence of free-thinkers and Protestants. The School of Law of the *Institut* boasted of the increase in the number of its students, a development that could only pain the soul of Mgr Bourget. Nor could he take comfort in the fact that a new faculty of medicine, affiliated with Bishop's College in Lennoxville, opened in Montreal in 1870.

The calm of 1871 carried over into the first months of the next year, perhaps because the newspapers were too preoccupied with their polemics regarding *le Programme catholique*. Pressures began to mount as the months passed, however, and Bourget was again subjected to requests from a substantial number of lawyers and doctors regarding the possibility of securing a Catholic university in Montreal. In addition, existing differences of doctrinal interpretation among the bishops—ultramontanism on the one hand, liberalism and Gallicanism on the other—became wider and wider. The New Brunswick school question, currently under consideration, brought about contradictory declarations in the two camps regarding the duties of Catholic deputies. Bourget suggested to his vicar-general in Rome that he might use the general situation to emphasize the necessity of establishing in Montreal another university "qui sera assez ultramontaine pour tenir en bride celle de Laval." Bourget suggested that it might be named Pius University and that it would have as its principal mission the extirpation from the country of all the errors condemned by Pius IX.

While awaiting a reply from Rome, Bourget reminded himself that Ottawa and Kingston had obtained degree-granting powers from the civil government without any protest from Laval. He therefore once again urged Collège Sainte-Marie to approach the provincial government in the hope of securing the power to confer degrees in law and in medicine.[12]

In October, 1872, Mgr Bourget celebrated his golden anniversary in the service of the Catholic Church and, as a part of the celebration, P. Antoine Nicolas Braun preached a sermon that was ultra-conservative and wholly reflective of the ultramontane point of view. The Jesuit's sermon created a furor among the clergy of a more liberal persuasion and in the newspapers.[13]

Amid the controversy over Braun's sermon there appeared in the *Gazette officielle* in early November, 1872, a list of the bills which were to be proposed during the next session of the legislature, among them one asking for degree-granting powers by Collège Sainte-Marie. The Rector of Laval, now Hamel, immediately wrote to P. Lopinto, expressing surprise at this public announcement of what he regarded as a request for the erection by the province of Quebec of a Catholic university in Montreal. Hamel then recalled the struggles of Laval to maintain its existence and he reminded Bourget of the decision by Rome to maintain the rights of the university. In the name of the Council of Laval, he called upon Bourget to use his influence to get Collège Sainte-Marie to desist from its quest.[14]

On November 10, P. Lopinto went to Quebec to deliver the official reply of Collège Sainte-Marie. He expressed disbelief that Laval had ever had the right to prevent for ever the erection of another university. There would come a time when it would be necessary to have other Catholic universities. Even the prohibition of Rome could not continue for ever. He reminded Hamel that Kingston and Ottawa were part of the ecclesiastical province of Quebec and that they had obtained university privileges, while Montreal, whose Catholic students were more numerous than Kingston and

Ottawa combined, had recourse only to Protestant universities. The Jesuits' college was therefore merely fulfilling its duty. If the legislature accorded it the requested privileges, they would use these without offence to Laval. On the same day, the Rector of Laval and Lopinto met with Pierre J. O. Chauveau and Gédéon Ouimet. Hamel left the meeting with the impression that the Jesuit fathers would withdraw their request from consideration by the legislature.

Meanwhile, Mgr Bourget communicated once again with his Vicar-General, Mgr Desautels, in Rome, bringing him up to date on the developments in the province. Desautels was told that Hamel had said that he would not object to the erection of a Catholic university in Montreal if the Holy See gave its consent. If Desautels could not get an indult authorizing a university, perhaps he could get the Sacred Congregation to agree that there was nothing to prevent the legislature from giving Collège Sainte-Marie the power to grant degrees. In Rome, Cardinal Barnabo promised to aid Desautels in a special plea to the Pope.

In the middle of November the Corporation of the Collège Sainte-Marie held an extraordinary session which approved a request to the legislature asking for a modification in the personnel of the Corporation, an augmentation in the real value of the property of the college, and university rights for it. In Quebec, Antoine Labelle went to work on behalf of the Order. Appearing before a committee of about fifteen members of the legislature, he countered the usual arguments against a second university with a strong statement regarding the needs in Montreal.

As a result of the Jesuits' request, there followed a considerable public turmoil stemming largely from the press. The University of Laval issued a brochure in which it reviewed the history of the question and its repeated offers of a branch for Montreal. The brochure also included letters from members of the hierarchy who were opposed to a separate university, that of Mgr Laflèche, who approved, being excluded. *Nouveau-Monde* defended Bourget against *Canadien* and *Journal de Québec* which constantly referred to the decision by Rome of 1865 that had declared it not expedient to establish a second university. *Nouveau-Monde* remarked that ten years had elapsed and that Bourget had had an understanding with Cardinal Barnabo that he might subsequently renew his appeal. It also called attention to a recent letter from Barnabo in which Bourget's agent was encouraged to appeal to the Pope regarding the need for a university in Montreal. Bourget's opponents asked that Barnabo's latest letter be released, but Bourget refused. Opponents to the proposed legislation advanced the idea that good Catholics could not conscientiously vote for it because of the 1865 decision, a contention vigorously and publicly denied by Bourget, and just as vigorously and publicly promoted by Mgr Taschereau.

Although the Jesuits themselves came in for some rather vicious attacks, including the impugning of their patriotism, Collège Sainte-Marie presented its petition to the legislature on November 25. Quebec opponents promptly wired Rome, asking two questions: Had the decrees regarding Laval University been revoked? Could Bishop Bourget address himself to the Parliament before formal revocation? A negative response to both questions was telegraphed on November 28, with an indication that an explanatory letter would follow. Bourget, without awaiting the letter or questioning the accuracy of the representation of the matter in Rome, called upon the Jesuits to suspend all proceedings concerning the securing of a provincial charter for the projected university in Montreal.[15]

Archbishop Taschereau, also without awaiting the explanatory letter, left for

Rome on December 5 to deal not only with the university question but also with the division of the parish of Montreal and the naming of a coadjutor for Mgr Bourget at Bourget's request. Bourget was not well enough to undertake a journey to Rome, but he decided to ask his chief ally, Mgr Laflèche of Trois-Rivières, to represent him there. Laflèche agreed but asked that P. Braun be permitted to accompany him. Laflèche and Braun arrived in Rome early in January and saw immediately that a strong case had been built up against Mgr Bourget. There were those who spoke of his abdication as the only possible way to resolve the difficulties in the province, alleging his incapacity because of his age, his infirmities, and even feebleness of mind. Laflèche and Braun ably defended Mgr Bourget, and in March Desautels reported that the parishes would remain as before, that the question of the university had been deferred, and that Mgr Fabre had been named coadjutor to Bourget.[16]

A decision on the university question was prolonged for another three years. Though the need for a university in Montreal was acknowledged, questions were raised concerning revenue, number of faculties, and the anxieties of Laval. In April, 1873, Cardinal Barnabo addressed these and other questions to the bishops of the province. Laflèche, writing to Bourget in May, urged Collège Sainte-Marie as a natural nucleus for a university in Montreal. Bourget followed up the suggestion, inquiring of P. Bapst, superior of the Mission, whether this suggestion would be agreeable and under what conditions. On the whole, Bapst's reply was quite favourable. There was a divided response to Barnabo's inquiry of the bishops. The Archbishop of Quebec, and the bishops of Rimouski, Saint-Hyacinthe, and Ottawa, argued for a branch of Laval in Montreal. Mgr Bourget, Mgr Laflèche, and Mgr Pinsonnault called for a completely independent university for the city, and they suggested that Collège Sainte-Marie would provide an adequate starting-point.

In the face of such divided opinion, Rome remained indecisive. During the summer of 1874 Cardinal Barnabo was succeeded by Cardinal Franchi who suggested to the interested bishops a way out. As the need for a university was grave and the provisions to date had proven inadequate, another university might be established along completely similar lines in order to avoid competition. Both would be under the supervision of a council composed of all the bishops of the province under the presidency of the Archbishop. Bourget saw in this an acceptable solution, but Laval regarded the proposal as impracticable.

The objections of Laval to Franchi's scheme prevailed in Rome. A year and a half later, on February 1, 1876, the Congregation of the Propaganda decided that a Laval branch should be established in Montreal. Though Bourget foresaw numerous difficulties, he unwillingly acquiesced. In order not to appear as an obstacle in the carrying out of the Congregation's mandate he submitted his resignation. His fears were soon to be realized: the Collège Sainte-Marie was destined to be implicated in the difficulties that subsequently arose.[17]

Another two years were to elapse before the first steps could be taken to establish the Laval branch. Mgr Taschereau was informed of the Congregation's decision on March 9, 1876, and was charged with making it known to his suffragants.[18] The cause of the delay arose out of the divergence of opinion that existed among the bishops. This was first manifested in 1871 when Mgr Taschereau publicly disavowed the *Programme catholique* that had been approved by Mgr Laflèche and Mgr Bourget. In 1875 differences were momentarily reconciled as the hierarchy closed ranks in the wake of the Guibord case and the charges of undue influence by the clergy in the provincial elections. The bishops had, in a unanimous gesture, defined the role of the Catholic Church in political questions, proclaimed its rights, and condemned Catholic liberalism. Taschereau had himself drawn up a pastoral letter which all his bishops were invited to sign in September of that year.[19]

The harmony thus established was not to last. The March decision of the Congregation of the Propaganda was followed in May by a pontifical bull, *Inter varias sollicitudines*, which accorded Laval its canonical erection. Supported by the two documents, the position of Laval was singularly affirmed, and its Chancellor, Mgr Taschereau, felt encouraged to proceed without the support of the other bishops. On May 25, 1876, Taschereau published a mandement in which he omitted all that the letter of the previous September had said concerning liberal errors current and condemned by the Holy See. Instead, the Archbishop put the two political parties ostensibly on the same footing, closing the mouths of the clergy by ordering them to read the mandement without comment. The mandement brought jubilation to the liberals, but it caused great consternation to those who were conservative in both politics and religion.[20]

Letters began to arrive from the Holy See indicating its concern at reports of dissension in the ranks of the clergy in Canada, and placing the odium for that dissension upon those who were opposed to the stance of the Archbishop. The suffragant bishops who opposed Taschereau therefore decided to delegate Mgr Laflèche to go to Rome to refute the charges being brought against them, specifically that of forbidding the professors of Laval to involve themselves actively in the political affairs of Canada when, in reality, they had only made a recommendation in that sense.[21]

Laflèche departed for Rome in July and there he obtained from Pius IX a brief which integrally approved the doctrine of the pastoral letter of September 22, 1875. He attempted to clarify the position of the bishops respecting Laval, declaring that they did not wish to have "any further crow to pick with that university."[22] Later, on February 5, 1877, the same bishops complained in a new supplication that they had no really practical means of effectively exercising the supervision of the doctrine and the discipline of Laval with which they had been charged by the decree of the Congregation of the Sacred Propaganda of February 1, 1876. Because of the refusal of the bishops to collaborate in the establishment of the Laval branch in Montreal and the contradictory reports that were being received from the spring of 1876 on into the following year, the Holy See decided to send a delegate to Canada whose mission would be to secure exact information concerning the relations of the clergy with the state and to press for the execution of the decree calling for the establishment of the Laval branch.[23]

When Mgr George Conroy, the delegate chosen to settle the religious difficulties in Canada, arrived in the spring of 1877, the new Bishop of Montreal, Mgr Edouard C. Fabre, was still deeply convinced of the impossibility of establishing the Laval branch. While the news of the sending of a delegate had generally been received with great favour by all who deplored the position in which the Canadian Church found itself, it soon became apparent after his arrival that he leaned toward the liberal or Gallican causes, an inclination that was evident from the fact that he on several occasions spoke very unfavourably of the conduct of Mgr Bourget. It was disquieting to many that he said nothing of the instructions he had received from Rome.[24]

Early in June Mgr Conroy paid a brief visit to Montreal where he was welcomed by Collège Sainte-Marie. Though he continued to be silent regarding his mission, P.

Braun had had notice from Fiesole to be ready to deal with the question of the Jesuits' estates. Furthermore, Conroy, who had stopped at Fiesole, had made it clear to the General's assistant that he maintained a distinction between Catholic liberalism, which he considered a very dangerous error, and political liberalism, which the Catholic Church tolerated. At Fiesole, Conroy had questioned the failure to use the opportunity to open a branch of Laval in Montreal.[25]

The summer passed and Mgr Conroy showed a more and more pronounced tendency not to recognize in Canadian political liberalism any trace of Catholic or religious liberalism. In September he returned to Montreal and it was only then that he raised the question of the establishment of the branch. Conroy's impressions of the Jesuits' part in the dissensions that were rending the province were revealed in an interview with P. Fleck on November 11. He correctly identified the Jesuits with a school of thought that ardently sought to have the civil code and constitution reformed in accordance with the *Syllabus* and canon law. That school, he contended, had been in error, had led the country into an impasse, and had irritated the Imperial government to the point that the latter had decided, if Rome did not bring about order, to break the federal pact and to establish a legislative union. Laval had better understood the situation and had let itself be guided by Rome as soon as a difficulty was encountered. It had done relatively well since it came into existence, despite the fact that the Jesuits in their mistaken zeal had continued to charge it with liberalism, even though Rome had taken it solemnly under its protection and had placed it under the surveillance of the bishops. Conroy concluded that the influential population of Montreal was decidedly hostile towards the Jesuits, though he himself was certain that their errors had been only from an excess of zeal of or devotion.[26] After considerable discussion the decision was reached, though reluctantly[27] on the part of the Rector of Laval, Mgr Hamel, that the Jesuits would have the faculties of law and the arts in their college. Towards the end of December Mgr Fabre announced that the various faculties of Laval would be established in Montreal, and that courses would begin in the fall of 1878. No mention was made of the decision to incorporate the Faculty of Law into the old school of Collège Sainte-Marie; notice was given only that the Faculty would give its courses in the facilities of the college until further notice.[28]

It must be remarked that the major initiative for the establishment of the branch had been taken by Mgr Conroy, who soon left the field open to Mgr Fabre and Rector Hamel. The announcement of Mgr Fabre was scarcely known when a change took place in the leadership of Collège Sainte-Marie. On December 24, 1877, P. François-de-Sales-Cazeau was named rector, a move that had been decided upon some time previously.[29] The change in leadership was crucial in determining the role the Jesuits ultimately played in the foundation of the Laval branch.

The new Rector soon reached the conclusion that Fleck had moved with too great precipitation in the negotiations with Conroy and Fabre on the matter of establishing the branch. Cazeau was of an entirely different temperament than Fleck. Upon taking charge of the college, one of his first acts was to seek directives from the Superior of the Mission. Charaux instructed him to get a copy of the regulations governing the future relationships between Collège Sainte-Marie and the mother university in order to determine exactly the extent of the authority of the rector of Laval with regard to the Jesuits.

On February 9, 1878, a document bearing the signature of Rector Hamel arrived from Quebec with an explanatory letter. After considerable consultation among the Jesuits in the province and between them and the Superior of the Mission as well as the General of the Order,[30] it was concluded that Collège Sainte-Marie should not take part in the branch. The General announced his decision regarding the Faculty of Arts in mid-June. Beckx was convinced that to accept what Laval proposed would be to sacrifice the *Ratio Studiorum* of the Company, the free disposition of the Jesuit members of the proposed faculty, as well as freedom in the governing of the students of the Faculty. Although Beckx was less categorical concerning the placing of the Faculty of Law in the college, Cazeau and his associates, with the manifest approval of Mgr Conroy and Mgr Fabre, finally declined that offer as well.[31]

There is evidence that both the foregoing decisions were received with relief by the authorities of Laval. During the course of the negotiations the Jesuits had concluded that the university did not want them and regarded them as having been forced upon Laval by the bishop of Montreal who desired that the Jesuits have all the influence they could.[32] Writing in 1882, Cazeau affirmed that Hamel told him: "We did not want the Jesuit fathers in the branch, but his excellence (Mgr Conroy) said that it would be better to give you the Faculty of Arts." Cazeau attested that he had also been told that one of the members of the university Council had said that if Laval had believed that the Jesuits might consent to be a part of the branch, it would have offered other conditions.[33] If Cazeau's word can be accepted, it is obvious that the university, instead of accepting the odium that a refusal would have had in the eyes of the apostolic delegate, had offered terms that put the Jesuits in the position of having to refuse.

As the debate between Laval and Collège Sainte-Marie continued, it became increasingly apparent that the question of which group would receive the compensation money for the estates was a central issue. By a papal indult of April 19, 1871, the General of the Order was made a delegate of the Holy See to supervise the reclamation of the Jesuits' estates,[34] and the Superior of the Mission for New York and Canada was authorized to negotiate at an opportune moment with the Canadian government. Toward the end of 1873 a chance of success rather abruptly presented itself. In 1869, after the departure of the English garrison, the former Jesuits' college became vacant, and the provincial government claimed it, supporting their claim on an agreement at the time of Confederation that placed all the properties of the Jesuits located within the province under the administration of the province. In October, 1873, after four years of discussion, the old college was tentatively transferred; titles of absolute proprietorship were not to be surrendered until May, 1876. Tentative possession placed the provincial government under an obligation to maintain the buildings in good condition.[35]

In the speech from the throne on December 4, the Lieutenant-Governor announced the intentions of the government regarding the newly acquired property by asking for appropriations necessary for the repair of the college in order to house public departments there. On the same day, the Deputy for Montreal-East, Ferdinand David, expressed the hope that this property would be returned, in part or in whole, to the Jesuits. Premier Gédéon Ouimet reminded David that the government had been in possession of the property only a few days, and asked for time to consider the questions that restitution of the property might raise.[36]

The Jesuits at Collège Sainte-Marie did not learn of this development until December 9 when they received a copy of an article from the Quebec *Chronicle*. Two days later the government made known its position regarding the estates. Its view, as expressed by the Premier and widely publicized, was that all the property of the old Order of the Jesuits, and the income therefrom, formed part of the funds for superior education in Canada. The college barracks were a part of the property and were therefore subject to the same purpose. Any indemnity taken from these funds would necessarily impose a reduction of grants in favour of superior education. In the view of the ministry, the appropriation of the properties conformed to their original purpose; the government was therefore not obliged to indemnify any corporation.

The Rector of Collège Sainte-Marie, P. Fleck, met with his advisers on December 12 and together they decided to send a telegram to their Superior, P. Théophile Charaux, asking him to come immediately to Canada. Charaux arrived in Montreal (from New York) several days later and engaged P. Braun, who had arrived from Europe early in December, to submit the manuscript of his *Mémoire sur les Biens des Jésuites* to three censors. The censors approved, except for some corrections of detail, and P. Charaux ordered the *Mémoire* to be printed as soon as possible.

Before this decision was taken, members of the episcopal hierarchy, including Mgrs Bourget, Laflèche, Fabre, and Pinsonnault, had been consulted, and all advised the Jesuits to act. Bourget told Braun that the circumstances demanded that the Jesuits reclaim their estates. Laflèche urged that the Jesuits must affirm and defend the principle underlying the property in question by insisting upon the rights of the Jesuit fathers and of the Canadian Church to the estates. He advised energetic efforts to get a settlement, but warned that the Jesuits ought to seek the support of the Archbishop of Quebec if they were to receive the support of the entire clergy. Promising the fathers his own support, Laflèche advised the publication of Braun's *Mémoire* as a means of arousing public opinion in their favour.[37]

In the first part of the *Mémoire* Braun treated the question of ecclesiastical estates in general, noting that it was a subject which had become almost foreign to modern jurists since the decline in the study of canon law. Braun's approach is revealed in his introductory statement: "The Church, which is a complete and independent society, has its law and its code of laws; and these laws are binding upon all conscientious Christians."[38] He argued that ecclesiastical property enjoys the protection of canon law and it cannot ever be appropriated by secular authorities without the permission of the church. As in his sermon on Bourget's golden anniversary, Braun developed an extreme concept of the subordination of the state to the church.[39]

In the second part of his *Mémoire*, Braun maintained that after the extinction of the Company of Jesus in Canada, the Jesuits' possessions remained, by their nature, estates of the Catholic Church. The state had no right to seize them, and, according to canon law, these estates must return to that church, represented by its visible head, who alone had the right to make a ruling on their destination and their use. In this part of the *Mémoire*, Braun followed the traditional argument that the British government had originally guaranteed to the Jesuits their proprietary rights;[40] he quite naturally ignored the adverse opinions of British and provincial legal experts to the contrary. In arguing that the Jesuits' estates were ecclesiastical property and that such property was specifically protected by canon law, Braun appears to have omitted the fact that the British monarchy was Protestant and that canon law could have a binding force only under those Catholic rulers who would recognize it.[41]

Braun's *Mémoire* was printed early in January, 1874, and circulated to the bishops and members of the legislature as quickly as possible. In a petition to members of the legislature that accompanied the memoir, Charaux indicated that it was not in the name of the Jesuits and for the Jesuits alone that he claimed the estates, but in the name of the Holy See and for the Church of Canada. He was acting as a delegate of the general of the Order and by virtue of special powers conferred upon him by the Holy See. In his view, a *fait accompli* could not prevail; the Catholic Church had never lost its rights over the properties. He declared, however, that he was provided with the necessary powers to negotiate a compromise, and he called upon the members, in the name of religion and of justice, to render to the church that which belonged to it. Catholic members were reminded of the inalienable rights of the church, while non-Catholics were reminded of their professed respect for legitimate property rights, for the capitulations and treaties, and for religious liberty sanctioned by the laws of the country. The bishops were plainly told that the moment seemed opportune to reclaim the rights of the church.[42]

The response of the bishops, with one exception, was encouraging. Mgrs Bourget, Laflèche, and LaRocque (Saint-Hyacinthe) enthusiastically endorsed the Jesuits' efforts. Taschereau suggested that a short résumé of Braun's *Mémoire* be prepared as the deputies were too busy to read such a lengthy piece. He took exception, however, to Braun's affirmation that the brief of suppression of the old Order had remained without effect because it had not been promulgated. Their divergence of interpretation on this matter eventually became a rallying point for opposition to the Jesuits' attempt, and ended by compromising their chance of success. The Bishop of Rimouski, Langevin, agreed in principle with the *Mémoire*, but wished to consult Archbishop Taschereau before committing himself.[43]

Langevin's reservations, expressed in a letter to Taschereau, caused a divergence of views among the bishops. He argued that the bishops should have an understanding on a question that was of interest to the entire province. The impending claim should have been presented to the bishops before being made public. They were entirely ignorant of the nature of the representations the Jesuits had made to the Holy See, as well as of the tenor of the indult Charaux claimed to have. Previous petitions, Langevin argued, had asked for the return of the estates to their original destination rather than exclusively to the Company of Jesus. Langevin asked that the episcopate examine the question and submit it to the Holy See before deciding on a course of action that would result in the removal of part of the revenues of the estates from the maintenance of their seminaries, colleges, and Catholic normal schools.[44]

In response to these reservations, Charaux insisted that the Jesuits were not trying to force the hands of the episcopate. Though fully authorized by the indult to act without the bishops, they were acting in the interests of the bishops as well as themselves. The Holy See had found their representations fully sufficient, and there were no grounds for suspicion regarding the mode of procedure. In previous petitions the clergy had unsuccessfully sought restoration of the estates. Now it appeared opportune for the Jesuits to make an attempt, backed by the strong support of the hierarchy, which stood to gain as much as they.[45]

Though Charaux sought to be conciliatory, he insisted upon a fundamental point: there had been a usurpation of ecclesiastical properties by the civil power; these had been unjustly detained and the civil power was under obligation to treat with the Holy See through the intermediary of the general of the Order or his delegate, the superior of the Mission. Langevin, supported by Taschereau and LaRocque, persisted in his objections and the three refrained from giving their concurrence. In addition to his initial objections, Langevin later agreed with Taschereau that the rights of the Jesuits had been extinguished by the promulgation of the brief of suppression. Questions were raised that gave pause to those who were inclined to favour the claims of the Jesuits. If the bishops assisted the Jesuits, would they not thereby formally recognize their exclusive rights to the estates? Was not the request of the Jesuits contrary to prior reclamations by the bishops themselves? Why suppose that the Jesuits had any better chance of success than the bishops? If the bishops assisted the Jesuits now, would it not appear strange for them to turn around and ask for the estates in their own name? These and other questions reflected the fear that the Jesuits would receive everything and the bishops would be left out.[46]

Faced by such opposition, Mgr Bourget firmly supported the claims of the Jesuits, convinced that for the episcopate the procedure provided a means to end a situation embarrassing to the consciences of both the clergy and the people.[47] Laflèche shared the views of Bourget and attempted to bring about a *rapprochement* with Langevin, who obdurately held that he could not consent to aid the Jesuits if they continued to claim that the brief of suppression had not been promulgated in Canada. If they would give up that pretension and claim the estates simply in the name of the church, and if they would come to a prior understanding regarding a suitable part of the estates for the support of the educational undertakings of the episcopate, he would not refuse to carry on discussions with them on the subject. He had no objection to the Jesuits having a reasonable part of the estates.[48]

The Jesuits, for their part, took the view that the question of the promulgation of the brief had nothing to do with the restitution, which they were seeking simply on the basis of the papal indult. Ouimet did not reply to Charaux's January petition.[49] Bourget, as before, counselled the Jesuits to attempt to mould public opinion in their favour, and, beginning on March 4, *Nouveau-Monde* published by instalments the *Mémoire* of P. Braun. In addition, Bourget suggested that lay persons be solicited to address requests to the government based on the *Mémoire*. He also advocated discourses on the subject—on the work and sufferings of the Jesuits in Canada—during the literary exercises marking the end of the school year. Further sympathetic interest might be generated by publishing extracts from the lives of Jesuit missionary martyrs, including the letters of pioneer missionaries.[50]

Charaux hesitated. Correspondence and supporting material from both sides had already made its way to Rome.[51] Nothing definitive could be done until the attitude adopted by the authorities there was known. The General of the Order had been regularly informed of the course of events in Canada, and, on January 24, 1874, he indicated to Charaux his approval of what had been done thus far by the Canadian Jesuits.[52] Charaux was further informed that Taschereau had complained to the College of the Propaganda that the Jesuits had made this ecclesiastical question public without warning the episcopate and that Braun's *Mémoire* made assertions that were false and contrary to the honour of the Canadian clergy. Taschereau was apparently offended by accusations of Gallicanism and liberalism which he assumed to be directed toward him. Charaux was advised to heed the advice of the Archbishop in publishing an abridgement of the *Mémoire*, and to avoid expressions that would be needlessly offensive.[53]

Charaux, as superior of the Company in Canada, was freshly charged with the task at hand on March 18. He was urged to do his utmost to secure the unanimous support of the archbishop and bishops of the province. The General of the Order,

Beckx, instructed him to give the hierarchy of the province an authentic copy of his supplication to the Sacred Penitentiary and of the indult. These documents would show that the Jesuits did not intend to obtain all the estates that the Company formerly possessed in Canada, nor to despoil the seminaries and other ecclesiastical establishments of what they presently received from the estates, but merely to have these grants by the lay authority sanctioned by the Holy See. The Company would be very accommodating about further concessions, and the Holy See would settle any disputed matters. The hierarchy was to be assured that no part of an indemnity would be used for any other end than for the good of the church in Canada.[54]

The General attached a private letter to the foregoing, in which he indicated the extent of the concessions that Charaux might make to the bishops. He proposed, as a last resort, to abandon to the bishops the greatest part of the non-alienated estates in their dioceses, and for the Jesuits to be content with a capital equalling $20,000. In general, Charaux was to seek for a harmonious relationship with the bishops.[55] Both Beckx and Charaux realized that the business of the estates would make no progress until it had been fully understood by the Roman Congregations.

In June, Beckx wrote from Fiesole that a memoir of the bishops had arrived. Though it stated that they had no quarrel with Beckx's request for the indult, they feared that the Company was seeking the lion's share of the estates. When the memoir was returned to the bishops by the Sacred Penitentiary, it informed them that it had given Beckx the power to recover the estates. As to the division of the recovered estates, the College of the Propaganda would look after that. Beckx decided that it would be useful to have Braun come to Rome to assist with any further difficulties that might arise, a move that met with the approval of the cardinal prefect of the Propaganda.[56]

A month later Charaux reported from Canada that the question of the estates remained in statu quo. The government was entirely silent; the newspapers of Quebec had orders from Archbishop Taschereau not to make the slightest allusion to the question, and all the bishops were on episcopal tour. The bishops of Montreal and Three Rivers (Bourget and Laflèche) were convinced, however, that public opinion in favour of the Jesuits' cause must be cultivated, though nothing had been yet delivered to the press because of uncertainty regarding the attitude of the Roman Congregations. Charaux was certain that Braun would be sorely missed in Canada but he acceded to Beckx's wish that he be sent to Rome.[57]

Braun met with Beckx at Fiesole on August 25, 1874. Five days later he went on to Rome where he learned that a person in the Quebec government had sent a document to the Propaganda complaining of the embarrassment that the Mémoire would cause the government and of the troubles which the Jesuits' claims would cause the country. More important, the document declared that the government did not wish to deal with the Jesuits but only with the Archbishop. If affirmed that the Jesuits would not get anything and asked that the Holy See retract the indult accorded to Beckx. Braun warned Beckx that however congenial the members of the government appeared to be in private interviews they would be hostile to the Jesuits when they acted as members of the government.[58]

In mid-September, Braun reported to Charaux concerning two important interviews he had had with Cardinal Franchi (prefect of the Propaganda) and Mgr Simeoni (secretary of the Propaganda). In an interview with Cardinal Franchi alone, Braun was hopeful that some restitution for the Jesuits' estates might be obtained from the existing government, provided the bishops, prodded by Rome, supported the claims of the Order. Complete restitution was out of the question, but there was a good chance for compensation. Braun thought the latter would probably take the form of a capital sum growing out of a transaction in which the Holy See would be invited to ratify everything by a brief. The Jesuits would have been satisfied to have the bishops take the lead in a reclamation but felt that because of the indult given to their General the Order should now proceed. The bishops had nothing to worry about as they would receive a good share of the desired restitution. Franchi had been led to believe that the claims would raise public opinion against the Jesuits and lead to factious troubles for the church and for the Company of Jesus. Braun assured him that though some Protestants and liberals would object, the Canadians were in general very sympathetic toward the Jesuits. As good Catholics they would follow the impulse of the direction of the bishops.[59]

In a second interview with Cardinal Franchi and Mgr Simeoni, Braun was made aware of their view that the bishops' fear of losing the grants they were presently receiving from the government was behind their opposition to the Jesuits' attempts to regain the estates. Furthermore, it appeared that the bishops feared that the steps taken by the Jesuits, even if successful in the provincial legislature, would be challenged by the Protestant minority who would ask for disallowance by the Dominion government. The possibility of such a set-back did not appear to trouble Braun, who concluded that, should such an event occur, the Jesuits would merely await better times. Simeoni, however, implied that too much furor had been made already, and he referred to the *Mémoire* that, several bishops had complained, had created a *fâcheuse* impression. Braun then admitted his authorship of the *Mémoire* and sought to justify it as a clarification of the rights of the church. Simeoni concluded that it would be necessary to submit the entire matter to the general Congregation.[60]

A short while after these interviews, Braun learned from Cardinal Antonelli (secretary of state and prefect of the Apostolic Palace) that the letter from the Quebec government official to Antonelli was from none other than Premier Gédéon Ouimet. Antonelli showed Braun the document, dated July, 1874, and the latter transcribed several passages. In the letter Ouimet referred to an act of 1856, definitively applying the Jesuits' estates to education, as a *concordat* between church and state, though the act had been passed without consulting any religious authority. The Premier asserted that the Jesuits' estates, by virtue of the law or *concordat* of 1856, became the common property of Catholics and Protestants for superior education. The government, then, was unable to give them to the Jesuits without violating the law. Moreover, argued Ouimet, why return the estates to the Jesuits? The Bull of Clement XIV, regularly signified at Quebec, had suppressed the Order. That being the case, the estates, if they were ecclesiastical, must be administered by the Ordinary of the diocese. Quebec being the only diocese at the time of suppression, the government of Quebec would presently deal only with the archbishop of Quebec if the question were to be treated. Ouimet declared that it was the "firm intention of the government not to treat this question with the Jesuits, but solely with the Archbishop of Quebec, whose prudence and wisdom gives the government the most complete confidence." He besought the intervention of the Holy See to arrest a movement whose results would interfere with the programme of the government and would gravely prejudice the interests of religion.[61]

Braun's reply to Antonelli concerning Ouimet's assertions was approved by Beckx.

It suggested that (1) it would be best that the three bishops in whose dioceses the estates were located be the principals in the cause; (2) the government might conserve the funds of the properties and give a suitable indemnity; (3) the Propaganda would divide that indemnity as it saw fit between the bishops and the Jesuits; and (4) the Holy See would sanction everything by a brief. Antonelli, reviewing the situation not only in Canada but in the rest of the world, concluded that governments everywhere were opposed to the Jesuits. His advice was that it would be wiser for the Jesuits to withdraw and let the bishops act. The entire matter, however, was to be left in the hands of the Propaganda. No answer was to be made to Ouimet—a needless decision because his government had just been defeated in Quebec.[62]

While Braun was thus being discouraged in Rome concerning the possibility of any favourable action on behalf of the Jesuits and the general milieu in which the contemporary church must act, the advent of Boucherville to power in Quebec gave rise to the hope of a legislative programme that would conform to the principles of the church as he saw them. On the matter of the estates, Bourget and Laflèche now suggested that the Jesuits defer all public claims and engage in extra-Parliamentary representations to the new ministers. Charaux informed Beckx in early December of the change and was encouraged to heed the advice of the friendly bishops.[63]

As the Jesuits ceased their public efforts, a rumour spread in Canada that the indult accorded to the Jesuits had been retracted. Charaux, however, was assured by Beckx that the rumour was without foundation. Despite this assurance from Rome, there were those in Canada and in Rome who felt that a claim by the bishops offered a better chance of success. In May, 1875, therefore, Charaux suggested to Beckx that he give up the indult and Beckx complied. On May 22 Beckx indicated to the Propaganda his willingess that the episcopate of Lower Canada treat with Boucherville in such a manner that the restored portion or compensations be remitted to the Holy See and disposed of by it according to the conditions expressed by Clement XIV. At the beginning of July Charaux received official notice that his powers of delegate had expired, but the Propaganda registered the renunciation of the indult without transferring it to the bishops or notifying them that the Jesuits had ceased to be delegated. As we shall see later, it was only in 1880 that Mgr Taschereau sought a new indult.

Early in June, the matter of compensation for the estates became complicated by the government's new project to demolish the old college of the Jesuits. Charaux asked P. Vignon of Quebec to ascertain from Boucherville the views of the government and to warn the Premier that a protest would be launched by the Order. Though Vignon was well received, Boucherville made it clear that the government was, in fact, planning to proceed with the demolition of the college.[64]

Boucherville then discussed the problem of a settlement of the Jesuits' estates question. He insisted that the old college could not be considered apart from the total estates. He claimed that he and his colleagues sincerely desired an arrangement with the church, but he warned that a public protest against the government's plans to demolish the college would be used by the opposition in the next elections, perhaps to the detriment of the Jesuits. Vignon was told that if the Boucherville ministry continued in power, the best procedure for the Jesuits to follow would be to present a request for a settlement, supported by the bishops of the province. Without such support, it was doubtful whether the Jesuits could secure a majority support for any proposal in the legislature. Despite Boucherville's advice, Charaux sent his letter of protest, addressed to the Premier alone, on June 10, 1875. There was silence on the question until the following year.[65]

About a year after Vignon's interview with Boucherville, Taschereau informed Charaux that he felt that the formal act of taking possession of the college would give the church a greater chance of securing a compensation. He stated that he would make no opposition to the demolition and to the proposed construction, but that he did not renounce the right the church might have to claim a compensation. Taschereau was under the impression that Charaux still had the apostolic indult and therefore sought an opinion from him. He reminded Charaux that the government knew the Jesuits only as Collège Sainte-Marie—a new creation, whose recent incorporation had no connection in its eyes with the former Company. On the other hand, the episcopal hierarchy represented the Catholic Church in a clear and unmistakable way in the eyes of the government.[66]

Charaux was surprised that Taschereau had had no notification from the Propaganda regarding the surrender of the indult by the Jesuits. He therefore informed the Archbishop that he had ceased to have the power to act directly in the matter and that it was up to the bishops of the province to reclaim this Catholic property. The least the government could and must do before proceeding with the demolition was to engage itself to treat with the bishops at an opportune time and, when it was able, to make a just compensation for all the Jesuits' estates, the use of which would be determined by the Holy See.[67] Intervention was made in the sense suggested by Charaux and once more the old college was saved.

However, those who wished to secure demolition counted upon winning the support of Mgr Conroy, the apostolic delegate, who arrived in Canada in the latter part of May. To counter that possibility, Fleck wrote to Conroy, protesting the solidity of the building and asking him to delay a decision until he came to Montreal. Conroy, however, did not see this letter until it was too late. On his arrival in Quebec, he was taken to the building and given the worst picture possible. Asked whether it might be demolished, with the rights of the church reserved, Conroy replied that since it threatened to fall on those passing by, natural law permitted its being razed. He warned, however, that the government had no right to dispose of a single stone without authorization by the Holy See. Despite subsequent efforts by P. Fleck to get Conroy and Boucherville to change their minds, the decision to demolish was not reversed.[68]

Demolition of the old college having been achieved, there now remained the question of disposing of the large vacant tract upon which it had stood. Five successive governments made this their project, while Laval and the Company of Jesus upheld their respective claims. The Jesuits hoped for a settlement in their favour because of the ever-pressing financial needs of Collège Sainte-Marie as well as the other mission projects in which they were engaged. Laval, operating only in Quebec, had experienced some of the same financial difficulties, and now it had the additional burden of the branch in Montreal. This conflict of interests between the Jesuits and the episcopate, in which each faction had its supporters among the hierarchy as well as among leading political figures, excited new problems and occupied the Roman court and public opinion for another decade after the demolition of the old college.

During his stay in Canada Conroy had broached the estates question with the bishops and with the Jesuits, but had deferred any attempt to solve the problem. Braun had urged upon him the view that the properties that formerly belonged to the

Jesuits were usurped ecclesiastical estates. They must be restored to the Holy See and disposed of by it. He also argued that no member of the episcopate had had an indult, nor had the hierarchy ever had possession of the estates; consequently, they had no right to them. Conroy appears to have agreed, though he felt that the time was inopportune to seek a settlement in view of Boucherville's declaration that there was nothing to restore. Braun reluctantly agreed to wait, feeling that the Jesuits would get only a small sum under the existing circumstances. Conroy wrote to Boucherville, making it clear that the Holy See reserved all its rights to make a claim at a more strategic time.[69]

In March, 1878, the *coup d'état* of Letellier de Saint-Just took place and Joly de Lotbinière succeeded Boucherville as premier. The college was in the process of being razed, and a plan had been prepared to divide the land into building lots. When the government announced in October that the lots would be offered for sale, Taschereau and the bishops sent a letter of protest to the government, reminding it of previous protests regarding the usurpation of the estates and renewing the church's claims to them. The government replied that it was determined to put the lots up for sale, since this was only a continuation of the plan decided upon by the preceding administration. The provincial secretary declared that since the land of the Jesuits' college had been ceded to the province by the federal government of Canada, it had been determined to forward the bishops' protest to Ottawa. On October 24 the under-secretary of state at Ottawa acknowledged receipt of the document and the matter rested there.[70]

Of the sale of building lots there was no further question during the ministry of Lotbinière. That Liberal ministry had too feeble a majority in the House to remain in power for very long, and it had to deal with a solidly Conservative Legislative Council. In October, 1879, the Council refused to vote subsidies; the ministry of Lotbinière was replaced by that of Joseph-Adolphe Chapleau. The new government announced no official project for disposing of the land of the old college, but it worked quietly to settle the estates' question. Chapleau, writing to Mercier in April, 1889, denied any exchange of correspondence with Taschereau or with anyone else. He recalled, however, that he had resolved to settle the question, though no fixed sum for any of the properties was discussed.[71]

Chapleau's scheme, which he submitted personally in the summer of 1881 to the cardinal prefect of the Propaganda, stipulated that an evaluation of the properties should be achieved in consultation with Archbishop Taschereau, that the interest (5 per cent) on the capital of this evaluation should be applied to superior education, and that some Protestant institution should be endowed with an annuity representing approximately one-sixth of the annuity accorded as interest from the estimation of the estates. In that way the church would regain possession of the estates and the Protestant minority would not have any recriminations. To this project, the cardinal prefect expressed only the opinion that the claim was with the Holy See; he thus apparently eliminated all the Jesuits' claims to the estates.[72]

On July 31, 1882, there was another change of government in the province. Chapleau entered the federal cabinet and was succeeded as premier by Joseph-Alfred Mousseau. Mousseau had scarcely assumed the position when a semi-official letter, dated August 1, was received by Archbishop Taschereau, in answer to his request concerning the intentions of the government regarding the Jesuits' barracks. After a brief sketch of steps taken since 1874, the writer stated that only the Imperial government could deal with the question of ownership of the terrain. If there was talk of returning it to the

Jesuits, the Imperial government might decide to reclaim it. However, there appeared to be no problem of using the area for a government building—a move that would enhance the value of all the surrounding area, the seminary and Laval included. The Archbishop, it was suggested, should give the government his approval, while reserving the rights of the church regarding proprietorship of the land. The writer warned that if the clergy opposed such a worthy project, discontent against the ecclesiastical authorities would inevitably result.[73]

Taschereau decided to seek the advice of the bishops concerning the proposal. Laflèche, as might have been expected, vigorously asserted the church's undisputed rights to the land in question. In his opinion, the church could not submit to the request of the letter without sacrificing the estates which the episcopate were obligated to protect, and without betraying the mandate it had received from the Holy See. The bishops had no right to treat with the government without positive guarantees, nor to make any concession under the insufficient safeguard of a declaration of principle.[74]

Confronted by the impossibility of getting the assent of all the bishops, the idea gradually took hold that the Archbishop alone might deal with the government in the name of the Holy See. In February, 1883, news reached the superior of the Mission that a memoir to that effect, drawn up by the Seminary of Quebec, was *en route* to Rome. P. Louis Saché, superior of the Residence at Quebec, reported the substance of the memoir, the aim of which was to claim the estates as the exclusive property of the Church of Canada, rather than as that of the Jesuits, and to portray the Seminary of Quebec as heir to the educational tasks of the old Order. Saché went on to state that one might then use any compensation from the government to aid the struggling Montreal branch of Laval University. It was reported that Taschereau had asked for sole authority to reclaim the estates to that end.[75]

The Jesuits sought the advice of Mgr Laflèche and decided to use the press to provoke a declaration from the government that would offset the memoir's assertion that the Jesuits were unpopular in Canada. The *Journal des Trois-Rivières* was chosen as the vehicle for this manœuvre. During February and March, articles appeared that depicted the Jesuits as the victims of a plot that would despoil them to the advantage of a rich institution, Laval University. Israel Tarte of *L'Etendard* undertook to defend the government against any suspicion of attempts to despoil the Jesuits. By March 9 the Jesuits had succeeded in provoking a ministerial declaration from Mousseau via *L'Etendard* that in no circumstance had he treated the question of the Jesuits' estates apart from the bishops. He declared that he had not taken part in Rome's decision to have the destination of the estates changed. Tarte himself declared that it was his opinion that the estates belonged to the Church Universal. It was with the church alone that the state could treat and it was the duty of Catholics to aid the church in the claiming of these estates. The church alone was mistress and judge of the mode and time for pressing its claims; it alone had the absolute right to dispose of the estates as it judged proper.[76] The Jesuits, however, had succeeded in extracting from Mousseau a declaration that the government would not exclude the Jesuits from any restitution.[77]

Meanwhile, mounting religious difficulties, including the troublesome question of the relationship of the Montreal School of Medicine and the Laval branch as well as that of the dismemberment of the diocese of Trois-Rivières, prompted Mgr Laflèche in May, 1883, to undertake another voyage to Rome to defend the interests of his diocese and to answer certain accusations brought against him. His intervention and the representations of other injured interests prompted the sending of a second apostolic commissioner. Dom Henri Smeulders, abbot in the Cistercian order and consultant of the Sacred Congregation for the Propaganda, arrived in Quebec on October 22.[78]

Smeulders had been in the country only a short while when a letter came from Beckx to the superior of the Mission verifying the rumours of the memoir and the supplication of Taschereau. Beckx had been informed that a letter had been sent to Smeulders for Taschereau and gave the latter the right to deal with the government concerning the restitution of the estates. According to information Beckx had received, Smeulders was not to give the letter to the Archbishop until Taschereau had committed himself to an understanding with the Jesuits on the share to be given them if the estates were returned.[79] It is doubtful whether Smeulders ever gave this letter to Taschereau for the Archbishop soon renewed his request at Rome for an indult to deal with the question of the estates alone, excluding both bishops and Jesuits. Undoubtedly Smeulders revealed the existence of the letter, but Taschereau abstained from taking any steps to conclude the prescribed *entente* with the Jesuits. Up to this point the sympathy of the government was apparently on the side of Laval and the causes defended by it.[80]

John J. Ross, who succeeded Mousseau as premier on January 23, 1884, showed no inclination to treat with Archbishop Taschereau on the estates question. Ross's attitude may be explained by his background. His father was English but his mother was French. After completing his studies in the Seminary of Quebec, Ross married a French Canadian, and was considered a *Canadien* as he used the French language. Originally from Sainte Anne de la Pérade, he was a compatriot and diocesan of Mgr Laflèche, the ardent ultramontanist, and likewise a disciple of Mgr Bourget of Montreal. Ross, then, kept close to the ultramontane group and naturally inclined to support the Jesuits in their endeavours.[81]

As Smeulders' inquiry progressed, it became clear that it was also turning to the disadvantage of the causes sustained by Laval and the Seminary of Quebec. Smeulders told Laflèche that the division of the diocese of Trois-Rivières was neither necessary nor useful; he showed himself favourable to the School of Medicine of Montreal, and even inclined to substitute an independent university for the Laval branch. As to the question of the Jesuits' estates, Smeulders met with Boucherville who suggested a project for settlement, though he told the commissioner that provincial finances would not permit it to be realized in the near future. Such inclinations on the part of the delegate prompted Taschereau to go to Rome to combat the decisions being effected. The Archbishop was successful. On May 31, Smeulders received a telegram telling him that the Sacred Congregation reserved to itself the question of the division of the diocese of Trois-Rivières. In August he was informed that the Holy See recognized Laval, including its branch, as the only Catholic university in Canada.[82]

Ross had protested to Smeulders against the division of the diocese of Trois-Rivières. Upon learning what was happening in Rome concerning the Jesuits' estates, he wrote a confidential letter to Smeulders, in which he called attention to a public rumour that there was a movement on foot to have the estates given by the Holy See to Laval. Though his government had not been approached on the matter, Ross stated that he desired that the estates question be settled in an equitable and definitive manner, and in such a way that the intentions of the donors be respected. A settlement that would give the estates to any institution or order other than the Jesuits would not be considered by many as a satisfactory settlement and would be difficult, if not impossible, to secure. If, however, Rome decided that a part of the indemnity claimed could be used otherwise, and the largest part was given to the Jesuits, it was possible that public opinion would be satisfied. In this letter Ross described the Jesuits as having numerous lay as well as clerical friends in the province.[83] Unfortunately for their cause, the letter was added to the numerous documents given to the apostolic commissioner which he did not make use of in Rome because of the ultimate set-back that his mission received.

Meanwhile in Rome Taschereau had been active and he soon gained a new victory. On October 11, 1884, the general of the Company received notice from the Congregation of Propaganda that the Archbishop would treat personally with the government on the matter of the estates. However, freedom to dispose of the estates was to be left to the Holy See, the Pope thinking it equitable that a part of them be returned to the Company of Jesus.[84] The Congregation had acted on the information that it was impossible for the Jesuits to recover the estates because the Protestant deputies were too strongly opposed to them to consent to restitution. Taschereau satisfied the Congregation that he might easily obtain them for his university and that he would then secretly pay to the Company a monetary compensation, a strange commitment in view of the fact that the Congregation had just reserved to itself expressly the free disposition of the indemnity.[85]

P. Antoine-Marie Anderledy had an interview with Taschereau at Cardinal Simeoni's request. He reported a cold reception. The Archbishop did nothing but complain about the Jesuits who, in his opinion, did not respect their bishops enough. No proposition was made at this time regarding the estates. Anderledy was left with the impression that Taschereau did not trust him, a feeling that was entirely mutual.[86]

Taschereau returned to Quebec on December 1. A month later the Archbishop informed Ross that by virtue of a papal indult of October 13, 1884, he was personally authorized by the Holy See to treat with the provincial government and, for a reasonable compensation, to settle the question of the ownership of the Jesuits' estates. Before proceeding, he wished to know whether the provincial government was disposed to negotiate.[87] Ross replied on January 7, 1885, that he would not fail to give every attention to this important communication, and, as soon as he could possibly do so, he would inform the Archbishop of the views of the government.[88]

After several subsequent interviews with Premier Ross and Lieutenant-Governor Rodrigue Masson, Taschereau wrote to Ross on April 8, reminding him that the Legislative Assembly had been in session for some time and that he would like to know the present position of the matter.[89] Ross replied on April 25, calling the Archbishop's attention to the fact that when the old Jesuits' college was transferred to the provincial government, the leader of the government had stated in the House that all the property of the Jesuit Order of which the government was in possession and the revenues thereof lawfully constituted the superior education fund in Canada, and that the government was not bound to indemnify anyone for the property. Ross also noted that this statement had received the tacit assent of the legislature. Therefore, before entering into negotiations about the property, the government must seriously consider whether it was possible or advisable to retract so formal and so precise a declaration. Ross regretted that it was impossible for him, in the midst of the pressing business of the moment, to give immediate consideration to Taschereau's request. If the lieutenant-governor decided to reopen and reconsider the question of the Jesuits' estates, he (Ross) would not fail to notify the Archbishop and the Reverend Jesuit Fathers, so that with his assistance and theirs, he might, if expedient, be able to submit to the legislature a measure that would settle the question in a definitive manner.[90]

Ross's letter brought an irate response from the Archbishop on April 27. Taschereau challenged the equity of the distribution of the superior education fund. According to him, in 1883–4 the fund consisted of $113,362, of which $27,110·01 was income from the Jesuits' estates. Of the total sum, $113,362, nearly one-third had been given to Protestant educational institutions. Since the Protestants, according to the Archbishop, were less than one-seventh of the whole population, this was hardly a just distribution. A Catholic could not admit that the government was not bound to indemnify *any* corporation. All that could be legitimately understood regarding the surrender of the Jesuits' college was that the federal government in turning it over to the provincial legislature did not impose upon it the obligation of indemnifying any corporation whatsoever. Taschereau called for the restoration to the Catholic Church of the property belonging to it.

The Archbishop expressed regret that, after a delay of three and a half months and in view of the fact that he had made his request before the session started and had had several interviews with the government, the matter could not be given immediate attention. He told Ross that he alone was authorized by the Holy See to deal with and settle the matter, and that the Reverend Jesuit Fathers had nothing to do with it. He therefore would cheerfully lend his aid to any measures that might settle the question satisfactorily. On the other hand, he was sure that the Catholic government of a Catholic province would make it a duty to settle it as soon as possible.[91] Ross replied that as soon as possible he would let the Archbishop know the views of the government on the subject.[92]

Meanwhile, the Jesuits had not remained inactive. To counter the effect of reports in Rome of their unpopularity, they had interviews with Lieutenant-Governor Masson and with Premier Ross. From Masson, who had studied in the Jesuit college of Georgetown (Washington, D.C.), they received a sympathetic hearing. Ross, while regretting their attitude on certain questions, was no less cordial. In response to a request of P. Turgeon, Ross gave him a copy of his correspondence with Taschereau, a documentation that would be useful in rehabilitating the reputation of the Order in Rome.

In addition to important interviews with Masson and Ross, the Company got Boucherville to describe in writing the project that he had made verbally to Smeulders the previous year. Boucherville expressed the hope that if the Imperial government did not object to the diversion of the revenues to ends other than those for which it had surrendered them to the province, and that if Protestants were not put in a position of being able to say that sums were being taken that had been appropriated to them, a settlement might be arrived at. The church would renounce all claims on the estates in Quebec in favour of the provincial government, provided that the government would capitalize the part of the funds for superior education belonging to Catholics after the last census as follows: (1) $400,000 to the Jesuits, which was nearly all of the capital of the revenues of their properties detained by the government of Quebec; (2) a part of said capital to each diocese where the college or seminary was not sufficiently endowed; and (3) the remainder to different institutions for Catholic superior education in the province. Boucherville's plan, though lacking immediate significance, appears to have provided the basis upon which the whole question was finally settled in 1888.[93]

In mid-December P. Hudon decided to take up the question of the estates with Rome. Reassured of the attitude of Ross's government, he sent a copy of the Boucherville project to Vicar-General Anderledy, along with a copy of the correspondence between Ross and Taschereau. Anderledy promised to forward this to Cardinal Simeoni as soon as possible.[94]

Recognizing the amount of prejudice that had been built up against the Order at the Roman court, the Jesuits decided to send a former Rector of Collège Sainte-Marie, P. Frédéric Lopinto, to Rome to act in their behalf and to keep them posted on developments there. In addition to having lived for twenty-five years in Canada, Lopinto spoke Italian, possessed a suppleness of mind, and also had carefully studied all the questions under consideration in connection with the Smeulders' mission. The Neapolitan, who went to Rome ostensibly for reasons of health, journeyed incognito under the name of Luis Gonzalès. Only certain members of the Company and Abbé Camille Caisse, curé of Sainte-Sulpice, knew the real reason for his going, and months were to elapse before Lopinto was identified as the secret informer who did so much to forward the interests of the Order in Rome.[95]

Lopinto arrived at Fiesole on March 22, 1886, and was briefed by Anderledy as to how to proceed in Canada as well as in Rome. Anderledy advised that a policy of working in silence and avoiding all direct involvement in the Canadian press would be greatly appreciated by the Holy See. In Rome, Lopinto was to depend principally on the advice of Smeulders who would decide whether he should declare himself openly. A few days later, upon his arrival in Rome and after visiting with Smeulders, Lopinto was forced to modify his plan. Smeulders, feeling keenly the manner in which his mission in Canada had been undermined, wished to reserve for a later time some of the documents that would have been immediately useful to Lopinto.[96]

Lopinto eventually found his greatest source of help in the Secretary of the Propaganda, Mgr Jacobini, who readily approved his remaining incognito at the Propaganda. It was clear from an early conversation with Jacobini that the Propaganda was under the impression that all was quiet in Canada since the division of the diocese of Trois-Rivières. Lopinto assured him that such was not the case and then raised the question of the Jesuits' estates, calling attention to the fact that Taschereau had failed to get the government to agree to a settlement. Lopinto then explained the Boucherville project to Jacobini, expressing a fear that nothing could be settled by bringing the matter before the provincial legislature. He suggested that it might be advantageous for the lieutenant-governor to come to Rome.[97]

Conversations between Jacobini and Lopinto continued throughout the month of April. Then, on April 26, a letter came to Anderledy from Hudon that exposed a new project for the settlement of the estates question. Taschereau had entered into new discussions with Ross and Masson and they were apparently on the verge of an understanding. The Archbishop's latest plan was to obtain from the general of the Order, directly or by the intervention of the Holy See, a legal quittance of the Jesuits' estates in Canada, and to get the Holy See to accord a major part of the estates to Laval. An effort would then be made to secure an order from the general for Collège Sainte-Marie to affiliate with Laval.[98]

Confronted by such ill news, Anderledy instructed Lopinto to do what he thought best *in Domino*. The latter decided to press for the Boucherville project and to urge

Masson to come to Rome if necessary. Any project involving a previous quittance and affiliation of the college with Laval was unacceptable, no matter what the cost. Lopinto also pointed out that the government did not legally recognize the Jesuits; consequently, it did not see them as legal successors to the fathers of the old Company. If Lieutenant-Governor Masson could come to a direct understanding with the Holy See—officially, semi-officially, or secretly—he would receive every concession desired by the government, particularly if he came to Rome himself.[99]

The new project subordinated the estates question to the two other very delicate questions of the civil incorporation of the Company and the affiliation of Collège Sainte-Marie with Laval. The rather heated debates that the first question provoked will be considered in Chapter x, though the matter of incorporation was not completely unrelated to the question of affiliation. Some of those who opposed incorporation felt that if the Jesuits succeeded here they would be in a better position to press their claims to the estates, thereby depriving Laval of what was regarded as a potential source of financial assistance. The Jesuits continued to resist affiliation because they feared the loss of administrative and academic freedom by becoming entirely subordinated to a Laval-controlled university council. They had concluded thus far that the advantages of university degrees for their students were not worth the sacrifice of the integrity of Collège Sainte-Marie.[100]

Faced by the hesitation of the legislature and perhaps the uncertainty of ever obtaining a settlement, Laval then thought of linking the question of affiliation to the question of the estates. If the Jesuits agreed to accept affiliation, or if they were constrained to do so by the Holy See, they would fall under the control of Laval. What the university called unity of Catholic instruction and its adversaries called university monopoly would thus be realized. If the Jesuits persisted in refusing to affiliate Collège Sainte-Marie with Laval, the college would be ruined and Laval would have thereby an assurance of the largest part, if not the whole, of any indemnity for the estates, at least, so it appeared to Lopinto and to the fathers in Montreal.

Discouraged by the lack of a prospective settlement in their favour, the Jesuits' anxieties were aggravated by the esteem that Taschereau enjoyed at the Roman court, which seemed to be ever on the increase. Rumours had been flying for some time of the approaching elevation of the Archbishop to a cardinalate. Lopinto confirmed the rumour from Rome, writing on April 23 that the nomination appeared to be certain and inevitable. On June 7, 1886, steps undertaken since the fall of the previous year culminated in Taschereau's becoming a member of the Sacred College. A week later, Mgr Fabre became Archbishop of Montreal, a move that offered no particular hope to the Jesuits because he was far more subservient to Taschereau than his predecessor, Mgr Bourget, had been.[101]

In the midst of such discouragement, Lopinto did his best to keep up the spirits of his colleagues in Canada, while at the same time moving discreetly to better the position of the Company at the Holy See. He sought to impress upon Cardinal Simeoni, prefect of the Propaganda, the poverty in which the members of the Order were forced to exist in Canada. More of his efforts, however, were directed toward the Secretary, Mgr Jacobini, who assured him that the Holy Father would never force the Jesuits to affiliate with Laval. While the Pope expressed irritation because the Jesuits made war on the university, he reassured them on the matter of the estates. In the Pontiff's opinion, the Jesuits, though suppressed in Canada, had major rights, at least of equity, and the Holy See would certainly take account of them. The Pope would not be the one to deprive them of the estates should they be returned. Moreover, he insisted that it was the Holy See that would make the division of any compensation and that Laval would not do as it wished.[102]

Because of the prevalent feeling in the Roman court that the Jesuits were unreasonably opposed to the affiliation of Collège Sainte-Marie with Laval, Anderledy decided to send a visitor to Canada. On September 9, P. Jean Lessman arrived there and spent the next few months listening and observing first-hand. Lopinto continued his work at the Holy See, submitting a programme for the Pope's consideration that upheld the interests of the Jesuits in any proposed settlement of the estates question. He received the encouraging word from Canada that Lieutenant-Governor Masson was willing to come to Rome in an attempt to arrive at a satisfactory arrangement with the Holy See concerning the properties, though the uncertain position of the government made the time of such a visit unpredictable. On December 8, Lopinto learned from Jacobini that the Pope would delay any final decision regarding the estates until he had had the opportunity of consulting with the new Cardinal, Taschereau, who would soon come to Rome.[103]

Once again the Jesuits in Montreal were greatly disconcerted by a fresh wave of rumours in the press, most of which augured well of success for Laval and its partisans on the question of affiliation and that of an estates settlement. In spite of reassurances that arrived periodically from Rome, they became again shaken in their confidence and troubled by the fear that Lopinto was being too optimistic. Anticipating more trouble from the impending visit of Cardinal Taschereau, it was decided that P. Lessman should return immediately to Rome, armed with sufficient documentation to serve as a champion of the Jesuits' cause.[104] Scarcely had Lessman left for Rome, bearing a lengthy memoir in which P. Turgeon sought to refute the charges being levelled against the Canadian Jesuits, when an event took place that would shortly change the entire situation.

In the Quebec election of 1886, Honoré Mercier capitalized on the wave of ill feeling that swept over the province because of what many considered to be the unjust conviction of Louis Riel for his participation in the North-west Rebellion of 1885. Mercier called for the formation of a *Parti National*, and, playing hard upon the religious and racial prejudices which had been stirred up by the fate of Riel, he won the election and became premier on January 29, 1887.[105] The Jesuits were particularly strong champions of Riel, and in the election they were openly "Merciéristes," contrary to Mgr Lafléche and the majority of the clergy.[106] The coming of Honoré Mercier to power in the province promised well for the interests of the Company of Jesus. Mercier was an alumnus of Collège Sainte-Marie, where he had been a fellow-student of P. Adrien Turgeon, now rector of the college. The moment seemed ripe for a Jesuit victory.

On January 27, 1887, the session of the legislature opened at Quebec. During its first sitting, the Conservative ministry, reconstituted for only a few days by Taillon, was forced to resign. Two day later Masson called upon Honoré Mercier, head of the new *Parti National*, to form a new government. With Mercier at the head of the government, the question of the Jesuits' estates entered its final phase.[107]

CHAPTER TEN

INCORPORATION AND THE ACT OF SETTLEMENT OF 1888

IT APPEARED URGENT to the Jesuits of Canada at the beginning of 1887 to assure Collège Sainte-Marie, on which rested the hope of the survival of the entire mission, privileges equal to those of the colleges affiliated with Laval without themselves submitting to affiliation. Measures were regularly being proposed in the legislature that would give special advantages to the student with a bachelor's degree. A combination of propitious circumstances now made it appear that the moment had come for them to act.

To those who might have had misgivings about the Pope's attitude toward the Order, a papal brief, *Dolemus inter alia*, was reassuring. Published in July, 1886, on the occasion of the reprinting of the *Institute* of the Company, the brief confirmed all their privileges, among which was that of conferring degrees in letters and in philosophy not only to students who were members of the Company but also to all those who attended their colleges.[1] Honoré Mercier, the new premier, gave clear evidence of his devotion to his Alma Mater. Writing to Turgeon in February, Mercier spoke of his deep attachment to Collège Sainte-Marie and to the good fathers of the Company of Jesus, for whom he had always had great admiration. He went on to say that his greatest desire was to seize the first opportunity to demonstrate his feeling of indebtedness toward the members of the Company.[2] The evident friendship of Lieutenant-Governor Masson, whose state of health made his tenure of office uncertain, was another reason for acting without delay.[3]

During February, 1887, preliminary discussions were held with the Premier to determine the nature of the request to the legislature. Instead of a simple amendment to the charter of the college which might permit it to grant degrees, it was decided to ask for civil incorporation of the Company of Jesus, introducing into the law a clause which would recognize all the Jesuits' privileges recently confirmed by Leo XIII. At the same time, the question of the estates was broached in order to determine the sentiments of Mercier's government. Preliminary inquiries were encouraging and an official request by P. Turgeon sought to determine whether Mercier shared the views of Ross as expressed to Mgr Smeulders in 1884. Mercier acknowledged the importance of the question but stressed the problem of dealing with the Jesuits alone on a question that canonically involved the provincial hierarchy as well. The government could not make itself the judge in a canonical matter. If the Jesuits themselves had canonical authorization to deal with the question the situation might be different.[4]

The results of these feelers were immediately communicated to the general of the Order and thence to P. Lopinto in Rome. Lopinto inquired about the possibility of obtaining papal authorization for the Jesuits rather than Cardinal Taschereau to seek a settlement with the government, but he was assured by Mgr Jacobini that such a decision could not be made in haste by the Pope, certainly not in time to be of use in the current session of the legislature. Cardinal Taschereau himself had just assured the Pope that the time was not ripe to reclaim the estates and had refused to commit himself regarding the proposal that he have a prior understanding with the Jesuits as to the distribution of the expected compensation.[5]

While Lopinto worked in Rome to keep the College of the Propaganda informed of events and attitudes in the province, steps were taken to secure incorporation. Details of a proposed law were carefully worked out, with an important emphasis upon the rights and privileges confirmed by the papal brief of July 13, 1886. Toward the end of March, Turgeon went to Quebec where he spent several days seeking the support of government ministers, legislative councillors, and the deputies. Mercier agreed to introduce the proposed law in the Legislative Assembly, while Boucherville accepted the same task in the Legislative Council. In general, Turgeon's efforts seemed to be successful, though he encountered the usual opposition from partisans of Laval.[6]

The policy regarding the bishops remained to be decided upon. Because the proposed measure was simply the civil recognition of a religious body already established in the country by pontifical law, a recognition that altered in no way the rules of canon law, it was felt that the intervention or permission of the bishops was not required. Out of deference to the Archbishop of Montreal, in whose diocese the principal house of the Order was located, the fathers decided to acquaint him with the decision. Mgr Fabre accepted the decision with goodwill but asked for a written declaration that the proposed bill had nothing to do with the Jesuits' estates, that colleges and universities could not be established without permission of the ordinaries, and that incorporation of the Jesuits on a basis similar to that of the other religious houses was all that was being sought. This declaration, designed primarily to prevent objections by Cardinal Taschereau, was drawn up by P. Lessman and sent to Mgr Fabre on April 12. Fabre, already aware of the Cardinal's anxieties, suggested that a copy be sent to each of the interested bishops.[7]

Cardinal Taschereau arrived from Rome on April 5, the same day Turgeon left Quebec to return to Montreal. Taschereau was soon made aware of the proposed law. Still preoccupied with his conversations with Simeoni and Jacobini on the subject of the estates, he saw that if the incorporation of the Jesuits was accorded and was supported by the pontifical brief, any decision of the Propaganda would be influenced significantly in their favour. For years Taschereau had striven to persuade Rome that the Jesuits were unsuited for the task of administering the estates because of their lack of civil recognition and their alleged unpopularity in Canada.[8] He therefore lost no time in seeking an interview with Mercier to ask him to delay presentation of the proposed law until the Cardinal had been able to study it and to consult his colleagues in the episcopate. Mercier accorded several days of delay and assured him that if the bishops were unanimous in their opposition, his duty was quite clear. During the course of the interview, Taschereau let something slip which gave clear expression to his attitude in the days ahead: If the question of the Jesuits' estates were settled, he would have no objection to the incorporation of the Company of Jesus.[9]

P. Hudon drew up a statement of the Jesuits' case and sent copies to all the bishops, as well as Taschereau, denying any ulterior motives or any intention to insult the bishops by moving ahead in efforts to secure incorporation without consulting them. The statement protested disbelief that the bishops might want to hinder the fulfilment of the brief, *Dolemus inter alia*, in which the Pope had confirmed the Jesuits in their numerous privileges and responsibilities. Taschereau, however, remained unconvinced, persisting in his belief that the Jesuits were acting hastily in order to make it impossible for the hierarchy to have time to deliberate and express its objection.[10]

Meanwhile, Turgeon returned to Quebec where he once more began making his rounds to secure support for the bill. Lieutenant-Governor Masson encouraged him to fight to the end. He was warned by L. O. Taillon, leader of the Conservative opposition, that the authorities of Laval felt that the government would be rebelling against the authority of the Cardinal and the bishops if it allowed the bill to pass.[11]

Finally, on April 14, 1887, a petition from the "Reverend Fathers of the Society of Jesus" asking for incorporation was read in the Legislative Assembly. Five days later Mercier was given leave to bring in a bill for that purpose, which, after being read a second time on April 23, was referred to the select standing committee on miscellaneous private bills.[12] Since incorporation implied that the Jesuits would obtain the right to confer diplomas in their college, there was immediate opposition from the University of Laval, whose Rector, Mgr Hamel, appeared before the committee to protest the incorporation. He is reported to have referred to the proposed incorporation as "un chef-d'oeuvre de style—Jésuite."[13]

Hudon now received answers of the bishops to his letter of April 16. Fabre of Montreal and Laflèche of Trois-Rivières approved without any reservation the steps taken by the Jesuits. Duhamel of Ottawa, hesitant at first, ended by promising his support. The other bishops reserved judgment until they could consult the Cardinal. On April 23, Taschereau himself drew up a lengthy memoir addressed to the bishops, in which he sought to demolish the arguments being used by the Jesuits. He questioned the need for the continued existence of Collège Sainte-Marie because of the numerous educational facilities in Montreal, and he again complained that this college was the only one in the province that had not affiliated with Laval, despite recommendations reiterated by the Holy See.[14] The response of the bishops to this memoir led Lessman and Hudon to stick to their proposed law. Of the ten archbishops and bishops of the province, three were entirely favourable, six were hesitant with no precise objections, while the tenth, Taschereau, was openly opposed, however, without having ever directly declared to the Jesuits the motives for his opposition.[15]

The Jesuits were satisfied that they had done everything possible to comply with the spirit of the telegram that Mercier had received from the Holy See, and that they would be able to justify their actions to the Roman authority. If the Cardinal remained adamant in his opposition to their incorporation, they were prepared to accept an amendment which would restrict the benefits of incorporation to the dioceses of the bishops who were supporting the Order.[16]

On April 22, Cardinal Taschereau reminded Mercier that only a fortnight previously the Premier had asked him (Taschereau) to consult the episcopate of the province on the subject of incorporation, and that he (Mercier) had then promised that the presentation of the bill would be delayed until later if the episcopate asked for time to examine it. He reported that the archbishop of Montreal and the bishop of Trois-Rivières had no objection to the bill, but that the others had asked for time to examine and discuss together the proposed law, and to have it referred to the Holy See if that were judged to be proper.[17] The Cardinal pointed out that, should the discussion not lead to the disappearance of all objections or to an agreement that would satisfy everyone, it might indeed be necessary to appeal to the Pope. Therefore, it was the

F

duty of each Catholic deputy to wait for the outcome of the discussions among the clergy and possibly of an appeal to Rome before voting on the matter.[18]

In acknowledging the foregoing letter, Mercier denied having asked Taschereau to consult the episcopate. According to the Premier, the Cardinal had asked him what he would do if the episcopate opposed the proposed law and he had replied that if the bishops were unanimously opposed to it, his duty was clear. Mercier argued that if the archbishop of Montreal and the bishop of Trois-Rivières had no objection to the bill, it could not be contrary to the laws of the church or to the intention of the Holy See. The archbishop of Montreal, having in his diocese more houses of the Jesuits than there were in the rest of the province, would have the greatest right to find objections to the bill. Mercier reminded Taschereau of all the other orders that had received civil recognition from the legislature. If there were difficulties between the ecclesiastical authorities and the Jesuits, the Holy See ought to be the arbitrator. The Premier did not feel, however, that the legislature would have any cause for regret in giving civil effect to the decrees of the Holy See itself concerning the Jesuits. Mercier closed his letter, a masterpiece, by expressing his pleasure at receiving the approval of his Archbishop, Mgr Fabre of Montreal, and his deep regret at being deprived of the Cardinal's approval.[19]

In presenting the bill to the Assembly, Mercier had decided to consult the Pope directly. A telegram was sent: "As a simple deputy, I have presented to the Quebec legislature a measure to give civil recognition to the Company of Jesus, with rights and privileges accorded by the popes. I dare to ask the blessing of your Holiness, and to pray that you will tell me if you see any objections to my request."[20] It was a very mild missive, which mentioned nothing of Taschereau's opposition. The Roman prelates must have known the whole situation, however, for they replied: "Holy Father blesses you. As to the subject of your telegram, listen to your archbishop." Mercier and the Jesuits shrewdly interpreted this to mean his own Archbishop, Mgr Fabre, who was favourable to the bill, as it said "archbishop" and not "cardinal."[21]

Opposition to the measure became more clearly circumscribed to the Cardinal's palace and to Laval University. P. Vignon wrote on April 21: "Laval is active against us. The shock will be rude, but we are hopeful. A large number of influential lay persons are giving us their support. But Laval has a powerful party, and a number of our former pupils, while wishing to favour us, dare not engage themselves in our behalf." The day following he reported: "Mercier is ever very devoted to our cause. He does not wish to deal with the cardinal; he knows him too well. As always, those whom we see agree that the cause is good, just, that it must succeed, and that it would certainly succeed without the cardinal."[22]

Turgeon reported on April 24 that the question was considered as the most important of the session—so much so that on the previous day the Cabinet had met for two and one-half hours to discuss nothing else. The ministers were unanimous except for Provincial Secretary Ernest Gagnon, who dwelt upon the Cardinal's opposition. He recognized the justice of the Jesuits' cause and agreed not to work against them, but he firmly insisted that if the Cardinal continued his opposition, he would not vote for them. In his report, Turgeon once again drew attention to Taschereau's remark to Mercier that if the estates question were settled he would have no objection to the bill.[23]

On April 29 the meeting of the committee on private bills took place in an atmosphere filled with tension. The meeting-place was filled with spectators, as well as a number of directly interested persons, among whom were Vignon and Turgeon and their lawyers, and the representative of Laval, Mgr Hamel. Mercier attempted to show that the Jesuits asked nothing more than had already been accorded to a number of other religious communities. He labelled as false the claim that the Cardinal and six other bishops were opposed to the bill; they were asking only for a delay. He then called upon Hamel to justify the requested delay. Hamel pled ignorance of the reasons but went on to say that the bill was of direct interest to the seven bishops who formed a majority of the episcopate. The Jesuits were asking certain civil powers but they were to be exercised for religious purposes in the different dioceses.[24]

After Hamel had spoken, P. Vignon indirectly questioned his insinuation that the opinion of the majority of the bishops should be imposed upon the members of the committee. He sought, however, to reassure the members by offering an amendment, previously considered by the fathers, that the incorporation be limited to the three dioceses (Montreal, Ottawa, and Trois-Rivières) whose bishops were favourable to it. This offer was enthusiastically received by the committee, and Hamel, completely taken by surprise, withdrew his objections. He left the room as soon as possible after this declaration, only to return shortly to report that he had been instructed by the Cardinal that he had exceeded his powers.[25] During Hamel's absence, however, the committee had adopted the preamble of the bill and consequently they had admitted the principle. They now proceeded to a study of the different clauses, despite the efforts of Hamel to assert the views of Cardinal Taschereau. Philippe Casgrain and Eugène Lafontaine, partisans of Laval, joined Hamel in opposing the bill, and though they were not successful in bringing a halt to discussion, the bill was soon reduced to simple civil recognition in its most elementary form. After more than four hours of debate, the bill was passed by the committee.[26]

After the lively discussion in the committee, the bill was finally submitted for debate on May 2. The order of the day being read for the House in committee to consider the bill, Mercier moved that the Speaker leave the chair. Thomas Chase Casgrain (Quebec) moved in amendment that the House, on that day six months hence, resolve itself into the committee. Casgrain based his amendment largely upon a consideration of Taschereau's letter of April 22 to Mercier, which he (Casgrain) read to the Assembly. Mercier spoke eloquently on behalf of the Jesuits, those "pauvres religieux," who were only seeking civil rights in the province. He reviewed the history of the incorporation of other orders, and then read his reply to Taschereau's letter, the contents of which have already been noticed.[27]

Other deputies followed the Premier, ranging themselves either on the side of Mercier, or on that of Casgrain. All of them denied having anything against the Society of Jesus, and those who opposed incorporation insisted that they were obliged to respect their religious authorities. However, N. H. E. Faucher de Saint-Maurice (Bellechase) said: "Let us consult Rome and next year I will be happy to give my most cordial and candid adherence to the cause of the Reverend Jesuit Fathers, if all difficulties have ceased." Eugène Lafontaine (Napierville) thought that each question must be considered on its own merits. He knew enough about theology to know that when a superior authority spoke, one must obey. To avoid additional religious strife in the province, he would vote in favour of Casgrain's amendment. Victor Gladu (Yamaska), who had been on the committee on private bills, reported that, due to protests from the Cardinal and Laval University, the proposed bill had been reduced to the very simplest act of incorporation. He was very respectful of ecclesiastical authority, but he felt obliged as a deputy to render justice to the Jesuits in this matter.[28]

As the debate continued, F. G. M. Dechène (L'Islet) affirmed that in the name of liberal principles he would vote in favour of the bill, though in so doing he might be giving the signal for the finish of his political career. William W. Lynch (Brome) spoke of the great degree of liberty which prevailed in the province and suggested that if there were anything in the proposed bill which was contrary to civil law, it should be withdrawn. In the name of "British fair play," however, he asked his colleagues to vote for it. The Secretary and Registrar of the Province, Ernest Gagnon (Kamouraska), stated that he was not against the Jesuits and that he would support them with all his efforts when they came before the Assembly with the backing of the religious authorities. He must, however, be guided by his judgment, his conscience, and the opinion of his bishop. All the archbishop of Quebec asked for was a delay; the wisest thing to do was to march with his bishop! He questioned whether a postponement of the discussion would be fatal to the future passing of the bill; if adopted under the circumstances, it would be a "blot on the statutes."

James McShane (Montreal-Centre), commissioner of agriculture and public works, reminded the House that Quebec was proud of being the freest of all the provinces of Canada. Why, then, refuse to these citizens (the Jesuits) what one accorded to others? Edmond Lareau (Rouville) emphasized that for the deputies the matter was a question of civil law only. He could not see how they would put themselves in opposition to the religious authorities by voting for the bill. It was simply a question of conferring civil rights on a religious association, and they could not refuse to do that without having very grave reasons.[29]

As the debate neared a close, Edmund J. Flynn (Gaspé) pictured the Assembly as a court of judgment. It must postpone hearings in order to give the dissenting bishops an opportunity to present their case. To this end he moved for a postponement of the debate. Mercier objected to Flynn's interpretation and then very shrewdly asked where the petitions against the proposed bill were. He reminded the deputies that the letters, having been read, had not been laid on the table and therefore could not be used as Parliamentary evidence of a particular point of view. The only official statement of dissent before the House was a resolution of a Protestant society in Montreal.[30]

Flynn's motion for adjournment of the debate was defeated by a vote of sixteen to thirty-four, and Casgrain's amendment, calling for a six months' hoist, was defeated by an identical vote. The motion to consider the bill in a committee of the whole House was then carried, and 50 Vict., c. 28, "An Act to incorporate the Society of Jesus," was passed on May 3.[31]

On May 4, the bill was sent to the Legislative Council for its consideration, and the opposition there continued unabated. The correspondence between Cardinal Taschereau and Mercier, begun on April 22, continued until May 9. Confidential at first, it became public when Casgrain, with the approval of the Cardinal, asked that it be produced in the legislature. Mercier argued that since the prelates of Montreal and Trois-Rivières had no objections, the measure could not be contrary to the laws of the church nor to the intentions of the Holy See. Taschereau countered that the lack of opposition by two bishops could not be interpreted to mean that the measure was not contrary to the laws of the church or to the intentions of the Roman authorities. If the witness of the two bishops was sufficient to prove the orthodoxy of a measure, the witness of eight others must be sufficient to cause it to be doubted.

Mercier contended that he had said that if the bishops were unanimously opposed, then his duty was clear; he had never engaged himself to follow blindly the opinion of the majority. A divergence among the hierarchy led him to conclude that the question was an open one and that the rights of the interested parties must be his guide. Taschereau stoutly maintained the religious as well as the civil nature of the bill and insisted upon the right of the hierarchy to be involved in its consideration. In a letter of May 2, Mercier hinted that the Cardinal's primary reason for seeking delay was the unsettled question of the Jesuits' estates. He reminded him that he had said as much in an interview on April 11, a reminder that was not denied by Taschereau in the subsequent exchanges. In a letter of May 5, Mercier cleverly contrasted conditions in France and Quebec:

In France, the legislators expel the Jesuits and refuse them the rights of other citizens; in the Province of Quebec, the legislators protect them and accord them civil rights. In France, the legislators are censured, and rightly, by the religious authorities, because of this iniquitous persecution. In the Province of Quebec, the legislators are threatened with incurring the disgrace of a prince of the Church because they have believed it their duty to sustain the religious. I avow, Eminence, not to be able to explain these strange anomalies.[32]

Meanwhile Turgeon and Vignon continued their visits with some of the Legislative Councillors and contradictory rumours circulated freely. On May 5 it was reported that letters from Rome had arrived and that the Jesuits were going to be forced to withdraw the bill. On May 8 word was spread that the opponents of the bill were going to bring all the influences of Quebec, Ottawa, and Rome into play against the Jesuits.[33]

In the Legislative Council delaying tactics were attempted in order to prolong consideration of the bill so that it would not be ready on the day of prorogation. On May 9, for example, when the second reading was to take place, nearly all the printed copies of the bill had disappeared from the chamber. Fortunately, Boucherville had some of them which he quickly distributed to those whom he suspected of being opponents. When Méthot, a nephew of the rector of Laval, protested the second reading on the ground that printed copies had not been distributed, Boucherville informed him that he personally had given him a copy. Méthot found his copy and, as there was no further protest, the reading took place.[34]

On May 11, when the Legislative Council was considering the bill as a committee of the whole, Mgr Hamel appeared and asked for a delay of twenty-four hours, which was granted. Hamel claimed to have new important documents. That evening Turgeon telegraphed Rome regarding rumours that the Pope was against the Order; he emphasized the urgency of an immediate reply because the next day would be the last for consideration of the bill.[35]

The meeting of May 12 took place before a sizeable gathering. Hamel spoke first and he read a lengthy memoir which sought to justify the actions of Cardinal Taschereau in the course of events since his interview with Mercier on April 11. He insisted upon the Cardinal's conviction that he was not going against the intentions of the Holy See. A councillor interrupted to ask if the rumour were true that the Pope had intervened to bring an end to all opposition to the bill. It was now Turgeon's turn. He explained the position taken by the Jesuits at the same time refuting certain insinuations of Mgr Hamel. The Jesuits had not consulted the episcopate because in similar cases the other religious orders had not. When the opposition of some of the bishops had become known, the Order had given them its solemn guarantee that it would not use its privileges without the assent of the Pope. Such assurances being of no avail, the Jesuits had addressed themselves to Rome where they had received favourable responses. Two telegrams from Lopinto were now used to advantage by Turgeon. The first, dated May 5, in response to news of the passing of the bill in the lower chamber had read: "Very good! The Sovereign Pontiff does not wish to place obstacle. Continue. I will write." On May 9, in response to another telegram saying that the opposition to the bill would be repeated in the upper house, Lopinto had wired: "Continue. A telegram from the pope has answered today: 'I cannot oppose myself to it.' " Thus encouraged, the members of the Order had persisted in their efforts. Turgeon reminded the House that it was on the merit of the bill that they were called upon to make a decision; since the bill affirmed nothing contrary to the laws of the church and to the laws of the state, the Order counted upon their spirit of justice.[36]

Hamel now attempted a stratagem that backfired, much to his chagrin. He produced another memoir that he had prepared in advance. He reported that the telegram received by the Jesuits was not unknown to the opposition, but Taschereau had received two on the same question, one not solicited, the other in response to a telegram sent by him. The unsolicited telegram (the first in the order of Mgr Hamel's reading) had stated that the Sovereign Pontiff could not oppose the incorporation of the Jesuits but that he reserved to himself absolutely the question of the estates. The second telegram, as translated by Hamel, told the Cardinal that the Pope did not judge it to be opportune to force the lay deputies, but invited him to try in his own name to secure a delay. On these two telegrams, the dates of which he was careful not to mention, Hamel built his argument that it was not against the opportunity of a delay that the Pope pronounced since he counselled Cardinal Taschereau to use his personal influence to try to obtain it. What the Pope did not judge opportune, said he, was his own intervention to dictate orders to the lay deputies.[37]

Unfortunately for Hamel, his argument, so laboriously built up, fell on two counts and rested upon an apparently calculated transposition of dates. Boucherville saw through the stratagem, and he asked for the dates and signees of the dispatches. Hamel then had to admit that the unsolicited telegram that he had cited first was dated May 9, while the other, which he did his utmost to complement and explain that of May 9, was dated April 30. Moreover, the Latin text of the April 30 telegram was "Eminentia tua *videat an* tuo nomine possis inducere (deputatos) ad supersedendum"; translated: "Let your Eminence see if he can in his own name persuade the deputies to a postponement." Hamel had translated *videat an* as if it were *videat ut*: "Let your Eminence *try* in his own name to lead them to a delay." From a simple suggestion of Cardinal Simeoni, who had signed the dispatch, the error in translation had nearly resulted in an order from the Holy Father himself.[38]

When Hamel had finished, Vignon added some remarks to highlight the contrast between the manner in which the Jesuits had been treated in their request and the treatment accorded to Laval. The public now withdrew to permit the councillors to deliberate behind closed doors and they very shortly adopted the bill unanimously.[39]

P. Jones kept Lopinto well supplied with all the documents relative to the question of incorporation. Letters of the Jesuits to the bishops and their responses, letters of the bishops among themselves, the correspondence between the Cardinal and Mercier, reports and commentaries of the press, Catholic as well as Protestant—all went to Rome where they were used to the great advantage of the Order. During the month of April, Lopinto had not been able to obtain information about the impact of the documents upon the Pope, but beginning May 1 he resumed his visits to the Propaganda and his opportune intervention, as well as the news that he gathered and telegraphed to Quebec, played a large role in the happy outcome of the incorporation project.[40]

On June 16 Lopinto had one of his most important and most useful visits with Mgr Jacobini. He brought him up to date on all that had happened on the subject of incorporation, particularly with regard to the private and public correspondence that it had evoked. It was decided that the principal materials should be printed in order to keep them as documents at the Propaganda. The bombshell that resulted from this interview was the unexpected suggestion of Mgr Jacobini that Lopinto propose to the general of the Order that he make a supplication to the Pope asking for the estates. Lopinto immediately drew up the request, which was approved by Jacobini, transcribed as such by the general, and brought to the Propaganda to be presented to the Pope.[41]

Even more encouraging perhaps was Lopinto's audience with Leo XIII on July 1, his first after a fifteen months' sojourn in Rome. He particularly thanked the Pope for the telegram of May 9 that had produced the unanimous vote in the Legislative Council. The latter acknowledged this gratitude, but urged a measure of restraint. "Let the Holy See act . . . it is necessary to deal with that episcopate!"—a remark that Lopinto interpreted to mean that the Pope regarded the episcopate, or whoever conducted it, as difficult.[42]

It is important to note that the subsequent clamour which was raised after the passage of the Act came primarily from Ontario Protestants who sought to have the measure, along with the Act of 1888 which provided for a settlement of the estates question, disallowed. But, according to Mercier's statement, only one official protest against the Act was received by the Assembly while it was under consideration.[43] This was a petition from the Protestant Ministerial Association of Montreal, asking that the bill incorporating the Society of Jesus might not become law, and the petition was read and received by the Assembly on April 29.[44] Other than Mercier's statement concerning it, the petition does not appear to have been mentioned in the debate. The opposition in 1887, then, came primarily from a part of the Catholic hierarchy and not from Protestants in Quebec.

The alumni of Collège Sainte-Marie arranged a meeting to honour P. Turgeon. Premier Mercier was doubly invited—as an alumnus and as the premier of the province. The alumni presented an address to the "heroes" of the occasion, to which P. Turgeon responded, asserting that the Jesuits had obtained justice, "thanks to the man Providence had placed at the head of the Province of Quebec." The Conservative newspapers *Minerve* and *Monde* protested, as the Liberal papers had already done, against this intrusion of the clergy into politics. Ironically, Mercier was called "l'homme providentiel." They added: "To the little ones of the castors he gives their pasture."[45]

During the summer of 1887, in accordance with a plan suggested by Lopinto, Turgeon had confidential talks on the question of the estates with Mgr Taché as well as with Masson and Mercier. Efforts to get Mgr Taché to go to Rome were of no avail because the state of his health had kept him away from his own diocese for a long time. Turgeon spoke to Mercier about resubmitting the incorporation bill to the legislature in order to restore it to its original text. He also raised the question of what the legislature would do if the Pope conferred the right to give academic degrees. Mercier replied that he could not answer in the name of the legislature but, saying nothing on the subject, the government would recognize the degrees. If legislative consent were necessary to make the degrees valid, he hoped that he would be able to secure it.[46]

Lieutenant-Governor Masson's devotion to the Jesuits' cause was assured. He expressed deep regret that the incorporation bill had been changed. He was also prepared to go to Europe after submitting his resignation as lieutenant-governor at the end of the provincial session (because of ill health). He accepted quite willingly Turgeon's plea that while he was in Rome he might air his views on the religious difficulties in Canada as fully as possible.[47]

Meanwhile, the activity of Laval and its partisans was relentless. During an election in the county of Laprairie, Mercier's opponents repeated that he had rebelled against the episcopate by pushing through the act of incorporation. To defend himself against the charge Mercier cabled Rome where, through the efforts of Lopinto, a reply was immediately sent that stated: "One cannot call you a rebel against the bishops because of the incorporation of the Jesuits since the Sovereign Pontiff himself permitted them to request this incorporation."[48]

In Rome, Lopinto had to defend the Order against charges that Collège Sainte-Marie was already conferring degrees contrary to papal orders. During the fall, fearing that a settlement of the estates question in favour of the Jesuits would follow swiftly upon their incorporation, Laval prepared what it reportedly called *un grand coup*. Briefly stated, a request was to be made to the provincial legislature for government subsidies that would render any request for compensation for, or restitution of, the Jesuits' estates ineffective. According to P. Fleck, such a request for subsidies was verbally made by the university. Mercier replied that the government would like nothing better than to be generous toward the university, but before making free gifts, it must pay its debts and restore the Jesuits' estates, in part at least, to whoever had the right.[49]

Laval had also decided to send a delegation composed of Mgr Gravel, Abbé Casgrain, and Judge Routhier to Rome. As news of the continuing efforts of Laval reached Lopinto in Rome he did his utmost to keep the Propaganda informed. Early in September he began to prepare for a worthy reception of Masson at the Holy See. He was assured by Jacobini that the Pope regarded the question of degrees as an open one, but that it would not be treated until after that of the estates. Jacobini assured Lopinto that the Jesuits would not be forced to affiliate with Laval; indeed, they must not affiliate. As to the delegates from Laval, he informed Lopinto that His Holiness was awaiting their visit in order to tell them to cease their opposition.[50]

Rodrigue Masson was replaced as lieutenant-governor in October. News of his replacement reached him only while he was visiting his sister in France. Despite his misgivings about his usefulness because of thus being relieved of his official capacity, Masson proceeded to Rome, arriving there on November 29. In the company of Lopinto he went first to visit Cardinals Rampolla, Simeoni, and Mazzella, who encouraged him to speak openly to the Pope. On December 11, despite a general suspension of private audiences, he was received at the Vatican and was able to speak with great frankness concerning the difficulties in Canada.[51]

Leo XIII received Masson and his family with goodwill and spoke of his affection for Canada, which he noted he had proved by giving it a cardinal. He remarked that it had been evident for a long time that things were not going well there. Masson then spoke freely of the situation. He assured the Pope that the Canadian people, both Catholic and Protestant, were fundamentally religious. Catholics, in general, were disposed to allow the clergy great influence and to let themselves be guided by them on all questions which concerned religion. If clerical influence was diminishing, it was the fault of the clergy themselves, though Masson painted a favourable picture of the clergy as a whole. Concerning the bishops, however, he reported that faithful and prudent public men had a right to complain of the lack of accord among them, and between them and the clergy on nearly all questions currently being discussed in the country. It was rare, he stated, to find accord even on questions of a very great religious importance. Moreover, their discords were often made public by the members of the clergy themselves, or by the newspapers which were generally recognized to be under their control. Such discord often caused confusion among well-disposed public men, and exposed them to the condemnation of the bishops and the clergy on questions where religious interests were concerned. Public officials, Masson insisted, had the right to the complete abstention or to the unanimity of the episcopate on such questions.

The Pope spoke of the duty of bishops to conform to orders coming from Rome. Masson acknowledged this and told His Holiness that the bishops should give an example of obedience and should not interpret these orders according to religious or political bias. To this frank statement, Leo replied, "The cardinal is there and must be able to bring about an understanding." Masson continued. The Cardinal was himself engaged in the conflict and the fact that the Jesuits had only a limited incorporation in the province was due almost exclusively to the opposition of His Eminence. There was apparently only one remedy—direct intervention by the Holy See. "Above all," begged Masson, "no more delegates; we have had enough of them." Masson reiterated the need of prior agreement among the hierarchy and the clergy upon religious matters. In exclusively political questions, a complete abstention on the part of the clergy would obviate the scandal of seeing acts of the governing body approved and condemned at the same time by the clergy and its organs.

While protesting the loyalty of the bishops to the Holy See, Masson called attention to conflicting schools of thought among them which, he felt, tended to accentuate divergencies of a political nature. Difficulties had been complicated for several years by quarrels on the subject of Laval University and more recently on the subject of the incorporation of the Jesuits and the material consequences that that incorporation might lead to. "Yes," remarked the Pope, "the question of the estates!" Masson, in response to the Pope's invitation, now revealed his views on the question. In his opinion, as long as the question remained a source of discord among the episcopate, a general understanding would be difficult; he alluded to the correspondence between Taschereau and Mercier as indicating clearly that the use of these estates had a great deal to do with the former's opposition to the Jesuits. Masson reviewed the developments regarding the estates, emphasizing Ross's unwillingness to deal with the question without the concurrence of the Jesuits and Taschereau's insistence that he alone was charged by the Pope and that the Jesuits had nothing to do with it. He remarked that the Pope's authority was not universally recognized in the province and that a discussion of the rights of the church would be inopportune if the question of the estates could be settled otherwise. A direct request by the Pope or by a papal delegate would not fail to raise a dangerous discussion that could be avoided by a direct request by the Jesuits as the donees of the estates. The estates were not given

F*

to the Sulpicians, to foreign missions, nor to any other religious corporation, but to the Jesuits. In the opinion of many, the state, in order to accomplish the intention of the donors, must give them to the Jesuits or to no one. Masson concluded that a request, if made, must in all fairness be made by the Jesuits as they were still engaged in the work for which the estates were given. In any case, if the government decided to deal with the question, it would insist that all arrangements be settled in advance in such a manner as to have the unanimous assent of the episcopate, in order to prevent subsequent embarrassment to public officials who might be involved in a settlement. Pope Leo ended the interview with the declaration that all would be settled; he would see to it.[52]

The visit of Masson to Rome was followed in February by that of Mercier. Between the two visits Pope Leo, at the Jesuits' request, appointed a special commission composed of five cardinals to pass judgment on the accusations that continued to mount against the Canadian members of the Order. This move on the part of the Order was in anticipation of a memoir that Hamel was reportedly directing to the Holy See. On December 8 Lopinto was warned of the efforts of Mgr Gravel, who had been in Rome since November 9 to undermine the mounting influence of the Jesuits in Rome. P. Désy of Quebec kept Lopinto posted on the activities of Hamel and other partisans of Laval. On December 18 he reported that Hamel, supposing that the fathers were working in Rome to have the indult accorded to the Cardinal revoked, had asked that the Holy See not settle anything definitively before taking cognizance of his memoir. Lopinto communicated this information not only to the Propaganda but to certain of the cardinals of the special commission as well. When the memoir finally arrived, Lopinto was able to write to Turgeon on April 17 of the following year that that "which threatened to be a machine-gun has been found to have neither iron nor powder, but only air making noise in the labyrinth of the ear."[53]

The coolness with which Hamel's memoir was received was due in no small measure to the impact that both Masson and Mercier made during their respective visits to Rome. In the early part of 1888 Mercier left for Europe. He was said to have gone to consult throat specialists. It was also reported that he was arranging for the participation of the province of Quebec in the Paris exposition in 1889. Of this the ultramontanes were highly critical since it was known that the exposition was being organized by the French Republic to celebrate the centenary of the Revolution. François Xavier Trudel, editor of the extremely Conservative L'Etendard, refrained from criticizing Mercier, however, and it is quite possible that this editor-friend of the Jesuits knew that the Premier was seeking to settle the question of the estates to the advantage of the Order.[54]

Upon his arrival in Rome in mid-February, Mercier met first with several cardinals and he chatted with Lopinto. He then was able to obtain an audience with the Pope who congratulated him upon having obtained the civil recognition of the Jesuits in Canada and for the example that he had been to other governments in their relations with the religious orders. During the course of a conversation concerning the question of the Jesuits' estates, Mercier indicated that he was willing to give the estates to whomever the Pope designated, on condition that the government receive a quittance signed by the Jesuits, now civilly recognized and the only proprietors of the estates as the successors of the old Jesuits. The Pope agreed that the condition was just and reasonable. Mercier said that he was prepared to settle the question when the Holy See wished. The question must be settled soon and he felt strongly motivated to deal with it. He protested a devotion to the Jesuits that some of his predecessors in office had not had, "car ce sont mes maîtres, mes professeurs et je les aime." Mercier spoke of an anticipated surplus which made the moment particularly opportune for awarding an indemnity for the estates. He proposed one further condition—that any action be taken with the Canadian fathers rather than with outsiders because there was anxiety that the compensation remain in Canada rather than pass into foreign hands.[55]

Mercier returned to Quebec at the beginning of March, bearer of an authorization to put the land of the old college of Quebec up for sale. This was a feather in his cap because for nearly twenty years his predecessors had tried in vain to dispose of this land in the heart of Quebec. Mercier's interviews with influential cardinals and his audience with the Pope undoubtedly precipitated a ruling by a special commission of cardinals, approved by the Pope, that the fathers of the Company of Jesus should treat with the government on the question of the estates.[56] Upon his return to the province, Mercier addressed a gathering at the Club National in Montreal on April 10. He announced the near settlement of the estates question and ended his address, in the midst of an ovation, with a call to rally around the national flag.[57]

The decision of the special commission reached Montreal on April 18. Meanwhile, subtle endeavours to discredit the Jesuit cause in Rome as well as in Canada, by the indiscreet leaking of questionable bits of information to the provincial press, prompted Lopinto to complain to Cardinal Simeoni. The upshot of this was a telegram from Cardinal Simeoni to Cardinal Taschereau that forbad the Catholic press to deal with the Jesuit question, which the Pope had reserved to himself, and to publish documents. This abstention, painful even to some well-meaning Catholic journalists, had the long-range effect of restricting opposition to the settlement that came about within a matter of weeks to the Anglo-Protestant milieu alone.[58]

For about three months prior to the presentation of the bill for the settlement of the estates question, Mercier carried on a correspondence with the Vatican and with the Jesuits of the province for the purpose of bringing the matter to a satisfactory conclusion. As the Premier insisted upon including this correspondence in the lengthy preamble to the bill which was finally submitted to the legislature, it is necessary to examine the contents of it in some detail. The correspondence began while Mercier was still in Rome. On February 17 he had written to Cardinal Simeoni reminding him of a dispatch from the Sacred Congregation of the Propaganda to Taschereau of May 7, 1887, in which it was indicated that the Pope reserved to himself the right of settling the question of the Jesuits' estates in Canada. Mercier reviewed the problem of disposing of the property on which the old college had been located. The Cardinal was asked if there were any serious objection to the government selling the property, pending a final settlement of the question. The government would look on the proceeds of the sale as a special deposit to be disposed of later in accordance with agreements to be entered into between the interested parties and sanctioned by the Holy See. As it would perhaps be necessary to consult the legislature of the province, which was to be convened very shortly, Mercier asked for an immediate reply.[59]

On March 1 Simeoni notified Mercier that the Pope was willing to grant permission to sell the property upon the express condition, however, that the sum to be received be deposited and left at the free disposal of the Holy See. To this letter Mercier replied by telegram on March 21 that the Quebec government objected to the condition imposed in the letter and that the settlement of the delicate question could not succeed unless permission was given to sell the property upon the conditions and in accordance with the exact terms of the Premier's letter of February 17. The Cardinal's response to this telegram is quoted exactly: "The pope allows the government to retain the proceeds of the sale of the Jesuit Estates as a special deposit to be disposed of hereafter with the sanction of the Holy See."[60]

Following this correspondence between Mercier and the Sacred Congregation there were several exchanges between the Premier and P. Turgeon, rector of Collège Sainte-Marie. On April 25 Turgeon informed Mercier that, by a letter of March 27 from the Sacred College, the Jesuit fathers were authorized to treat with the provincial government in the matter of the estates. Turgeon announced that on April 2, at a meeting of the Society, he had been appointed general and special attorney for that purpose.[61] He had likewise been given the power of attorney by the superior of the Jesuits in Canada, with full power to treat with the government upon the conditions expressed in the letter of the Sacred College.[62] In the letter to which Turgeon referred, it was announced that the cardinals had decided to permit the Jesuits to treat in their own name with the civil government, in such a manner, however, as to leave full liberty to the Holy See to dispose of the property as it deemed advisable. The Jesuits were warned to be careful that no condition or clause should be inserted in the official deed of concession that could in any manner affect the liberty of the Holy See to dispose of the property. Furthermore, whatever might be the sum which the fathers received from the government, they should be obliged to deposit it in a place of safety to be determined by the Sacred College. The Pope's concurrence with the foregoing decisions of the cardinals was announced.[63] The letter from Turgeon and that from the Sacred College were now submitted to the Cabinet by Mercier.

On May 1 Mercier notified Turgeon of the terms upon which the government was willing to negotiate. In consenting to treat with the Jesuits, the government did not recognize any civil obligation, but simply a moral obligation with respect to the estates. There could not be any question of a restitution in kind, that having been abandoned by those concerned, but only a compensation in money, to be agreed upon amicably with the Jesuits. The compensation was to be expended exclusively in the province. The Jesuits would grant to the provincial government the complete and perpetual concession of all the property which might have belonged to them in Canada, and they would renounce all rights upon such property and the revenues thereof in the name of the Pope, of the Sacred College of the Propaganda, and of the Roman Catholic Church in general. Any agreement between the Jesuits and the government would be binding only in so far as it should be ratified by the Pope and the legislature of the province. The amount of the compensation would remain in the possession of the government as a special deposit until the Pope had ratified the settlement and made known his wishes respecting the distribution of this money in the province. Finally, the statute would provide for a grant, in proportion to population, to the Protestant minority for its educational work in the province.[64] Mercier gave copies of the letter of March 27 from the Sacred Congregation, that of April 25 from Turgeon, and his own response of May 1, to Cardinal-Archbishop Taschereau on May 3, and received simply an acknowledgment from Taschereau on May 4.[65]

On May 8 Turgeon indicated general agreement with the government's terms. He thought that if it were necessary to arbitrate in order to determine the amount of the compensation, none of the interested parties could object. Referring to Mercier's stipulation in favour of the Protestants, Turgeon remarked that since that clause did not touch the question which he was instructed to treat with the government he wished to be relieved from replying to it.[66] On May 14 Mercier asked Turgeon for a written claim as to the amount of the compensation to be allowed, expressing the hope that it would be very reasonable and moderate, "in view of the financial and other difficulties of the province."[67]

Turgeon made his reply on May 20. He felt that the official valuation of the estates at $1,200,000 was too modest. After suggesting that he considered $2,000,000 to be a more correct estimate of the total value of all the properties, he indicated a willingness on the part of the Jesuits to settle for half the sum of $990,009, which was a valuation placed upon the pieces of property in the City of Montreal. In addition to this monetary compensation he suggested that as soon as the settlement was reached the fathers should be given "a lot of land which would be a monument to commemorate the eminently Catholic and conservative act which Mercier was about to perform." Turgeon suggested the Common of Laprairie as a suitable grant. He reasoned that as the government would use the estates to encourage teaching, education, industries, arts and settlement by other institutions, the Jesuits ought to have a lasting share from the estates with which they had enriched the province.[68]

Mercier replied that in view of the difficulties surrounding the question and the situation of the province the government could not offer more than $400,000. The government did not take the intrinsic value of the property as a basis for this figure since the religious authorities had long ago abandoned the claim for a restitution in kind and had invariably limited their claim to a compensation. The amount of the compensation had been described to Rome as acceptable by the religious authorities of Canada. The Premier informed Turgeon that it was therefore impossible for the government to exceed that sum, which it was ready to offer the Jesuits upon the conditions contained in his (Mercier's) letter of May 1. As to Turgeon's request for an additional grant, the government would retrocede to the Jesuits the rights which it might have in the Common of Laprairie.[69]

On June 8 Turgeon reluctantly accepted the government's offer of $400,000 as the sum of the compensation to be awarded. Mercier acknowledged this acceptance on the same day, indicating to Turgeon that there now remained only the task of preparing the necessary documents and to submit them to the proper persons.[70]

Mercier moved on June 12 that on the following day the House resolve itself into a committee to consider certain proposed resolutions respecting the settlement of the question of the Jesuits' estates.[71] The schedule on June 13 was apparently too full to permit this to take place, and it was not until June 28 that a consideration of the proposed resolutions was begun in a committee of the whole House. The resolutions were preceded by a lengthy preamble in which the history of the confiscation of the estates and the subsequent efforts of the church to regain control of them was reviewed, and the correspondence of 1888 with the Holy See and the Society of Jesus was included *verbatim*. The resolutions themselves were a ratification of the arrangements which had been stipulated in various parts of the correspondence between Mercier and Turgeon. The arrangement between Mercier and Turgeon was thereby ratified and the lieutenant-governor-in-council was authorized: (1) to carry it out according to its form and tenor; (2) to pay out of any public money at his disposal the sum of $400,000 in the manner and under the conditions mentioned in the documents, and to make any deed that he might deem necessary for the carrying out of the settlement; (3) to transfer to the Society of Jesus all the rights of the province to Laprairie Common; (4) to pay a sum of $60,000 to the different Protestant and dissentient universities and educational institutions, according to instructions from the Protestant Committee of the Council of Public Instruction; (5) to enforce whenever necessary all claims that might become due to the provincial government owing to the fulfilment of the other terms; (6) to freely dispose of the property, the proceeds of which might be used in fulfilling the terms of the settlement or for any other purpose approved by the legislature.[72]

After consideration in the committee of the whole House, the resolutions were taken up in the Assembly.[73] In the debate Mercier went at great length into the history of the estates and of the efforts of the church to regain control of them. Needless to say, his recitation was one in which the claims of the Jesuits appeared in a manner calculated to evoke the full sympathy of the deputies. Evidence from P. Braun was cited in their favour, which tended toward the debatable conclusion that the Jesuits had not in fact been suppressed in Canada. Mercier drew from statistical reports of the commissioner of Crown lands to prove that the sum of $400,000 was by no means excessive. The Premier also anticipated the questions which would later be raised regarding the position of the Pope in the transactions. He denied that the authority of the legislature was being vacated in the interests of a foreign power. The Pope had been asked to participate in the settlement to prevent dissension in the ranks of the interested religious authorities over the allocation of the compensation. Since both the Jesuits and the Quebec hierarchy had advanced claims to the estates, only the intervention of the superior of both, the Pope, could bring about an agreement which would be absolutely final. With reference to the matter of Protestant acceptance of the Pope as an arbitrator, Mercier cited the example of Bismarck's use of the Pope as an arbitrator in a controversy between Germany and Spain. The Pope would be acting in the role of statesman rather than as head of the Catholic Church.[74]

Mercier came finally to the question of why the government must sanction the proposed arrangements. He reviewed the history of the confiscation of the estates and came to the conclusion that it was "an act of spoliation."[75] In Mercier's opinion, the proprietary rights of the Jesuits had been on an identical footing with those of any of the other inhabitants of Canada, in which case the seizure of their property on the basis of the right of conquest was contrary to international law. The British government, in taking possession of the estates in 1800 on the basis of the right of conquest, had invoked a right that did not exist. It had violated the Capitulations, the Treaty of Paris, and the law of nations. He ended his discourse by urging that the settlement ought to be accepted because it would put an end to a question that had plagued the province for a long time. In true Mercier fashion, there was a final note of praise for the work of the Jesuits in the province, with the mention that the Jesuits proposed to use the Laprairie Common as a location for an agricultural college.[76]

After Mercier's lengthy disquisition on the proposed settlement of the estates question, there were only two dissenting voices against the resolutions, both English Protestants. John Smythe Hall (Montreal-West) objected on principle to any opening of the question. In his opinion, it had been settled and fixed on many occasions by various statutes, and the opening of it under such circumstances was a dangerous precedent. He would not accept the lengthy argument of the Premier setting forth the Jesuits' legal claim. No one had ever pretended there was any legal claim, Hall asserted. He was surprised that Mercier characterized the act of taking possession under the sheriff's writ in 1800 as an act of spoliation. The matter had been before many people for nearly a century and the Premier was the first, said Hall, to make any such statement. Hall objected that the authority of the Pope, which was claimed to be necessary, had been brought before the legislature in advance, and that the resolutions were subject to his ratification. The deputy from Montreal-West also raised the question of how the Protestants would be affected by the settlement. The province was now to disburse $400,000 for distribution by the Pope among the Roman Catholics, and $60,000 for distribution by the Protestant Committee. This was approximately the customary distribution and if the sum of $460,000 was replaced by funds from the estates, reasoned Hall, the situation for the Protestants would not be changed. On principle he would object to a distribution of the funds by any authority outside the recognized institutions of the province, and it appeared to him that the Roman Catholic Committee was the proper authority to distribute the $400,000.

William Owens (Argenteuil) was a more formidable opponent. He pointed out that to refer to the proposed resolutions as "resolutions respecting the settlement of the Jesuits' estates" was to imply that the Jesuits had an unsettled claim to these estates. The legal documents that he had been able to obtain led Owens to conclude that the Jesuits had no claim, legally or morally, to the property. The most devastating legal opinion to this effect was that expressed by James Marriott in his letter to the attorney- and solicitor-general of Great Britain of May 12, 1765, which Owens quoted at length. Owens also quoted from the British government's instructions to Governor Carleton of January 3, 1775, which supported the view that he took regarding the Jesuits' legal or moral claims. These instructions called for the suppression and dissolution of the Order, and for the allowance of sufficient stipends and provisions for the remainder of the Jesuits' lives. "Why not remove the veil," queried Owens, "and bring down these resolutions in their proper form, intituled: 'Resolutions to endow the Society of Jesus to the extent of $400,000.00?' " Owens chided Mercier for wanting to pay the $460,000 out of the funds of the province, when he had been constantly reminding the deputies of the financial difficulties with which it was confronted. His final objection to the proposed resolutions was the role assigned to the Pope in the matter. He criticized Mercier, a Liberal, for providing "for a fourth branch of our Legislature having for its head His Holiness the Pope," instead of abolishing the Legislative Council as Liberals had hitherto talked of doing.

Owens also called the attention of the House to certain specific portions of the correspondence attached to the resolutions and forming part of them. He objected to the stipulation that any agreement made between the government and the Jesuits would be binding only in so far as it should have been ratified by the Pope and the legislature of the province, as well as to the provision that the compensation should remain in the possession of the government of the province as a special deposit until the Pope had ratified the settlement and made known his wishes respecting the distribution of the amount.[77]

In spite of the objections of Hall and Owens, the resolutions were agreed upon by the committee of the whole House, and Mercier was permitted to bring in a bill respecting the settlement of the Jesuits' estates.[78] After further consideration, the bill was passed in the Legislative Assembly on July 3.[79] It was then considered by the Legislative Council which passed it, without amendment, on July 10. Royal assent to "An Act respecting the settlement of the Jesuits' Estates" (51-2 Vict., c. 13) was given by the lieutenant-governor in the Queen's name on July 12, 1888.[80] Thus, in the words of Rumilly, the bill passed "comme une lettre à la poste."[81]

For the success of the bill Mercier got all the credit; the roles of Lopinto, Turgeon, and Masson were unknown or unheralded. Turgeon left shortly for Rome where the distribution of the $400,000 would be settled only after protracted and sometimes acrimonious discussions. Mercier expressed a desire to see the Pope award the entire sum to the Company of Jesus. In the midst of the proceedings which led to the final passing of the Jesuits' estates bill, a telegram arrived from Rome on July 4 which announced that the Pope had conferred upon Mercier the grand cross of the Order of St. Gregory, the highest distinction ever accorded to a layman in the New World.[82]

The involved story of the efforts by the partisans of the Company of Jesus as well as those of Laval to influence the Pope in the division of the indemnity is not essential to this study which has dealt only with the background for the settlement. If it were pursued, however, it would serve only to further document the cleavages in the Canadian Church that had made papal participation in the Act of Settlement absolutely necessary.[83] A papal brief of January 15, 1889 (published on February 18), awarded $160,000 and Laprairie Common to the Company of Jesus, $100,000 to Laval, $40,000 to its branch in Montreal, with the other $100,000 to be divided among the bishops of the province. The university question, which we have seen as a problem intricately related to the estates question, was laid to rest by the Constitution, *Jamdudum*, dated February 2. By it, Laval University was required to give diplomas to the students of Collège Sainte-Marie after they had successfully completed examinations given by the college.[84]

The sequel to the "Act respecting the settlement of the Jesuits' estates" is too well known to need retelling.[85] In the Province of Quebec there was some small stir immediately following the passing of the Act, primarily over the role assigned to the Pope in the settlement. The real storm broke in Ontario after the Dominion government refused to yield to pressures to disallow the Act, and announced on January 19, 1889, that it would be left to take its course. The British North America Act of 1867 gave the Dominion government the right to disallow provincial legislation within a year after the receipt of such legislation from the province. The Jesuits' Estates Act was received on August 8, 1888, which meant that the government would have had until August 9 of the following year to decide whether to allow or disallow it. Following the January 19 announcement attempts to induce the government to reverse itself and to disallow the Act became a *cause célèbre* in Ontario, and, to a much less extent, in Quebec. The question of disallowance of the Act was debated in the Dominion House of Commons between March 26–8, and the government was sustained in its decision not to disallow by an overwhelming majority (188–13). John A. Macdonald jestingly referred to the thirteen who voted against the government as the "devil's dozen." Anti-Catholic sentiment which was awakened by over-zealous Protestant clergymen, Orangemen, newspapers like the Toronto *Mail*, the "noble thirteen," including Dalton McCarthy, and the Equal Rights Association, which was born of the Ontario agitation against the Act, shook the Dominion. The tragedy of it all was that McCarthy and others like him were not content to confine their agitation to the question of the Jesuits' Estates Act; they called for an all-embracing attack on Catholic "aggression" and "encroachment" because, it was alleged, the Act recognized the sovereignty of the Pope in a part of Canada and it "endowed" the religious organization of the Jesuits and was therefore contrary to the principle of separation of church and state. McCarthy carried the campaign westward into Manitoba and added fuel to the fires of the troublesome school question there. He insisted that the French nationality must be completely submerged in order for the development of a unified Canada to take place. In a word, the Jesuits' estates question, coming so shortly after the bitter feelings aroused by the hanging of Riel (1885), contributed in a major way to bitter racial and religious strife in Canada. The readiness of certain firebrands to use one issue to kindle a host of others had tragic consequences for the efforts of moderate statesmen who were trying to build a unified Canadian nation.

In retrospect, it is difficult to see how the provincial government could have settled the thorny estates question otherwise. The historical narrative of this study should indicate that the question of the right to the properties was not a matter of black and white. Certain historical, if not legal, circumstances seem to warrant the conclusion that the Society of Jesus, or the Catholic Church, had at least a moral right to some compensation for the estates which had been enjoyed under *bona fide* titles during the French régime. Recourse to the Pope to distribute the compensation seems to have been absolutely necessary in view of the conflicting claims of the provincial church hierarchy and the Society of Jesus which were vastly complicated by the university question. In the light of the intensity of the controversy within the church, it would seem that the Pope alone could have silenced it.

NOTES

ABBREVIATIONS USED IN NOTES

D.L.P.Q.—Débats de la Législature de la Province de Québec
J.H.A.L.C.—Journal of the House of Assembly of Lower Canada
J.L.A.P.C.—Journals of the Legislative Assembly of the Province of Canada
J.L.A.P.Q.—Journals of the Legislative Assembly of the Province of Quebec
J.L.C.P.L.C.—Journals of the Legislative Council of the Province of Lower Canada

CHAPTER ONE

1. Marcel Trudel, *L'Eglise canadienne sous le régime militaire* (Québec, 1956–7), I, p. 89; II, p. 135.
2. *Ibid.*, pp. 128–9.
3. Adam Shortt and Arthur G. Doughty, eds., *Documents Relating to the Constitutional History of Canada, 1759–1791* (Ottawa, 1918), I: 1, p. 67.
4. Trudel, *L'Eglise canadienne*, I, p. 80; II, pp. 129–30, 141.
5. *Ibid.*, I, p. 214; II, p. 130.
6. Shortt and Doughty, eds., *Documents*, I: 1, pp. 15–16, 30.
7. *Ibid.*, pp. 17–18, 31–2.
8. R. G. Thwaites, ed., *The Jesuit Relations and Allied Documents* (Cleveland, 1896–1901), LXX, p. 313, n. 36.
9. *Ibid.*, p. 314, n. 36.
10. J. H. Pollen, "Society of Jesus," *Catholic Encyclopedia* (New York, 1913), XIV, pp. 96–100; Ludwig, Freiherr von Pastor, *The History of the Popes from the Close of the Middle Ages* (St. Louis, Missouri, 1913–53), XXXV, chaps. v, vi; XXXVI, chaps. i, vii, viii; XXXVII, chaps. i and ii; Leopold von Ranke, *The History of the Popes* (London, 1907), II, pp. 479–98.
11. François Philibert Watrin, "Banissement des Jésuites de la Louisiane" (written in Paris, Sept. 3, 1764), *Jesuit Relations*, LXX, pp. 211–301.
12. *Ibid.*, p. 317, n. 40; and vol. LXXI, p. 389, n. 9.
13. Trudel, *L'Eglise canadienne*, II, p. 135; see *Jesuit Relations*, LXXI, pp. 137–81, for a chronological list of missionaries (entries 195, 208, 217, 226, 271, 283, 302, 305, 308, 314, and 316). Father Claude-Joseph Viret was killed by Iroquois in July, 1759. Three (Fathers Joseph-Pierre de Bonnecamp, Siméon Le Bansais, and Pierre Audran) had returned to France, while two of the aged members, Fathers Nicolas Degonnor and Jacques-François Le Sueur, died in Canada. During the same period, death had claimed two of the ten brothers, and the three scholastics (Charles-Alexandre Morlière, Pierre de Phleugny, and René Rivalin) had returned to France.
14. Trudel, *L'Eglise canadienne*, I, pp. 108–11, 93–108 (list of remaining Jesuits among other clergy); II, pp. 136–9 (list of Jesuit priests and brothers); *Jesuit Relations*, LXXI, pp. 137–81, entries 190, 199, 214, 236, 247, 250, 257, 258, 260, 262, 265, 266, 274, 276, 279–82, 284, 291–3, 295, 296, 306, 307, 309–12, 317–19.
15. Trudel, *L'Eglise canadienne*, I, pp. 338–43, 349–57 (list of Jesuits among other clergy at end of 1764); II, pp. 135, 171–3 (list of Jesuit priests and brothers alone), 173–5; *Jesuit Relations*, LXXI, pp. 137–81, entries 190, 236, 247, 257, 266, 280, 281, 292, 295, 296, 307, 311. Death claimed Jean-Baptiste Denouville, Etienne Lauverjat, Alexis-Xavier de Guyenne, and Simon-Pierre Gounon. The decrees of expulsion in the Illinois region forced the return to France of Jean-Baptiste Lamorinie, Jean-Baptiste de Salleneuve, Philibert Watrin, and Julien Devernai. Pierre-Antoine Roubaud was lost to the Order through a combination of defection and expulsion. Three of the eight brothers

(Charles-Philippe Dohen, Etienne-Marin Racine, and Julien Pernelle) disappeared from the Order, whether by death or return to France it is unknown.

16. Shortt and Doughty, eds., *Documents*, I: 1, p. 100, French text; pp. 115–16, English translation.

17. *Ibid.*, Instructions to Governor Murray, Dec. 7, 1763, pp. 191–3.

18. Trudel, *L'Eglise canadienne*, II, pp. 131–3.

19. Shortt and Doughty, eds., *Documents*, I: 1, pp. 67–8, 71, 73, 79.

20. Q. 1, pp. 253–4, Murray to Halifax, Oct. 23, 1763; Trudel, *L'Eglise canadienne*, II, p. 159.

21. Trudel, pp. 159–61.

22. Q. 1, p. 121; Trudel, p. 161, n. 39.

23. Q. 1, pp. 262–3, address dated at Quebec, Oct. 24, 1763.

24. Trudel, pp. 164–5.

25. Gray to Murray, June 11, 1764, C.O. 42, I. 2: 366, cited in Trudel, p. 167.

26. Murray to Gray, June 14, 1764, C.O. 42, I. 2: 371 f., cited in Trudel, p. 167.

27. Murray to the Board of Trade, Aug. 22, 1764, C.O. 42, I. 2: 380, cited in Trudel, p. 168.

28. Trudel, p. 147.

29. *Ibid.*, pp. 147–52; Murrary to the Earl of Halifax, June 26, 1764, Murray Papers, II, pp. 139–40.

30. "Statement of the Case as Between Roubaud and the Jesuits," Feb. 8, 1786, enclosed in Hope to Sydney (No. 15), Feb. 10, 1786, Q. 26: 1, pp. 125–6.

31. Murray to Hillsborough, Murray to Halifax, Murrary to Ross, all dated June 26, 1764, Murray Papers, II, pp. 138–9, 141–2.

32. "Statement of the Case as Between Roubaud and the Jesuits," Q. 26: 1, p. 126.

33. Roubaud to Mr. Marteith, Jan. 17, 1765, *ibid.*, pp. 127–8.

34. Statement of Feb. 8, 1786, *ibid.*, pp. 128–9. See also Q. 5: 2, p. 599, de Glapion's statement of April 7, 1768, enclosed in Carleton to Shelburne (No. 35), April 14, 1768.

35. Q. 25, pp. 253–5.

36. Statement of April 7, 1768, enclosed in Carleton to Shelburne (No. 35), April 14, 1768, Q. 5: 2, pp. 598–9.

37. Carleton to Shelburne, *ibid.*, pp. 591–2.

38. Trudel, II, p. 155.

39. Hope to the Jesuits, Jan. 30, 1786, and statement of Feb. 8, 1786, enclosed in Hope to Sydney (No. 15), Feb. 10, 1786, Q. 26: 1, pp. 120–32.

40. "Thoughts upon the Ecclesiastical Establishment in Canada," April 11, 1764, Shelburne Manuscripts, vol. 59, pp. 33–4.

41. *Ibid.*, pp. 35–6.

42. Q. 18A, pp. 88–103; A. L. Burt, *The Old Province of Quebec* (Minneapolis, 1933), p. 99.

43. *Ibid.*

44. Legislative Council, vol. B, p. 178.

45. François Xavier Garneau, *Histoire du Canada* (Montreal, 1944–6), VI, pp. 87–8.

46. A. Rankin, *Jesuits' Estates of Canada, Public Property* (Montreal, 1850), p. 80; see pp. 78–81 for Marriott's opinion in its entirety. See also *J.H.A.L.C.*, 1823–4, XXXIII, App. "Y," pp. 44–5.

47. Shortt and Doughty, eds., *Documents*, I: 1, p. 377, n. 3.

48. *Ibid.*, p. 236.

49. "Considerations on the Expediency of Procuring an Act of Parliament for the Settlement of the Province of Quebec," *ibid.*, p. 261.

50. Camille Rochemonteix, *Les Jésuites et la Nouvelle France au 18e Siècle* (Paris, 1906), II, p. 206, refers to a letter from Shelburne to Carleton, dated London, Nov. 14, 1767. See also Shortt and Doughty, eds., *Documents*, I: 1, p. 311.

51. Q. 5: 2, p. 600. The entire report, including the statement on Roubaud, is found in Q. 5: 2, pp. 593–600.

52. *Ibid.*, p. 590, Carleton to Shelburne (No. 35), Quebec, April 14, 1768.

53. Trudel, *L'Eglise canadienne*, II, p. 141.

54. *Ibid.*, I, p. 214.

55. *Ibid.*, II, p. 142.

56. *Ibid.*, II, p. 135.

57. *La Gazette de Québec*, July 4, 1765, p. 3; cited *ibid.*, II, p. 164, n. 43.

58. De Glapion to Shelburne, Nov. 12, 1766, Q. 3, pp. 416–19.

59. Briand was consecrated on March 16, 1766.

60. Rochemonteix, *Les Jésuites*, II, p. 208; Henri Têtu, *Les Evêques de Québec* (Quebec, 1889), pp. 314–17 for letter from Briand to Carleton, 1771.

61. Têtu, pp. 315–17.
62. Rochemonteix, *Les Jésuites*, II, p. 208; Garneau, *Histoire*, VI, p. 284.
63. Shortt and Doughty, eds., *Documents*, I: 1, p. 377 and n. 3.
64. *Ibid.*, pp. 387–8.
65. See *ibid.*, p. 377, n. 3, and p. 424, n. 1, regarding the nature of this fact-finding.
66. *Ibid.*, pp. 427–9.
67. *Ibid.*, p. 429. An abstract of such regulations as the provincial legislature of Quebec might carry into effect was inclosed in Wedderburn's report; p. 435 relates to the Society of Jesus.
68. *Ibid.*, p. 443.
69. Rochemonteix, *Les Jésuites*, II, p. 211 and n. 3.
70. See Pastor, *History of the Popes*, XXXVIII, chap. I, for the history of the conclave of the cardinals of 1769. Chap. III gives the full story of the Bourbons' demands for the abolition of the Society and of Clement XIV's resistance during the first years of his pontificate. The work of Moñino is described in chap. IV, *ibid.*
71. *Ibid.*, p. 286. Pastor does not include the brief in its entirety.
72. *Ibid.*, pp. 287–8.
73. *Ibid.*, p. 239,
74. *Ibid.*, pp. 236–8, 289.
75. Briand to Mesdames de Pontbriand, quoted in Rochemonteix, *Les Jésuites*, II, p. 214.
76. *Ibid.*, pp. 214–15, n. 2, 216. Rochemonteix quotes from Briand's letter to Cardinal Castelli, located in the Archives of the Propaganda in Rome (Canada, vol. I, fol. 323).
77. See Rochemonteix, App. VIII, pp. 279–301, for that historian's attempt to build such a case.
78. Translated from *ibid.*, pp. 216–17, n. 3.
79. By Rankin, in *Jesuits' Estates in Canada*, p. 29.
80. Shortt and Doughty, eds., *Documents*, I: 1, p. 569, "Queries re Government of Quebec."
81. *Ibid.*, p. 568, citing a few notes endorsed "Genl Carleton's Memoranda"; the chief item refers to the subject of religion as indicated in the "Queries."
82. *Ibid.*, p. 573.
83. *Ibid.*, I: 2, 604–5.
84. *Ibid.*, p. 697.
85. *Ibid.*, p. 825.
86. *Ibid.*, pp. 1043–4.
87. Arthur G. Doughty and Duncan A. McArthur, eds., *Documents Relating to the Constitutional History of Canada, 1791–1818* (Ottawa, 1914), p. 25.

CHAPTER TWO

1. *Arpent* is an obsolete French measure of land—a hundred square *perches*, varying with the value of the *perch* from about an acre and a quarter to about five-sixths of an acre.
2. Q. 26: 1, p. 240a, enclosure in Hope to Sydney, March 6, 1786.
3. Q. 86: 1, p. 98.
4. C.O. 42: 74, p. 75; C.O. 42: 75, p. 78.
5. *J.L.A.P.C.*, 1858, XVI: 5, App. 18.
6. William Kingsford, *The History of Canada* (Toronto, 1887–98), VII, p. 286.
7. Amherst Papers, Packet 47, "Sir Jeffery Amhert's Situation relative to the Grant of the Jesuits Estate. 1774." Transcript is noted: "in Amherst's hand." The papers in the Amherst Packets are not numbered by pages, but they are listed in order in the front of each packet.
8. The motives of the various grants will be discussed in chap. V.
9. Amherst Papers, Packet 69, "Memoire justifieant de la donation Royalle des biens des jesuites, en faveur de Mr. le General Amherst by Père Roubaud."
10. *Ibid.*, Packet 47, "Eclaircissemens sur les jesuites du Canada," Feb. 13, 1770, consisting of twelve unnumbered pages.
11. *Ibid.*, Amherst to Robertson, March 31, 1770.
12. *Ibid.*, Ross to Amherst, April 4, 1770.
13. *Ibid.*, "Mem. relating to the Jesuits' Estates by A. Wedderburn," April, 1770.
14. *Ibid.*, T. Moncrieffe to Amherst, New York, April 24, 1770.
15. *Ibid.*, Robertson to Amherst, New York, April 25, 1770.

16. *Acts of the Privy Council of England: Colonial Series*, V, p. 24; *Abstract of Proceedings in Council, Relative to the Grant, to the late Jeffery Lord Amherst, of the Estates, Belonging to the Jesuits, in Canada*, p. 1; *J.H.A.L.C.*, 1823–4, XXXIII, App. "Y," p. 4.

17. Amherst Papers, Packet 47, "Copy of the Report from the Board of Trade to the Council, on Sr. J. A⁸ Petition of a Grant of the Jesuits' Land in Canada," Whitehall, June 7, 1770.

18. *Ibid.*, Robertson to Amherst, New York, June 20, 1770.

19. *Ibid.*, William Smith to Robertson, New York, June 20, 1770, enclosed in a letter from Robertson to Amherst of the same date.

20. *Ibid.*, Robertson to Amherst, New York, June 20, 1770.

21. *Acts of the Privy Council of England: Colonial Series*, V, p. 242.

22. Amherst Papers, Packet 47, Henry Davidson to Jeffery Amherst, London, July 5, 1770.

23. *Ibid.*, H. S. Conway to Amherst, Park Place, July 7, 1770.

24. *Ibid.*, Davidson to Amherst, London, July 12 and 14, 1770.

25. *Ibid.*, Amherst to Conway, Riverhead, July 16, 1770.

26. *Ibid.*, Davidson to Amherst, July 26, 1770.

27. *Ibid.*, Wedderburn to Davidson, Lincoln's Inn, July 30, 1770.

28. *Ibid.*, Robertson to [Amherst], Quebec, Aug. 21, 1770.

29. *Jesuit Relations*, LXXI, pp. 105, 107, 172, 179, 180.

30. Amherst Papers, Packet 47, Robertson to Amherst, Quebec, Aug. 21, 1770.

31. *Ibid.*, Amherst to Robertson, Sept. 3, 1770.

32. *Ibid.*, Robertson to [Amherst], New York, Sept. 24, 1770.

33. *Ibid.*, Amherst to Conway, Riverhead, Oct. 26, 1770.

34. *Ibid.*, Roubaud to [Amherst], London, Oct. 31, 1770.

35. *Acts of the Privy Council of England: Colonial Series*, V, p. 243; *Abstract of Proceedings in Council, relative to the Grant*, p. 1, See also MS "Copy of His Majesty's Order in Council of the 18th of August, 1786," in a file in the Public Archives, Ottawa, marked "Appendice au Rapp. du Comité des Commissaires," p. 2. This MS is hereafter referred to as "Order-in-Council of 18 Aug. 1786."

36. Amherst Papers, Packet 47, Robertson to Amherst, Nov. 7 and 9, 1770, and Jan. 14 and Mar. 7, 1771.

37. *Ibid.*, Robertson to Amherst, New York, Nov. 7 and 9, 1770, and Jan. 14, 1771.

38. *Abstract of Proceedings in Council, relative to the Grant*, pp. 1–2; "Order-in-Council of 18 Aug. 1786," p. 2.

39. *Ibid.*, p. 2; *Acts of the Privy Council of England: Colonial Series*, V, pp. 242–3.

40. Amherst Papers, Packet 47, Robertson to Amherst, May 7 and Aug. 6, 1771.

41. *Ibid.*, Robertson to Amherst, Dec. 12, 1771.

42. *Ibid.*, Maseres to Amherst, Inner Temple, July 2, 1772.

43. *Ibid.*, [Amherst] to Maseres, Riverhead, July 17, 1772.

44. *Ibid.*, Robertson to [Amherst], New York, Oct. 19, 1772, and same to same, Feb. 4, 1773.

45. *Ibid.*, Robertson to [Amherst], New York, April 6, 1773.

46. *Ibid'*, "Sir Jeffery Amherst's Situation relative to the Grant of the Jesuits Estate, 1774," in Amherst's hand.

47. *Ibid.*

48. Shortt and Doughty, eds., *Documents*, I: 1, p. 573.

49. *Ibid.*, I: 2, pp. 604–5.

50. *Ibid.*, I: 1, p. 568, n. 1. The editors cite a few notes endorsed "Gen¹ Carleton's Memoranda."

CHAPTER THREE

1. Jeffery Amherst was the recipient of a succession of offices and honours: in 1761 he was made a knight of the Bath; in 1770, governor of Guernsey; in 1772, a privy councillor and officiating commander-in-chief; and in 1776, a baron; *Dictionary of National Biography*, I, pp. 358–9.

2. *Acts of the Privy Council of England: Colonial Series*, V, p. 244; "Order-in-Council of 18 Aug. 1786," p. 3.

3. *Ibid.*; *Abstract of Proceedings in Council, relative to the Grant*, pp. 2–3. The exact date on which Amherst submitted this information is not indicated in the documents, but it appears to have been in the early part of 1786.

4. *Ibid.*, p. 3; "Order-in-Council of 18 Aug. 1786," pp. 3–4.

5. *Ibid.*, p. 5. The date of the petition is not indicated in the order-in-council, in which these proceedings are reviewed.

6. *Ibid.*, pp. 5–6; *Abstract of Proceedings*, p. 1.

7. "Order-in-Council," p. 6.

8. Shortt and Doughty, eds., *Documents*, I: 2, p. 825.

9. See "Appendice au Rapp. du Comité des Commissaires," pp. 8–9, for a copy of the letter to Dorchester.

10. State Book, vol. D, p. 317.

11. *Ibid.*, p. 320.

12. Monk to Dorchester, Oct. 16, 1787, "Appendice au Rapp. du Comité des Commissaires," p. 11; see also pp. 11–13 for the draft commission.

13. State Book, vol. D, p. 347.

14. Monk to Dorchester, Nov. 1, 1787, "Appendice au Rapp. du Comité des Commissaires," p. 14.

15. *Ibid.*, p. 16.

16. State Book, vol. D, p. 348.

17. The minutes of the meeting of the Quebec nominees are printed in *J.H.A.L.C.*, 1823–4, XXXIII, App. "Y," p. 12.

18. *Ibid.* The minutes of the Quebec and Montreal meetings of the nominees are also to be found in "Appendice au Rapp. du Comité des Commissaires," pp. 18–21.

19. State Book, vol. D, p. 353.

20. Q. 35, p. 1, Dorchester to Sydney (No. 48), Dec. 10, 1787.

21. State Book, vol. D, p. 353.

22. Q. 35, pp. 64–5, Dorchester to Sydney (No. 50), Jan. 9, 1788, translation of the petition enclosed.

23. *Ibid.*, p. 70, translation of the memorial.

24. *Ibid.*, pp. 71–106. Extracts from the titles of the estates indicating the motives and conditions of grant are given pp. 80–93, *ibid.*

25. *Ibid.*, pp. 74–7, for the statement of authorities in the memorial. See also pp. 102–3 for the statement of the conclusion at which the memorialists arrived.

26. *Ibid.*, pp. 78–9, 104.

27. *Ibid.*, pp. 105–6.

28. *Ibid.*, pp. 106–10.

29. *Ibid.*, pp. 109–10.

30. *Ibid.*, pp. 110–12.

31. *Ibid.*, pp. 113–15.

32. *Ibid.*, pp. 62–3 for Dorchester's letter. He had mentioned earlier that the petition was under consideration by the provincial Council; Q. 35, p. 1, Dorchester to Sydney, Dec. 10, 1787.

33. Panet was appointed in place of Descheneaux, who had declined to serve; C.O. 42: 72, p. 6.

34. C.O. 42: 74, p. 9; C.O. 42: 81, p. 8.

35. *J.H.A.L.C.*, 1823–4, XXXIII, App. "Y," p. 13, minutes of the meeting of Jan. 23, 1788. A copy of the letter to the Jesuits is included.

36. *Ibid.*, pp. 13–14, minutes of the meetings of Jan. 30, Feb. 2, and Feb. 14, 1788.

37. *Ibid.*, p. 14, minutes of the meeting of Feb. 9, 1788.

38. *Ibid.*, minutes of the meeting of Feb. 14, 1788.

39. *Ibid.*, p. 15, minutes of March 31.

40. See *Jesuit Relations*, LXXI, pp. 65–95.

41. *J.H.A.L.C.*, 1823–4, XXXIII, App. "Y," p. 15. The letter from the Montreal commissioners to Chandler, dated March 26, 1788, is included in the minutes.

42. *Ibid.* The letter from the Quebec commissioners to those at Montreal, dated March 31, 1788, is included in the minutes of March 31.

43. *Ibid.*, p. 14, minutes of March 17, 1788.

44. *Ibid.*, minutes of March 18, 1788.

45. *Ibid.*, pp. 15–16.

46. *Ibid.*, p. 15, Panet's statement of motives is included in the minutes of April 17.

47. "Appendice au Rapp. du Comité des Commissaires," pp. 57–8.

48. *Ibid.*, pp. 58–9. The temporary report appears in the minutes of Council of May, 1788; State Book, vol. E, pp. 290–1.

49. State Book, vol. E, p. 291.

50. "Appendice au Rapp. du Comité des Commissaires," pp. 60–1. See pp. 60–4 for the entire report of the law officers.

51. *Ibid.*, pp. 61–2.

52. *Ibid.*, p. 65.

53. State Book, vol. E, p. 348.

54. MS "A Reference on the affairs of the Jesuites. Minutes of the Committee appointed on the 22d July 1788 by His Excellency Lord Dorchester in Council to Report on the due Course required by Law for the execution of His Majesty's Order of the 18th August 1786 issued on the Petition of the Right Honorable Lord Amherst," p. 1 (pages un-numbered throughout). This document is found in a book marked "Jesuit Estates 1790. Appendix to Commission's Report," in the Public Archives in Ottawa. It is hereafter referred to as "Minutes of the Committee of July 22, 1788."

55. *Ibid.*, p. 3, minutes for Aug. 21, 1788.

56. *Ibid.*, p. 4, for a signed statement of objections by Mabane and de Léry.

57. *Ibid.*, p. 5, Hugh Finlay to P. de Glapion, Aug. 26, 1788, and a letter to the commissioners of the same date.

58. *Jesuit Relations*, LXXI, pp. 97–9. A copy of de Glapion's letter is also included in "Minutes of the Committee of July 22, 1788," pp. 6–7, minutes of Sept. 15.

59. *Ibid.*, pp. 7–8.

60. *Ibid.*, pp. 12–13, 15.

61. *Ibid.*, pp. 17–18.

62. *Ibid.*, p. 18.

63. *Ibid.*, p. 21, minutes of Oct. 21, 1788.

64. *Ibid.*, pp. 18–19.

65. *Ibid.*, pp. 19–20.

66. *Ibid.*, pp. 20–2.

67. MS. "Letter from The Chief Justice [Wm. Smith] to His Excellency Lord Dorchester, 13 Dec. 1788," in P.A.C.; file marked "Sir Guy Carleton."

68. *J.H.A.L.C.*, 1823–4, XXXIII, App. "Y," p. 16.

69. *Ibid.*, minutes of April 23, 1789.

70. C.O. 42: 74, p. 9.

71. *J.H.A.L.C.*, 1823–4, XXXIII, App. "Y," p. 16.

72. C.O. 42: 72, p. 7.

73. *J.H.A.L.C.*, 1823–4, XXXIII, App. "Y," pp. 16–17, minutes of June 17, 1789.

74. *Ibid.*, pp. 17, 21.

75. *Ibid.*, p. 17.

76. C.O. 42: 72, p. 9.

77. *J.H.A.L.C.*, 1823–4, XXXIII, App. "Y," pp. 22–9.

78. See *ibid.*, under columns headed "Parties échues à Sa Majesté."

79. *Ibid.*, p. 31.

80. *Ibid.*, p. 30.

81. C.O. 42: 74, pp. 11–12; the objections of Taschereau and Panet are summarized in a report of attorney- and solicitor-general of May 18, 1790.

82. *Ibid.*, pp. 12–14.

83. In April, 1789, Dorchester was informed that Monk was dismissed and that Alexander Gray was to be attorney-general; Burt, *Old Province of Quebec*, p. 444.

84. C.O. 42: 74, pp. 14–16.

85. *Ibid.*, p. 17.

86. *Ibid.*, pp. 17–18.

87. *Ibid.*, p. 18.

88. *Ibid.*, pp. 10–11.

89. *Ibid.*, p. 14; C.O. 42: 81, p. 8.

90. C.O. 42: 74, pp. 19–20.

91. See "Aveu et Dénombrement des Terrains des Pères Jésuites en Canada, 1781–88," in *Jesuit Relations*, LXXI, pp. 65–95.

92. *Ibid.*, p. 93.

93. C.O. 42: 74, p. 20.

94. *Ibid.*, pp. 20–1.

95. C.O. 42: 72, pp. 1–2, Dorchester to [Grenville], duplicate (No. 65), Quebec, Nov. 10, 1790.

96. *Ibid.*, p. 2.

97. *Ibid.*, pp. 2–3.

98. *Ibid.*, pp. 3–4.

CHAPTER FOUR

1. Trudel, *L'Eglise canadienne*, I, pp. 338–43, 349–57; II, pp. 135, 171–5.
2. See *ibid.*, p. 173, n. 83, regarding Amherst; *Jesuit Relations*, LXXI, pp. 137–81, entries 199, 214, 260, 274, 306, and 310.
3. During the last quarter of the century the remaining Jesuits were removed, one by one, from the ranks of the Order by death: P. Alexis Maquet, March 2, 1775; P. Marin-Louis Lefranc, May 25, 1776; P. Sebastien Louis Meurin, August 13, 1777; P. Antoine Gordan, June 30, 1779; P. Charles Germain, August 5, 1779; P. Pierre Du Jaunay, July 16, 1780; Frère Jean-Baptiste Nicolas Demers, after 1780; P. Pierre Potier, July 17, 1781; P. Jean-Baptiste de La Brosse, April 11, 1782; P. Pierre-René Floquet, October 18, 1782; P. Joseph Huguet, May 5, 1783; P. Augustin-Louis de Glapion, February 24, 1790; P. Bernard Well, March 1791; P. Etienne-Thomas-de-Villeneuve Girault, October 8, 1794; and P. Jean-Joseph Casot, March 16, 1800. *Ibid.*, entries 250, 258, 262, 265, 276, 279, 282, 284, 291, 309, 312, 317–19. See also *ibid.*, p. 400, n. 49, regarding Frère Demers.
4. State Book, vol. D, p. 317.
5. Hilda Neatby, *The Administration of Justice Under the Quebec Act* (Minneapolis, 1937), pp. 243–55.
6. *J.H.A.L.C.*, 1823–4, XXXIII, App. "Y," p. 36, journal of a committee of the Council, Nov. 26, 1789.
7. *Ibid.*, pp. 39–40.
8. Têtu, *Les Evêques de Québec*, p. 393.
9. Burt, *The Old Province*, pp. 464–5.
10. Jean François Hubert, born in Quebec in 1739, ordained in 1766, and consecrated bishop in 1786. He remained coadjutor till 1788, when, on the death of Desglis, he succeeded to the headship of the church; *ibid.*, p. 463, n. 41.
11. Hubert's letter, dated Nov. 18, 1789, is printed in Têtu, *Mandements*, II, pp. 385–96, and in *J.H.A.L.C.*, 1823–4, XXXIII, App. "Y," pp. 37–9.
12. State Book, vol. G, pp. 232–43.
13. Rochemonteix, *Les Jésuites*, II, pp. 224–5, and n. 2, pp. 225–6.
14. Têtu, *Mandements*, II, pp. 398–409, "Mémoire de Mgr Bailly au Sujet de l'Université," April 5, 1790.
15. C.O. 42: 72, p. 14, Dorchester to Grenville (No. 66), Nov. 10, 1790.
16. Têtu, *Mandements*, II, pp. 414–21.
17. *Ibid.*, pp. 421–3, "Lettre de Monseigneur Briand à Lord Dorchester au sujet de Monseigneur Bailly," May 2, 1790.
18. *Ibid.*, pp. 347–8.
19. *J.H.A.L.C.*, 1823–4, XXXIII, App. "Y," p. 33.
20. *Ibid.* See also L. P. Audet, *Le Système Scolaire de la Province de Québec* (Quebec, 1950–2), II, part III, chaps. I–IV. In chap. III, Audet suggests that Charles Inglis, the first Anglican bishop of Nova Scotia, who visited Quebec during the summer of 1789, played a major role in the project for a university. Thomas R. Millman, in *Jacob Mountain: First Lord Bishop of Quebec* (Toronto, 1947), p. 169, also suggests an influence by Bishop Inglis.
21. C.O. 42: 72, p. 12, Lord Dorchester to W. W. Grenville, Quebec (No. 66), Nov. 10, 1790, enclosed in No. 65 of the same date.
22. *Ibid.*, pp. 12–13.
23. *Ibid.*, p. 13.
24. *Jesuit Relations*, LXXI, pp. 101–7, "Letter of Reverend Father de Glapion to Monsieur Louis Germain [Langlois], *fils*," Quebec, Dec. 31, 1789.
25. Rochemonteix, *Les Jésuites*, II, pp. 233–4.
26. *Abstract of Proceedings in Council*, p. 4.
27. Garneau, *Histoire*, VII, p. 21.
28. *J.H.A.L.C.*, 1792–3, I, p. 288.
29. Q. 84, pp. 140–6, Milnes to Portland (No. 16), Quebec, Jan. 31, 1800.
30. *J.H.A.L.C.*, 1792–3, I, pp. 288, 292, 294, 324, 346, 348, 350, 352, 354, 356, 358, 360, 362, 364.
31. *Ibid.*, p. 356.
32. *Ibid.*, pp. 356, 358, 360.
33. *Ibid.*, p. 364.
34. *Ibid.*, pp. 366, 368, 372, 374, 376, 378, 382, 384, 386.
35. *Ibid.*, p. 374.

36. *Ibid.*, pp. 382, 384, 386.
37. *Ibid.*, p. 386.
38. *Ibid.*, pp. 406, 408, 410, 412, 464, 466, 468.
39. *Ibid.*, p. 408.
40. *Ibid.*, p. 468.
41. *J.L.C.P.L.C.*, I, pp. 198, 200.
42. *Ibid.*, pp. 206, 208.
43. *Ibid.*, pp. 208, 220, 224, 226, 228.
44. See *ibid.*, pp. 224, 226, 228, for a copy of the address of the Legislative Council.
45. *J.H.A.L.C.*, 1800, pp. 46–8.
46. *Ibid.*, p. 48.
47. William Pitt Amherst, Earl Amherst of Arracan (1775–1857).
48. *Abstract of Proceedings in Council*, p. 5.
49. *Ibid.*, pp. 5–6.
50. Q. 84, pp. 48–9, noted in an order of reference to a committee of the Council (Quebec), Dec. 24, 1799.
51. *Ibid.*, pp. 59–62.
52. *Ibid.*, p. 64; italics in original.
53. *Ibid.*, p. 65.
54. *Ibid.*, p. 67, enclosure: Ryland to attorney- and solicitor-general, Quebec, Nov. 16, 1799.
55. *Ibid.*, pp. 69–70, enclosure: attorney-general's report on the provincial claims to the Jesuits' estates, Nov. 28, 1799; relevant parts of the Jesuits' constitution are cited pp. 70–1.
56. *Ibid.*, pp. 72–3.
57. *Ibid.*, pp. 83–6, enclosure: appendix to the attorney-general's report, Nov, 28, 1799.
58. *Ibid.*, pp. 74–5; relevant articles of the edict of suppression of July 28, 1763 are quoted pp. 75-6.
59. *Ibid.*, pp. 76–9.
60. *Ibid.*, p. 79.
61. *Ibid.*, p. 80; see pp. 87–148 for copies of various petitions and memorials.
62. *Ibid.*, pp. 149–51, enclosure: memorial of Jean-Joseph Casot, Dec. 5, 1799.
63. *Ibid.*, pp. 152–3, enclosure: attorney-general's report on Casot's memorial, Quebec, Dec. 7, 1799.
64. *Ibid.*, pp. 38–40, 48–9, Milnes to Portland (No. 15), Dec. 19, 1799, and Ryland to the chairman of the committee, Dec. 24, 1799.
65. *Ibid.*, pp. 50–5.
66. *Ibid.*, pp. 43–4, Milnes to Portland (No. 16), Quebec, Jan. 31, 1800.
67. *Ibid.*, pp. 44–6.
68. *Ibid.*, p. 154, Milnes to Portland (No. 17), Quebec, Feb. 13, 1800.
69. *J.H.A.L.C.*, 1800, pp. 32–4.
70. *Ibid.*, pp. 42–4.
71. *Ibid.*, pp. 46, 48.
72. *Ibid.*, pp. 162, 164, 166, 168.
73. Q. 84, pp. 270–1, Milnes to Portland (No. 21), Quebec, April 5, 1800.
74. *Ibid.*, pp. 271–3.
75. *Ibid.*, pp. 302–3, Milnes to Portland (No. 25), June 21, 1800.
76. *Jesuit Relations*, LXXI, p. 180, entry 317; Rochemonteix, *Les Jésuites*, II, p. 235; Q. 84, p. 270, Milnes to Portland (No. 21), Quebec, April 5, 1800.
77. *Ibid.*, pp. 301–10, copy of the commission.
78. *Ibid.*, p. 300.
79. G–I, vol. 1, pp. 227–xli-xliii, Duke of Portland to Milnes, Whitehall, July 12, 1800.
80. Q. 86: 1, pp. 94–98A, Milnes to Portland (No. 42), Feb. 23, 1801.
81. *Ibid.*, pp. 95–7.
82. *Abstract of Proceedings in Council*, p. 6.
83. *Ibid.*, pp. 6–7.
84. Q. 91, p. 61, J. S. [John Sullivan] to Milnes, on Lord Hobart's behalf, Feb., 1803. The document in the Q series is a transcript of a draft of the letter. According to Q. 92, Milnes to Sullivan (No. 2), June 21, 1803, the original was dated Feb. 9.
85. Q. 92, pp. 2–3.
86. *Ibid.*, pp. 3–4.

87. *Journals of the House of Commons*, 1802–3, vol. 58, p. 597; *Journals of the House of Lords*, 1802–4, vol. XLIV, p. 331a.

88. For the deliberations in the House of Commons, see *Journals*, 1802–3, vol. 58, pp. 597, 613, 617, 621, 623, 628, 668, 675, 677, 681. For the same in the House of Lords, see *Journals*, 1802–4, vol. XLIV, pp. 331a, 347b, 385a, 391a, 398b, 400a. The action was also reported in *J.H.A.L.C.*, XXXIII, 1823–4, App. "Y," pp. 5–6.

CHAPTER FIVE

1. William B. Munro, *The Seigniorial System in Canada* (New York, 1907), pp. 179–80.

2. *Ibid.*, p. 181. Munro's figure of 880,705 is at variance with that of 794,863, the latter representing the total of the estates as included in a report by the Commissioner of Crown Lands submitted on January 30, 1858; *J.L.A.P.C.*, 1858, XVI: 5, App. 18. See Munro, p. 180, for his listing of the estates, which he drew from J. C. Taché, *A Plan for the Commutation of the Seigniorial Tenure* (Quebec, 1854).

3. *Ibid.*, p. 182.

4. C.O. 42: 76, pp. 21–4; Q. 50–C, pp. 33–8.

5. Munro, *Seigniorial System*, p. 22.

6. C.O. 42: 76, pp. 25–7, 29–31; Q. 50–C, pp. 39–43, 47–53.

7. Grants *en franc aleu noble* were not really feudal grants, but rather allodial grants; only fealty and homage were required from the grantee, and only two grants of this type were made throughout the French régime, both to the Jesuit Order—one of a small strip of land at Trois Rivières in 1634, the other of Notre Dame des Anges; Munro, *Seigniorial System*, pp. 52–3.

8. C.O. 42: 76, pp. 13, 34; Q. 50–C, pp. 54–6.

9. C.O. 42: 75, p. 4; Q. 50–C, p. 33.

10. Q. 50–C, pp. 34–5.

11. *Ibid.*, pp. 39, 41–2.

12. *Ibid.*, pp. 7, 11–12, 54–5.

13. C.O. 42: 74, p. 28.

14. C.O. 42: 76, pp. 45–6, 48–9; Q. 50–C, pp. 72–4, 76–8.

15. C.O. 42: 74, pp. 29–30.

16. C.O. 42: 76, pp. 61–2.

17. Q. 50–C, pp. 86–8.

18. C.O. 42: 74, pp. 31–2.

19. C.O. 42: 76, pp. 68–70; Q. 50–C, pp. 101–4.

20. C.O. 42: 76, pp. 72–4, 76–83; Q. 50–C, pp. 105–22.

21. C.O. 42: 74, p. 34.

22. C.O. 42: 76, pp. 84–92; Q. 50–C, pp. 124–38.

23. C.O. 42: 74, p. 34; C.O. 42: 76, pp. 17–19.

24. C.O. 42: 76, pp. 101–2; Q. 50–C, pp. 150–3.

25. C.O. 42: 75, p. 34; C.O. 42: 76, pp. 107–8; Q. 50–C, pp. 157–61.

26. C.O. 42: 74, pp. 24, 37–8.

27. *Ibid.*, pp. 38–9; C.O. 42: 75, p. 37; C.O. 42: 76, pp. 107–8, 110–11; Q. 50–C, pp. 158–60, 162–4.

28. C.O. 42: 76, p. 121; Q. 50–C, pp. 172–3. "Grants *en franche aumône*, or *frankalmoign*, were made in considerable number, invariably to religious, educational, or charitable orders or institutions. The sole obligations imposed upon the holders of such grants, in addition to that of rendering fealty and homage, was the duty of performing some specified religious, educational, or charitable service in return for the grant. Usually this latter obligation was definitely set forth in the title deed"; Munro, *Seigniorial System*, pp. 53–4.

29. C.O. 42: 74, p. 41; C.O. 42: 76, p. 14, article 27.

30. Q. 50–C, pp. 174–80; C.O. 42: 76, pp. 122–4.

31. C.O. 42: 74, p. 43; C.O. 42: 75, p. 48; C.O. 42: 76, p. 14; Q. 50–C, pp. 176–9.

32. C.O. 42: 74, pp. 43–4; C.O. 42: 75, p. 72; C.O. 42: 76, pp. 156–7; Q. 50–C, pp. 214–16; *Jesuit Relations*, LXXI, p. 71.

33. C.O. 42: 74, p. 44; C.O. 42: 76, pp. 55–7; Q. 50–C, pp. 86–90, 261–5.

34. C.O. 42: 74, pp. 44–5; C.O. 42: 76, pp. 17–19, 66; *Jesuit Relations*, LXXI, p. 89.

35. French text is in Q. 50–C, p. 266.

36. C.O. 42: 74, pp. 45–8; C.O. 42: 75, p. 75; Q. 50–C, pp. 266–8, 272–5.

37. C.O. 42: 74, pp. 24, 46–8; C.O. 42: 75, pp. 75–6; Q. 50–C, pp. 277–82.

38. The date of August 9, 1634, is apparently in error. Such a grant was made by Governor Mézy on August 8, 1664; it consisted of four or five *arpents* in front by 25 in depth; Q. 50–C, p. 282.

39. C.O. 42: 74, pp. 48–9; C.O. 42: 75, p. 75; *Jesuit Relations*, LXXI, pp. 85, 87.

40. C.O. 42: 74, pp. 22–3, 78–9; C.O. 42: 75, p. 80; C.O. 42: 76, pp. 21–2, 25–6, 29–31; Q. 50–C, pp. 33–6, 39–43, 54–7.

41. Q. 50–C, pp. 33, 39, 54–5. The law officers reported that only approximately 10 acres of the farm appeared to be subject to *cens et rentes* and other feudal obligations, the remainder being a *franc aleu roturier*, or tenure somewhat resembling free and common soccage; in other words the remainder of the farm was free from all seigniorial dues and acknowledgments, but at the same time possessed none of the rights of seigniory: C.O. 42: 74, pp. 79–80.

42. The Seminary of Quebec had received it from the bishop of Petrée, who had in turn received it as a grant from Jean de Lauzon; C.O. 42: 75, p. 81.

43. C.O. 42: 74, p. 81; C.O. 42: 76, pp. 127–43; Q. 50–C, pp. 184–200.

44. C.O. 42: 74, pp. 81–2, C.O. 42: 75, p. 83.

45. C.O. 42: 74, pp. 23–4, articles 13–15, 27; C.O. 42: 75, pp. 83–4; C.O. 42: 76, pp. 144–50, 153–4; Q. 50–C, pp. 201–13.

46. C.O. 42: 74, p. 84.

47. *Ibid.*, pp. 23, 51, 85; C.O. 42: 76, pp. 161–2; Q. 50–C, pp. 220–1.

48. C.O. 42: 74, pp. 95–7; C.O. 42: 75, pp. 94–5; C.O. 42: 76, pp. 164–7; Q. 50–C, pp. 222–32, 253–8.

49. C.O. 42: 74, pp. 97–8.

50. *Ibid.*, p. 98.

51. *Ibid.*, pp. 98–9; C.O. 42: 75, p. 92; Q. 50–E, pp. 88–9.

52. C.O. 42: 74, p. 99; C.O. 42: 75, p. 92.

53. C.O. 42: 74, pp. 23, 85–6; C.O. 42: 75, p. 86; C.O. 42: 76, p. 29; Q. 50–E, pp. 2–3.

54. C.O. 42: 74, pp. 23, 51–2, 86–90, 92; C.O. 42: 75, pp. 87–8; Q. 50–E, pp. 5–6, 10–11, 13–21, 24–25, 29–30, 34–5, 40–1, 47–50.

CHAPTER SIX

1. Q. 84, p. 300, Milnes to Portland (No. 25), June 21, 1800, with the commission enclosed.

2. For the work of the commission, see Q. 97, pp. 271–306A; Q. 101: 1, pp. 6–71; Q. 171, pp. 139–52; "Transcript of the Minutes of the proceedings of the Commissioners for managing the Estates heretofore belonging to the late Order of Jesuits," in file marked "Reports on Jesuits' Estates, 1790–1842," in Public Archives, Ottawa; and Dalhousie Papers, III: 2, pp. 1–40.

3. Robert Christie, *A History of the Late Province of Lower Canada*, I, p. 214. See also George W. Parmelee, "English Education," *Canada and its Provinces*, XVI, p. 451.

4. *Provincial Statutes of Lower Canada*, III, pp. 128–38.

5. *Ibid.*, p. 128.

6. Q. 97, pp. 169–71, Milnes to Camden (No. 28), July 4, 1805.

7. *Ibid.*, p. 172.

8. *Ibid.*, pp. 313–18.

9. Christie, *A History*, VI, p. iv.

10. *Ibid.*, p. v.

11. Dalhousie Papers, III: 2, pp. 9, 14.

12. See Christie, *A History*, I, chaps. XI–XIII, for an account of Craig's governorship, which is generally favourable to him and hostile to the House.

13. *Ibid.*, V, pp. 391–418. Copy of a dispatch from Sir James H. Craig, governor-in-chief, to Lord Liverpool, Quebec, May 1, 1810; see pp. 380–90 for a report of the Chief Justice, J. Sewell, which was included in the dispatch of Craig, and was of the same general tone.

14. *Ibid.*, VI, p. vi.

15. *Ibid.*, V, p. 422, Quebec, "Letter of Instructions from Sir J. H. Craig to Ryland," June 10, 1810.

16. *Ibid.*, VI, p. 119, "Observations Relative to the Political State of Lower Canada, by Mr. Ryland."

17. *Ibid.*, p. 192, Ryland to Peel, London, Feb. 11, 1811.

18. *Ibid.*, p. 194, as related in Ryland's statement.

19. *Ibid.*, pp. 195–6.

20. *Ibid.*, pp. 218–19, Ryland to Peel, London, May 9, 1811.

21. *Ibid.*, pp. 263–4, Ryland to Peel, Oxford, Feb. 1, 1812.

22. *Ibid.*, p. 264.

23. *Ibid.*, pp. 272–5, 292–3.

24. Q. 119, pp. 170–2, Ryland to Peel, Poet's Corner, March 2, 1812; Also printed in Christie, *A History*, VI, pp. 266–8. See Christie, *A History*, VI, p. 269, for the order of the Lords Commissioners of the Treasury to Caldwell.

25. Christie, *A History*, VI, pp. 295–6.

26. *Ibid.*, p. 304.

27. *Ibid.*, p. vi.

28. The petition of the Council is given in its entirety in *J.H.A.L.C.*, 1812, XX, pp. 594, 596. Kempt, in a "Memorandum relative to the Estates in Lower Canada heretofore belonging to the late Order of Jesuits" (Dec. 30, 1829), reported that the address was sent to the Assembly for their concurrence but that they did not act upon it; Q. 190: 2, p. 461, Kempt to Murray (No. 131), Dec. 30, 1829.

29. GᴸL-7, pp. 120–3, Bathurst to Drummond, Downing Street, Dec. 30, 1815.

30. *J.H.A.L.C.*, 1816, p. 134.

31. Q. 190: 2, p. 461, Kempt to Murray (No. 131), Dec. 30, 1829; Christie, *A History*, II, pp. 255–62.

32. During the closing days of February or early in March, Drummond received notice of the appointment of Sir John Coape Sherbrooke as governor. On May 21, Drummond sailed for England, the administration of the government devolving upon Major General John Wilson until Sherbrooke's arrival from Nova Scotia on July 21; Christie, *A History*, II, pp. 263–5.

33. GᴸL-9, pp. 65–7, "Bathurst to the Officer Administering the Government of Lower Canada," Downing Street, May 10, 1816.

34. *Ibid.*, pp. 75–6, Bathurst to Sherbrooke, Downing Street, May 31, 1816.

35. GᴸL-9, pp. 100–1, Bathurst to Sherbrooke (No. 81), Downing Street, April 14, 1817.

36. Parmelee, "English Education," p. 495; Millman, *Jacob Mountain*, p. 173.

37. GᴸL-10, pp. 127–8, Bathurst to Richmond (No. 20), Downing Street, March 9, 1819.

38. Q. 170, pp. 556–7.

39. Q. 198: 1, pp. 45–56, Aylmer to Goderich (No. 43), May 9, 1831, with enclosures.

40. Q. 171, pp. 50–4; cited in Millman, *Jacob Mountain*, p. 177.

41. *J.H.A.L.C.*, 1831–2, XLI: 2, App. "I.I.," Table A.

42. Q. 170, pp. 627–30, Stewart to Horton, Sept. 8, 1823, enclosed in J. Stuart to Horton, Nov. 28, 1824.

43. *Ibid.*, pp. 523–6; cited in Millman, *Jacob Mountain*, p. 178.

44. *J.H.A.L.C.*, 1823, XXXII, p. 217.

45. *Ibid.*, pp. 222–3.

46. *Ibid.*, p. 219.

47. Christie, *A History*, III, pp. 24–5.

48. Kingsford, *History of Canada*, IX, pp. 296–7.

49. *Ibid.*, p. 300; Christie, *A History*, III, pp. 28–32.

50. Q. 171, pp. 95, 99, 101, Burton to Bathurst (No. 29), May 16, 1825.

51. Christie, *A History*, III, p. 32.

52. In the session of the legislature from Nov. 23, 1823, to March 9, 1824.

53. *J.H.A.L.C.*, 1823–4, XXXIII, App. "Y," pp. 6–7.

54. *Ibid.*, pp. 7–8 for the report of Secretary Mills. The other documents can be found on pp. 9–12; list of the students (p. 12) in the Royal Grammar School at Quebec (as of Jan., 1824) includes predominantly English names.

55. A. L. Burt, *A Short History of Canada for Americans*, pp. 143–4. Extensively documented in Abbé Lionel Groulx, *L'enseignement Français au Canada*, I, chaps. III–V. See also Audet, *Le Système Scolaire*, IV, pp. 379–92, for a final evaluation of the actual functioning of the Royal Institution that is less harsh than that of Groulx.

56. *J.H.A.L.C.*, 1823–4, XXXIII, App. "Y," p. 1. For brief accounts of the history of education in the province from 1763 to 1824, see Adelard Desrosiers, "French Education," *Canada and its Provinces*, XVI, pp. 397–411, and Parmelee, "English Education," pp. 445–69; see Parmelee especially, pp. 452–5, for criticism of the Royal Institution.

57. *J.H.A.L.C.*, 1823–4, XXXIII, App. "Y," p. 1.

58. *Ibid.*, p. 6. The report comprises approximately fifty folio pages of small print, most of which related to the Jesuits' estates problem rather than to education *per se*.

59. *Ibid.*, 1825, XXXIV, p. 124.

60. *Ibid.*, p. 143.

61. *Ibid.*, p. 183.
62. *Ibid.*
63. *Ibid.*, p. 184.
64. *Ibid.*, p. 184–5, 196–7, 217–18, 220, 230, 305, 326.
65. Q. 171, pp. 54, 61–5, Burton to Bathurst (No. 24), Quebec, March 25, 1825, with the address from the Assembly enclosed.
66. *J.H.A.L.C.*, 1826, XXXV, p. 23.
67. *Ibid.*, p. 39. See also Q. 190: 2, p. 462, Kempt to Murray (No. 131), Dec. 30, 1829, enclosure 5: "Memorandum relative to the Estates."
68. *J.H.A.L.C.*, 1826, XXXV, pp. 351, 368. See also Q. 190: 2, p. 463.
69. Q. 176: 3, pp. 780–1, Wilmot Horton to Dalhousie, Aug. 29, 1826, enclosed in Dalhousie to Horton, Nov. 10, 1826.
70. Which was generally though not strictly true, as already observed.
71. Dalhousie Papers, XI: 2, Dalhousie to Horton, Nov. 10, 1826. See also Q. 176: 3, pp. 772–4.
72. *J.H.A.L.C.*, 1827, XXXVI, pp. 148–9, 174.
73. *Ibid.*, p. 313. See also Christie, *A History*, III, p. 125, note (*).
74. *J.H.A.L.C.*, 1827, XXXVI, p. 319; Christie, *A History*, III, pp. 127–8.
75. Christie, *A History*, III, p. 132; Kingsford, *History of Canada*, IX, pp. 345–9.
76. Christie, *A History*, III, p. 137.
77. *Ibid.*, pp. 141–6.
78. *Ibid.*, pp. 146–9; Kingsford, *History of Canada*, IX, pp. 360–5.
79. Christie, *A History*, III, p. 61; also pp. 157–62, for the petition in its entirety. A *précis* of the address from Montreal to the king in the *Quebec Mercury* indicates that it was more pointed in its attack upon the Governor himself than was the Quebec petition; see Christie, pp. 163–4, for this *précis*.
80. *Ibid.*, pp. 158–60.
81. Kingsford, *History of Canada*, IX, pp. 372–3, for the views of Huskisson; pp. 374–5, for those of Mackintosh. The House of Assembly passed a vote of thanks to the latter in 1829; Christie, *A History*, III, p. 240.
82. Christie, *A History*, III, p. 190; see pp. 184–202, for the report in its entirety, and Kingsford, *History of Canada*, IX, pp. 372–84, for an analysis.
83. Christie, *A History*, III, p. 192.
84. Kingsford, *History of Canada*, IX, p. 384.
85. *Ibid.*, p. 388. Kempt was Administrator from Sept. 8, 1828, to Oct. 20, 1830.
86. Christie, *A History*, III, pp. 216–17.
87. Duncan McArthur, "Papineau and French-Canadian Nationalism," *Canada and its Provinces*, III, p. 308.
88. Christie, *A History*, III, p. 217; Kingsford, *History of Canada*, IX, p. 397.
89. *J.H.A.L.C.*, 1828–9, XXXVIII, pp. 9, 28–31, 107–9; Christie, *A History*, III, n. (*), pp. 224–8, 232–4.
90. *J.H.A.L.C.*, 1828–9, XXXVIII, pp. 109, 665, 680; Christie, *A History*, III, n. (*), p. 234, n. (*), p. 253; GI–21, p. 23, Murray to Kempt (No. 132), Downing Street, June 2, 1830.
91. Lord Aylmer arrived at Quebec on October 13, 1830, relieving Sir James Kempt, who sailed for England on October 20. Aylmer assumed the office of administrator, his commission as governor-in-chief not having been prepared at the time of his leaving England. This he received in February, 1831; Christie, *A History*, III, p. 295.
92. *Ibid.*, pp. 324–7.
93. *Ibid.*, p. 332.
94. *Ibid.*, pp. 332–6; Kingsford, *History of Canada*, IX, pp. 440–1, for a resumé of the resolutions.
95. Kingsford, *History of Canada*, IX, p. 442.
96. *Ibid.*, p. 443.
97. *Ibid.*, pp. 444–5.
98. Christie, *A History*, III, p. 351.
99. GI–22, pp. 542–4, Goderich to Aylmer (No. 51), Downing Street, July 7, 1831. In the dispatch of December 24, 1830, Goderich had recognized that the Jesuits' estates revenues were regularly applied to education and could not properly be diverted from that purpose; an extract of the part of the dispatch which related to the Jesuits' estates is printed in *J.H.A.L C.*, 1831–2, XLI: 2, App. "I.I.," pp. 15–16.
100. GI–22, pp. 544–5. It should be observed that the transfer of the Jesuits' estates to the Assembly was part of a more general arrangement provided by the Howick Act, which also transferred the

revenue from the acts of 1774 and 1791; Kingsford, *History of Canada*, IX, p. 467; Christie, *A History*, III, pp. 316–23; Garneau, *Histoire*, VIII, pp. 156–8.

101. G^I-22, pp. 545–8.

102. Christie, *A History*, III, p. 363.

103. *J.H.A.L.C.*, 1831–2, XLI, p. 205; see App. "D.D.," XLI: 1, for a list of the documents, and App. "I.I.," XLI: 2, for the documents themselves.

104. *Ibid.*, XLI: 2, App. "I.I.," Table A.

105. Christie, *A History*, III, p. 319, "List of Items of Expenditure objected to by the house of assembly of Lower Canada, in the Supply Bill for the year 1830" includes pensions to the Misses De Salaberry for 1829 and 1830 in the amount of £200, but does not indicate circumstances.

106. Tables 4 and 5, referred to in this resumé, are found in *J.H.A.L.C.*, 1831–2, XLI: 2, App. "I.I"; explanations are from Table A of XLI: 2, App. "I.I."

107. G^L-9, Bathurst to Sherbrooke (No. 87), Downing Street, April 14, 1817. See Christie, *A History*, II, pp. 155–62, for the seventeen articles of impeachment against Sewell.

108. See Q. 181, pp. 211 ff., Ryland to Horton, April 20, 1827, and enclosures. See also Dalhousie Papers, XI: 1, Cochran to Dalhousie, Quebec, May 18, 1826; Ryland to Dalhousie, May 19, 1826; Ryland to Dalhousie, June 1, 1826; XI: 2, Dalhousie to Bathurst, June 19, 1826, for the details concerning the quarrel. Ryland claimed that his separate commission as treasurer entitled him to special consideration.

109. G^L-29, Aberdeen to Aylmer (No. 19), Feb. 13, 1835, pp. 157–8.

110. G^L-17, p. 71, Murray to Dalhousie, Downing Street, June 2, 1828.

111. G^L-16, pp. 70–1, Bathurst to Dalhousie, April 10, 1827.

112. G^L-17, pp. 70–1. This arrangement was apparently carried through. See *J.H.A.L.C.*, 1831–2, XLI: 2, App. "I.I.," Table A, which shows no expenditures for the school at Kingston for the years 1828, 1829, 1830.

113. *J.H.A.L.C.*, XLI, pp. 417, 446–7, 479, 490.

114. *The Provincial Statutes of Lower Canada*, XIV, p. 570.

115. G^L-22, pp. 546–7, Goderich to Aylmer (No. 51), Downing Street, July 7, 1831.

116. *J.H.A.L.C.*, 1831–2, XLI: 2, App. "I.I.," p. 4.

CHAPTER SEVEN

1. *J.H.A.L.C.*, 1832–3, XLII, pp. 170, 178.

2. *Ibid.*, 1834, XLIII, pp. 124, 138, 162.

3. *Ibid.*, XLIII: 1, App. "X," p. 1.

4. *Ibid.*

5. *Ibid.*, XLIII, p. 222.

6. W. P. M. Kennedy, ed., *Statutes, Treaties and Documents of the Canadian Constitution, 1713–1929* (Toronto, 1930), p. 288; the Resolutions are given in their entirety, pp. 270–90, and in Kingsford, *History of Canada*, IX, pp. 544–54; see pp. 528–42 of Kingsford for his discussion of the Resolutions.

7. *J.H.A.L.C.*, 1835–6, XLV, p. 48.

8. The Earl of Gosford performed the duties of governor-in-chief and high commissioner from Aug. 24, 1835 to March 30, 1838.

9. *J.H.A.L.C.*, 1835–6, XLV, p. 148.

10. *Ibid.*, p. 155.

11. *Ibid.*, p. 20. The first such standing committee on the Jesuits' estates had been appointed on March 2, 1835; *ibid.*, 1835, XLIV, p. 58.

12. *Ibid.*, 1835–6, XLV: 3, App. "X.X.," p. 1.

13. *Ibid.*, p. 2.

14. *Ibid.*, pp. 2–6, for the "Minutes of Evidence," upon which the committee based its conclusions.

15. McArthur, "Papineau and French-Canadian Nationalism," *Canada and its Provinces*, XVI, pp. 318–19.

16. Christie, *A History*, IV, pp. 258–9; see chap. xxxvii concerning the operations of the Montreal and Quebec Constitutional Associations and their branches throughout the province.

17. Adam Shortt, "General Economic History, 1763–1841," *Canada and its Provinces*, IV, p. 529. For a more comprehensive study, see Benjamin Sulte, *Les Forges Saint Maurice* (Mélanges Historiques VI), (Montreal, 1920).

18. *Ibid.*, chap. xviii.

19. *J.H.A.L.C.*, 1835–6, XLV: 1, App. "S," p. 10, Aylmer to Goderich, March 23, 1832; p. 11, Bell to Col. Craig (civil secretary), March 12, 1832.

20. *Ibid.*, p. 10, Aylmer to Goderich (No. 29), April 9, 1831.

21. *Ibid.*, 1834, XLIII: 1, App. "X," pp. 2–3.

22. Christie, *A History*, III, pp. 304–5.

23. *J.H.A.L.C.*, 1835–6, XLV: 1, App. "S," p. 11, Bell to Craig (civil secretary), March 12, 1832.

24. *Ibid.*, p. 10, Aylmer to Goderich (No. 30), March 23, 1832.

25. *Ibid.*, pp. 11–12, Goderich to Aylmer (No. 111), June 2, 1832.

26. *Ibid.*, pp. 12–13, Bell to Civil Secretary, April 8, 1833.

27. *Ibid.*, p. 12, Aylmer to Goderich (No. 39), April 13, 1833.

28. *Ibid.*, p. 13, Stanley to Aylmer (No. 9), May 25, 1833.

29. *Ibid.*, pp. 6–7.

30. *Ibid.*, pp. 1–2.

31. *Ibid.*, pp. 2–3.

32. *Ibid.*, 1831, XL, pp. 237, 265.

33. *Ibid.*, 1831–2, XLI, p. 115, for an address of Nov. 30, 1831, and pp. 116–17 for the Governor's answer; see also 1834, XLIII, pp. 35, 39–40, 117, for references to addresses of Dec. 22 and 28, 1832.

34. *Ibid.*, pp. 35, 40.

35. *Ibid.*, pp. 42, 43, 62.

36. *Ibid.*, p. 117.

37. *Ibid.*, XLIII: 1, App. "X," third report, pp. 2–4, for the committee's analysis of the situation.

38. *Ibid.*, pp. 4–5.

39. *Ibid.*, p. 5; for the "Minutes of Evidence" pertaining to Bell's lease of the forges and of the reserve in Cap de la Magdeleine, see pp. 11–14.

40. Appointed March 2, 1835; *ibid.*, 1835, XLIV, p. 58.

41. *Ibid.*, 1835–6, XLV, p. 20.

42. *Ibid.*, pp. 48, 124.

43. *Ibid.*, p. 148.

44. *Ibid.*, p. 250.

45. See *ibid.*, XLV: 3, App. "S," for the documents relating to the lease of the forges and the reserve of Cap de la Magdeleine.

46. See *ibid.*, App. "X.X.," "Minutes of Evidence," pp. 3–53. There are many scattered references concerning the lease of the forges and of the reserve.

47. *Ibid.*, XLV, pp. 424, 432.

48. McArthur, "Papineau and French-Canadian Nationalism," p. 317.

49. Kennedy, ed., *Statutes*, p. 276.

50. *Ibid.*, p. 288.

51. Sulte, *Les Forges*, p. 186.

52. Q. 176: 2, Dalhousie to Bathurst, June 18, 1826; Q. 176: 3, Dalhousie to Horton, Nov. 10, 1826, with enclosures.

53. *J.H.A.L.C.*, 1835–6, XLV: 3, App. "X.X.," p. 52; in addition to this appendix of over fifty pages, see also "Minutes of Evidence," 1834, XLIII: 1, App. "X."

54. *Ibid.*, p. 6.

55. *Ibid.*, 1835–6, XLV, p. 494.

56. C. P. Lucas, ed., *Lord Durham's Report on the Affairs of British North America* (Oxford 1912), III, p. 304.

57. Kennedy, ed., *Statutes*, pp. 276–7.

58. *J.H.A.L.C.*, 1835–6, XLV: 3, App. "X.X.," "Minutes of Evidence," p. 29.

59. Christie, *A History*, IV, p. 219.

60. "Rapport du Comité permanent sur les Biens des Jésuites—Régie actuelle et future," dated Feb. 20, 1836; Box 17, No. 1071, Archives du Collège Ste. Marie, Montreal. Original not signed, but written in the hand of R. J. Kimber.

61. René Joseph Kimber, "Dilapidation des Biens des Jésuites de 1826 à 1843: Mémoire sur la Mauvaise Administration de l'honorable John Stewart, Commissaire des Biens des Jésuites," dated Feb. 7, 1843; Box 17, No. 1073, Archives du Collège Ste. Marie, Montreal, copy by A. E. Jones, S.J., and original.

62. W. P. M. Kennedy, *The Constitution of Canada* (London, 1922), p. 114.

63. Kennedy, ed., *Statutes*, pp. 350–2.

64. Kennedy, *Constitution*, p. 115.

65. Lucas, ed., *Lord Durham's Report*, III, p. 310, Glenelg to Durham, Jan. 20, 1838; see also pp. 311–19, Glenelg to Durham, April 3, 1838.

66. *Ibid.*, II, p. 136.

67. *Ibid.*, I, p. 4.

68. *Ibid.*, III, p. 241, "Report of the Commission of Inquiry into the State of Education in Lower Canada," Nov. 15, 1838.

69. *Ibid.*, pp. 242–3.

70. See Q. 194: 1, pp. 152–65, Kempt to Murray (No. 47), May 3, 1830, with enclosures, and Q. 194: 2, pp. 221–30, Kempt to Murray (No. 53), May 13, 1830, with enclosures.

71. Q. 194: 1, p. 165; Q. 194: 2, p. 221.

72. Q. 194: 2, p. 223.

73. G^L-22, pp. 548–9, Goderich to Aylmer (No. 51), July 7, 1831.

74. Lucas, ed., *Lord Durham's Report*, III, pp. 243–4.

75. *Ibid.*, p. 244.

76. *Ibid.*, pp. 244–5.

77. *Ibid.*, pp. 245–91.

78. *Ibid.*, p. 291.

79. *Ibid.*, pp. 294–304.

80. *Ibid.*, p. 303.

81. *Ibid.*, pp. 303–4.

CHAPTER EIGHT

1. Mason Wade, *The French Canadians* (London, 1955), p. 224; Kennedy, *Statutes*, pp. 433–45, for the Union Act (3 & 4 Vict., c. 35).

2. *Ibid.*, p. 433, and n. 1.

3. *J.L.A.P.C.*, 1841, I, pp. 361–2.

4. *Ibid.*, pp. 418–19.

5. *Ibid.*, p. 418.

6. *Ibid.*, p. 432.

7. *Ibid.*, pp. 468–9.

8. *Ibid.*, 1842, II, p. 17.

9. *Ibid.*, p. 18.

10. *Ibid.*, pp. 29–30.

11. *Ibid.*, p. 49.

12. *Ibid.*, p. 111.

13. *Ibid.*, 1844–5, IV, pp. 36, 56.

14. Paul Desjardins, S.J., *Le Collège Sainte-Marie de Montréal* (Montreal, 1940, 1945), II, p. 51.

15. *Ibid.*, pp. 46–7.

16. *Ibid.*, I, pp. 17–19.

17. Archives du Collège Sainte-Marie, 3184–2, Mgr Bourget à Mgr Gaulin, 25 avril 1841.

18. Desjardins, *Le Collège Sainte-Marie*, I, chap. I.

19. Archives du Collège Sainte-Marie, File A–3–3, extract of a letter from Mgr Power to P. Chazelle (Letter No. 16), Dec. 1, 1843; Box 17, No. 1080, P. Félix Martin to P. Peter Chazelle, Jan. 15, 1845 (original).

20. Desjardins, *Le Collège Sainte-Marie*, II, pp. 48–50.

21. *Ibid.*, pp. 49–59.

22. *Ibid.*, pp. 50, 51.

23. *Ibid.*, I, p. 37.

24. Comte de Vatimesnil, *Memoir upon the Estates which the Jesuits Possessed in Canada, and the Objects to which these Estates Should be at Present Applied* (Montreal, 1845), pp. 2–4.

25. *Ibid.*, pp. 5–13.

26. *Ibid.*, p. 13.

27. *Ibid.*, pp. 15–24.

28. *Ibid.*, pp. 29–30.

29. *Ibid.*, p. 34; italics in the original.

30. Desjardins, *Le Collège Sainte-Marie*, I, p. 38.

G

31. Archives du Collège Sainte-Marie, Document No. 1743, "Notes confidentielles de l'Evêque de Montréal aux Honbles Membres du Ministère."

32. Desjardins, *Le Collège Sainte-Marie*, II, pp. 51–4; P. Antoine–N. Braun, *Mémoire sur les Biens des Jésuites en Canada, par un Jésuite* (Montreal, 1874), pp. 120–4.

33. *Ibid.*, pp. 120–1.

34. Desjardins, *Le Collège Sainte-Marie*, I, pp. 38–9.

35. *J.L.A.P.C.*, 1846, V, pp. 284–5.

36. *Ibid.*, p. 285.

37. A. Gérin-Lajoie, *Dix Ans au Canada de 1840 à 1850* (Quebec, 1888), p. 357.

38. Desjardins, *Le Collège Sainte-Marie*, I, pp. 39–40.

39. Gérin-Lajoie, *Dix Ans*, p. 356.

40. Archives du Collège Sainte-Marie, File 1759, "Biens des Jésuites: Discussion au parlement, 1846: Extraits du *Canadien*," p. 1.

41. *Ibid.*, p. 2.

42. Gérin-Lajoie, *Dix Ans*, pp. 357–8.

43. "Extraits du *Canadien*," pp. 3–4.

44. *Ibid.*, pp. 3, 7, 17.

45. *Ibid.*, pp. 1–21, for sampling of other newspapers as they were reported in *Le Canadien*.

46. Archives du Collège Sainte-Marie, Box 17, No. 1081, "Protestation des Evêques du Canada contre le vote de l'Assemblée Législative, au sujet des Biens des Jésuites," June, 1846.

47. *J.L.A.P.C.*, 1846, V, p. 346.

48. *Provincial Statutes of Canada*, II, pp. 919–20.

49. Braun, *Mémoire*, pp. 124–5; *J.L.A.P.C.*, 1847, VI, p. 48.

50. Archives du Collège Sainte-Marie, Box 17, No. 1083, "Lord Elgin's Answer to the Petition of the Catholic Clergy of the Diocese of Quebec & Montreal," p. 1.

51. *Provincial Statutes of Canada*, 1847, II, pp. 1929–33.

52. Wade, *French Canadians*, p. 253.

53. Sir Arthur G. Doughty, ed., *The Elgin-Grey Papers, 1846–1852* (Ottawa, 1937), I, p. 94.

54. Comte de Vatimesnil, *A Note, in Addition to that of 1845, on the Jesuits' Estates* (published in English and in French), p. 19.

55. *J.L.A.P.C.*, 1848, VII, p. 7.

56. *Ibid.*, pp. 29–30.

57. Doughty, ed., *Elgin-Grey Papers*, IV, pp. 1361–4.

58. A. Rankin, *Jesuits' Estates of Canada: Public Property* (Montreal, 1850).

59. *Ibid.*, p. 29.

60. *Ibid.*, chaps. VIII and IX.

61. *Ibid.*, p. 111.

62. *Ibid.*, p. 71.

63. *Ibid.*, pp. 122–3.

64. *Ibid.*, p. 123.

65. *Ibid.*, pp. 60–4.

66. *Ibid.*, p. 129.

67. *Ibid.*, pp. 124–34.

68. *J.L.A.P.C.*, 1852–3, XI: 1, pp. 490, 494, 495, 536, 562, 591, 596.

69. Rankin, *Jesuits' Estates*, p. 64.

70. Archives du Collège Sainte-Marie, Box 17, No. 1085, article in *L'Ordre Social*, Sept. 12, 1850, p. 386.

71. Desjardins, *Le Collège Sainte-Marie*, I, pp. 124–6.

72. See John Lewis, *George Brown*, VII, *Makers of Canada*, pp. 44 ff., 121 ff., for an account of Brown's stand *vis à vis* the Catholic Church.

73. Desjardins, *Le Collège Sainte-Marie*, I, pp. 126–7.

74. *Ibid.*, pp. 126–8.

75. *Ibid.*, pp. 128–30; see also *J.L.A.P.C.*, 1852–3, XI: 1, pp. 52, 189, 290, 379, 388, 400, 460, 472.

76. *A Complete and Revised Edition of the Debate on the Jesuits' Estates Act in the House of Commons* (Montreal, 1889), pp. 177–8.

77. *Statutes of the Province of Canada*, 1856, pp. 229–34.

CHAPTER NINE

1. See Ranke, *History of the Popes*, II, pp. 522–45 on the papacy of Pius IX, and pp. 546–71 for the work of the Vatican Council. On the subject of ultramontanism among Canadian Catholics, the following are helpful: Wade, *French Canadians*, chap. vii; Robert Rumilly, *Histoire de la Province de Québec*, I–VI, and *Monseigneur Laflèche et son temps*; J. S. Willison, *Sir Wilfrid Laurier and the Liberal Party*, I, chaps. x–xi; O. D. Skelton, *The Life and Times of Sir Alexander Tilloch Galt*, chap. xv; Arthur Savaète, *Voix canadiennes, vers l'abîme*, I–V, IX; Laurier L. LaPierre, "Joseph Israel Tarte: A Dilemma in Canadian Politics (1874–96)," chap. ii (M.A. thesis, University of Toronto); H. Blair Neatby, "Laurier and a Liberal Quebec: A Study in Political Management," chaps. i and ii (Ph.D. thesis, University of Toronto); and Barbara J. L. Fraser, "The Political Career of Sir Hector Langevin" (M.A. thesis, University of Toronto).

2. Wade, *French Canadians*, p. 343.

3. Desjardins, *Le Collège Sainte-Marie*, II, pp. 160–4.

4. *Ibid.*, pp. 164–77.

5. *Ibid.*, pp. 180–1, Bourget to Mgr Pinsonnault, July 11, 1863.

6. *Ibid.*, p. 183, Bourget to Cardinal Barnabo, Feb. 5, 1863.

7. *Ibid.*, pp. 183–5.

8. *Ibid.*, pp. 185–7, Bourget to Baillargeon, Oct. 31, 1864, and Baillargeon to Bourget, Nov. 3, 1864.

9. *Ibid.*, pp. 191, 194–8.

10. *Ibid.*, pp. 269–74.

11. *Ibid.*, pp. 274–82. Desjardins cites letters between Bourget and Taschereau from a document entitled *Suite aux remarques de l'Université Laval*.

12. *Ibid.*, pp. 282–5.

13. *Ibid.*, pp. 286–7; see especially notes 21 and 22 in which Desjardins gives many of the details concerning this controversial sermon, and also Wade, *French Canadians*, pp. 357–8, and Rumilly, *Histoire*, I, pp. 230–1.

14. *Quelques remarques sur l'Université Laval*, Nov., 1872, pp. 1–2, cited in Desjardins, *Collège Sainte-Marie*, II, pp. 286–7; Rumilly, *Histoire*, I, pp. 235–6.

15. Desjardins, *Collège Sainte-Marie*, II, pp. 288–98; Rumilly, *Histoire*, I, pp. 237–41.

16. Desjardins, *Collège Sainte-Marie*, II, pp. 298–302.

17. *Ibid.*, pp. 304–9.

18. Cardinal Franchi to Mgr Taschereau, March 9, 1876; Paul Desjardins, "Le Collège Sainte-Marie de Montreal," III (unpublished Ms., hereafter referred to as Desjardins Ms.), chap. i, pp. 1–2.

19. *Ibid.*, pp. 2–3.

20. *Ibid.*, pp. 3–4, and ns. 6, 7.

21. *Ibid.*, pp. 4–5, and ns. 8–12.

22. *Ibid.*, p. 5, n. 13.

23. *Ibid.*, pp. 5–6, and n. 14.

24. *Ibid.*, pp. 9–10, and n. 25.

25. *Ibid.*, pp. 10–11, and ns. 26, 27.

26. *Ibid.*, pp. 16–17, and ns. 32, 33.

27. *Ibid.*, p. 17. At one point Hamel had complained of the thousand miseries the Jesuits had caused the university.

28. *Ibid.*, p. 19.

29. *Ibid.*, p. 21.

30. *Ibid.*, pp. 22–36 for detailed discussion.

31. *Ibid.*, pp. 36–8, Beckx to Charaux, May 31, 1878.

32. *Ibid.*, p. 29. Desjardins quotes P. Hippolyte Lory to this effect.

33. *Ibid.*, p. 39.

34. Archives Collège Sainte-Marie, File 17, Documents 1097a and 1097b.

35. See *Sessional Papers of the Dominion of Canada*, 1877, X: 8, No. 26, pp. 1–21 for complete correspondence between the provincial and federal governments concerning the barracks; Desjardins, *Collège Sainte-Marie*, II, pp. 349–50.

36. *Ibid.*, p. 350; Braun, *Mémoire*, p. i.

37. *Ibid.*, p. ii; Desjardins, *Collège Sainte-Marie*, II, pp. 351–3.

38. Braun, *Mémoire*, p. iv.

39. *Ibid.*, pp. 1–56.

40. *Ibid.*, chaps. ii and iv of part II.

41. *Ibid.*, pp. 57–178, for Braun's discussion of the disposal of the Jesuits' estates which offered no new argument in favour of the Jesuits.

42. Desjardins, *Collège Sainte-Marie*, II, pp. 354–5; Archives du Collège Sainte-Marie, File 17, Document No. 1111: 1, Petition to the legislature and letter to the bishops that accompanied Braun's *Mémoire*.

43. Desjardins, *Collège Sainte-Marie*, II, pp. 355–6.

44. *Ibid.*, pp. 356–9; Archives du Collège Sainte-Marie, File 17. Document No. 1111: 1, Langevin to Taschereau, Jan. 27, 1874.

45. *Ibid.*, Charaux to Bourget, Feb. 2, 1874; Desjardins, *Collège Sainte-Marie*, II, p. 360, n. 5. Charaux's remarks were used by Bourget in a response to Taschereau in connection with a second letter to Mgr Langevin.

46. *Ibid.*, pp. 360–1; Archives du Collège Sainte-Marie, File 17, Document No. 1111: 1, Langevin to Taschereau, March 11, 1874.

47. *Ibid.*, Bourget to Taschereau, March 31, 1874.

48. *Ibid.*, Langevin to Laflèche, end of March, 1874; cited in Laflèche to Fleck, April 3, 1874; Desjardins, *Collège Sainte-Marie*, II, pp. 363–4.

49. *Ibid.*, p. 365, n. 9.

50. *Ibid.*, pp. 368–9; Archives du Collège Sainte-Marie, File 17, Document No. 1111: 1, Bourget to Charaux, April 15, 1874.

51. *Ibid.*, Bishops of Montreal to Pope Pius IX, May 30, 1874.

52. Desjardins, *Collège Sainte-Marie*, II, p. 369, Beckx to Charaux, Jan. 24, 1874.

53. *Ibid.*, p. 370, Rubillon to Charaux, Feb. 13, 1874.

54. Archives du Collège Sainte-Marie, File 17, Document No. 1112, Beckx to Charaux, March 18, 1874; Desjardins, *Collège Sainte-Marie*, II, pp. 371–2.

55. *Ibid.*, p. 372.

56. *Ibid.*, p. 373, Beckx to Charaux, June 13, 1874.

57. *Ibid.*, Charaux to Beckx, July 7, 1874.

58. *Ibid.*, p. 374, Report by Braun, Sept. 7, 1874.

59. *Ibid.*, pp. 374–7, Braun to Charaux, Sept. 14, 1874, report of the first interview; Archives du Collège Sainte-Marie, File 17, Document No. 1113, pp. 35–7.

60. *Ibid.*, pp. 37–9, Braun's report of the second interview; Desjardins, *Collège Sainte-Marie*, II, pp. 377–8.

61. *Ibid.*, pp. 379–80; Archives du Collège Sainte-Marie, File 17, Document No. 1113, extracts from Ouimet's letter, p. 23.

62. *Ibid.*, pp. 43 ff., Braun's explanation to Cardinal Antonelli; Desjardins, *Collège Sainte-Marie*, II, pp. 380–1.

63. *Ibid.*, pp. 382–3.

64. *Ibid.*, pp. 383–4, Beckx to Charaux, Jan. 30, 1875.

65. *Ibid.*, pp. 384–5, Vignon to Fleck, June 18, 1875.

66. *Ibid.*, p. 386, Taschereau to Charaux, May 13, 1876.

67. *Ibid.*, pp. 386–7, Charaux to Taschereau, May 19, 1876.

68. *Ibid.*, pp. 387–92, P. Fleck, *Démolition de notre ancien collège de Québec* (memoir drawn up at the request of the superior of the Mission, Nov. 20, 1886); see Archives du Collège Sainte-Marie, File 17, Document No. 1118, pp. 21 ff., for copies of official action of the provincial government.

69. Desjardins Ms., chap. II, pp. 3–4, Braun to Charaux, Oct. 2, 1877.

70. *Ibid.*, pp. 4–6.

71. *Ibid.*, p. 6.

72. *Ibid.*, p. 7, Chapleau to Mercier, April 10, 1889.

73. *Ibid.*, pp. 7–8; Rumilly, *Histoire*, IV, pp. 63–5.

74. Desjardins Ms., chap. II, pp. 9–10, Laflèche to Taschereau, Aug. 10, 1882.

75. *Ibid.*, pp. 10–11, Saché to Charaux, Feb. 15, 1883.

76. *Ibid.*, pp. 12–15; Rumilly, *Histoire*, IV, p. 65.

77. Desjardins Ms., chap. II, p. 15, P. Vignon to Saché, March 12, 1883.

78. *Ibid.*, pp. 16–17.

79. *Ibid.*, Beckx to Henri Hudon, Dec. 25, 1883.

80. *Ibid.*, p. 18.

81. Rumilly, *Histoire*, I, p. 317.

82. Desjardins Ms., chap. II, pp. 18–19.

83. *Ibid.*, pp. 20–1, Ross to Smeulders, Aug. 26, 1884.

84. *Ibid.*, p. 22, Secretary of the Congregation of Propaganda to the general of the Order, Oct. 11, 1884.

85. *Ibid.*, pp. 23–4; *Débats de la Législature de la Province de Québec*, 1888, X, pp. 1257–8. Mercier's account during the debate on the Settlement of 1888.

86. Desjardins Ms., chap. II, p. 24.

87. *Sessional Papers of the Province of Quebec*, 1886, XIX: 3, return No. 74, p. 4, archbishop of Quebec to Ross, Jan. 2, 1885.

88. *Ibid.*, p. 5, Ross to archbishop of Quebec, Jan. 7, 1885.

89. *Ibid.*, archbishop of Quebec to Ross, April 8, 1885.

90. *Ibid.*, p. 6, Ross to archbishop of Quebec, April 25, 1885.

91. *Ibid.*, pp. 8–9, archbishop of Quebec to Ross, April 27, 1885.

92. *Ibid.*, p. 10, Ross to archbishop of Quebec, May 5, 1885.

93. Desjardins Ms., chap. II, pp. 27–8.

94. *Ibid.*, p. 29, Hudon to Anderledy, Dec. 14, 1885.

95. *Ibid.*, pp. 29–30.

96. *Ibid.*, p. 31, Lopinto to Turgeon, March 25, 1886.

97. *Ibid.*, p. 32, Lopinto to P. A. E. Jones, April 28, 1886.

98. *Ibid.*, pp. 33–4, Hudon to Anderledy, April 26, 1886.

99. *Ibid.*, pp. 34–5, Lopinto to Jones, no date.

100. *Ibid.*, pp. 36–8.

101. *Ibid.*, p. 38.

102. *Ibid.*, pp. 39–44.

103. *Ibid.*, pp. 47–9.

104. *Ibid.*, pp. 49–56.

105. See Wade, *French Canadians*, pp. 416–22 and Rumilly, *Histoire*, V, chaps. I–III, on the repercussions of the Riel execution.

106. *Ibid.*, pp. 69, 239.

107. Desjardins Ms., chap. II, p. 57.

CHAPTER TEN

1. Desjardins Ms., chap. III, p. 2–3.

2. *Ibid.*, p. 3, Mercier to Turgeon, Feb. 18, 1887.

3. *Ibid.*, n. 2, P. Fleck, *Exposé chronologique de ce qui s'est passé à l'occasion de l'incorporation de la Compagnie de Jésus en 1887*.

4. *Ibid.*, pp. 3–6, Turgeon to Mercier, March 9, 1887, and Mercier to Turgeon, March 11. Turgeon had included the letter of Ross to Smeulders, dated Aug. 26, 1884.

5. *Ibid.*, pp. 7–8, Hudon to Anderledy, March 14, 1887, and Lopinto to Turgeon, April 4.

6. *Ibid.*, pp. 10–12.

7. *Ibid.*, pp. 13–14, Lessman to Fabre, April 12, and Fabre to Lessman, April 13, 1887.

8. *Ibid.*

9. *Ibid.*, pp. 14–15, interview of Taschereau with Mercier, April 11, 1887.

10. *Ibid.*, pp. 15–17.

11. *Ibid.*, p. 17.

12. *J.L.A.P.Q.*, *1887*, XXI, pp. 72, 97, 123.

13. Rumilly, *Histoire*, V, p. 240.

14. Desjardins Ms., chap. III, pp. 20–1.

15. *Ibid.*, p. 22.

16. *Ibid.*, pp. 23–4.

17. *D.L.P.Q.*, *1887*, IX, pp. 951–2. The eight included the bishops of Rimouski, Sherbrooke, St. Hyacinthe, Chicoutimi, Nicolet, the apostolic vicar of Pontiac, and the archbishops of Ottawa and of Quebec.

18. *Ibid.*, p. 952.

19. *Ibid.*, pp. 956–8.

20. Desjardins Ms., chap. III, p. 18.

21. *Ibid.*, p. 19; Rumilly, *Histoire*, V, p. 242. The reply to Mercier's telegram was made on April 18.

22. Desjardins Ms., chap. III, pp. 24–5.

23. *Ibid.*, p. 25.

G*

24. *Ibid.*, pp. 26–7.

25. *Ibid.*, pp. 27–8; *D.L.P.Q.*, *1887*, IX, pp. 959–60.

26. Desjardins Ms., chap. III, p. 28.

27. *J.L.A.P.Q.*, *1887*, XXI, p. 171; *D.L.P.Q.*, *1887*, IX, pp. 950–9.

28. *Ibid.*, pp. 962–6.

29. *Ibid.*, pp. 968–75.

30. *Ibid.*, p. 977.

31. *J.L.A.P.Q.*, *1887*, XXI, pp. 172–3, 177.

32. Desjardins Ms., chap. III, pp. 33–6. Desjardins includes extracts from the Cardinal's letters of April 22, 27, 30, and May 4, 7, and 9, along with Mercier's replies of April 23, 28, and May 2, 5, and 9.

33. *Ibid.*, p. 37.

34. *Ibid.*, n. 16.

35. *Ibid.*, p. 38.

36. *Ibid.*, pp. 39–40, and n. 17, p. 40.

37. *Ibid.*, pp. 40–1. According to a report in *La Vérité* of May 21.

38. *Ibid.*, p. 41 and n. 18.

39. *Ibid.*, p. 41.

40. See *ibid.*, pp. 42–4, for a documentation of the activities of Lopinto.

41. *Ibid.*, p. 45.

42. *Ibid.*, and n. 22 for Lopinto's report of the conversation in Italian.

43. *D.L.P.Q.*, *1887*, IX, p. 977.

44. *J.L.A.P.Q.*, *1887*, XXI, p. 157.

45. Rumilly, *Histoire*, V, p. 246. Castors (beavers) was the name applied to the ultramontane wing in the province.

46. Desjardins Ms., chap. IV, p. 1. Rumilly states erroneously that Turgeon himself went to Rome; *Histoire*, V, pp. 278–9.

47. Desjardins Ms., chap. IV, pp. 1–2.

48. Mercier cabled on July 21 and received the reply in time to read it on July 23; *ibid.*, p. 2, and n. 1.

49. *Ibid.*, p. 3.

50. *Ibid.*, p. 5.

51. *Ibid.*, pp. 5–6; Masson Papers, Masson to Mercier, Oct. 28, 1887.

52. Masson Papers, Masson to Mgr Taché, Feb. 14, 1888 and Masson to P. Désy, Jan. 3, 1889. The letter to Taché is quoted rather fully in Desjardins Ms., chap. IV, pp. 6–10; see also n. 5 for Lopinto's enthusiastic reaction to Masson's mission.

53. *Ibid.*, pp. 11–12, Anderledy to Lopinto, Dec. 8, 1887, Désy to Anderledy, Dec. 18, and Lopinto to Turgeon, April 17, 1888.

54. Rumilly, *Histoire*, V, pp. 281–2.

55. See "Notes sur la Visite que fit le R. P. Turgeon, recteur du Collège Sainte-Marie, à l'honorable H. Mercier, Premier Ministre, à son retour de Rome, le 17 mars 1888," in Léon Pouliot, "Au Sujet des 'Biens des Jésuites,'" *Le Bulletin des Recherches Historiques*, XLIV: 6 (June, 1938), pp. 173–5.

56. Desjardins Ms., chap. IV, p. 14.

57. Rumilly, *Histoire*, V, p. 292.

58. Desjardins Ms., chap. IV, p. 16.

59. *D.L.P.Q.*, *1888*, X, pp. 1209–10, Mercier to Simeoni, Feb. 17, 1888.

60. *Ibid.*, pp. 1210–11, Simeoni to Mercier, March 1, Mercier to Simeoni, March 21, and Simeoni to Mercier, March 24, 1888.

61. *Ibid.*, p. 1226.

62. *Ibid.*, pp. 1211–12, Turgeon to Mercier, April 25, 1888; see pp. 1227–8 for the legal instrument.

63. *Ibid.*, pp. 1212–13, Simeoni to the procurator of the Jesuits, March 27, 1888, enclosed in Turgeon to Mercier, April 25, 1888.

64. *Ibid.*, pp. 1213–15, Mercier to Turgeon, May 1, 1888.

65. *Ibid.*, pp. 1225–6, Mercier to Taschereau, May 3, and Taschereau to Mercier, May 4, 1888.

66. *Ibid.*, pp. 1215–18, Turgeon to Mercier, May 8, 1888.

67. *Ibid.*, p. 1218, Mercier to Turgeon, May 14, 1888.

68. *Ibid.*, pp. 1219–22, Turgeon to Mercier, May 20, 1888.

69. *Ibid.*, pp. 1222–3, Mercier to Turgeon, June 4, 1888.

70. *Ibid.*, p. 1223, Turgeon to Mercier, and Mercier to Turgeon, June 8, 1888.

71. *J.L.A.P.Q.*, *1888*, XXII, p. 172.

72. *Ibid.*, pp. 269–84. The resolutions are on p. 284.

73. *Ibid.*, pp. 285–300.

74. *D.L.P.Q.*, *1888*, X, pp. 1235–7, 1248–64.

75. *Ibid.*, p. 1264.

76. *Ibid.*, pp. 1264–70.

77. *Ibid.*, pp. 1742–52.

78. *J.L.A.P.Q.*, *1888*, XXII, p. 300.

79. *D.L.P.Q.*, *1888*, X, pp. 1284–7, for the very brief debate the second time in the committee of the whole House.

80. *J.L.A.P.Q.*, *1888*, XXII, pp. 231, 237, 242, 254, 285.

81. Rumilly, *Histoire*, VI, p. 27. The *Journals* of the two Houses do not indicate the vote on the bill, but Rumilly states that it passed unanimously.

82. *Ibid.*, p. 28. The former Lieutenant-Governor, Rodrigue Masson, was a commander in the Order.

83. Desjardins Ms., chap. v, gives a detailed account of the developments that led to the final distribution of the $400,000.

84. *Ibid.*, p. 23.

85. The following accounts may be profitably consulted: John P. Heisler, "Sir John Thompson, 1844–1894" (Ph.D. thesis, University of Toronto, 1955), chap. VIII; John F. O'Sullivan, "Dalton McCarthy and the Conservative Party, 1876–1896" (M.A. thesis, University of Toronto, 1949), chaps. IV–IX, inclusive; J. Castell Hopkins, *Life and Work of the Rt. Hon. Sir John Thompson* (Toronto: London and Brantford: United Publishing Houses, 1895), chaps. VII–VIII. The debate in the House of Commons is very revealing of the strong feeling that developed against the Act. See *Debates of the House of Commons, 1889*, XXVIII, pp. 811–910, or *A Complete and Revised Edition of the Debate on the Jesuits Estates Act in the House of Commons, Ottawa, March, 1889*. Volume XCIV of the Macdonald Papers contains a miscellaneous collection of papers (letters, pamphlets, newspaper clippings, a few petitions) that deal with the agitation against the Act throughout 1889.

BIBLIOGRAPHY

A. Manuscript Material

1. *Archives du Collège Sainte-Marie, Montreal*

These archives have probably the best single collection of documents relating to the history of the Jesuits' estates question. Begun by A. E. Jones, S.J., and ably maintained by Paul Desjardins, S.J., several of its files of correspondence, unpublished memoirs, newspaper clippings, government documents, and other miscellaneous materials were useful to this study.

2. *Colonial Office Documents*

C.O. 42 Series. This series consists of original papers at the Public Record Office, London. It is composed of correspondence of the governors and other administrative officers of Quebec (Lower Canada) and Upper Canada from the first years of British rule until 1841. Dispatches and enclosures from Canada form the major portion of this material. The enclosures are numerous and often both important and bulky. Volumes 74–81 are particularly pertinent to the study of the Jesuits' estates because they include the vast documentary results of the investigation of the estates which was concluded in 1790. Microfilm copies of these particular volumes are available in P.A.C.

3. *Public Archives of Canada*

"A Reference on the affairs of the Jesuites. Minutes of the Committee appointed the 22nd July 1788 by His Excellency Lord Dorchester in Council to Report on the due Course required by Law for the execution of His Majesty's Order of the 18th August 1786 issued on the Petition of the Right Honorable Lord Amherst," in book marked "Jesuit Estates 1790. Appendix to Commission's Report."

Amherst Papers, Packets 47 and 69. Transcripts in P.A.C. The whole of Packet 47 deals with Amherst's attempts to obtain a grant of the Jesuits' estates.

"Appendice au Rapp. du Comité des Commissaires," found among a collection of papers entitled, "Jesuits Estates 1790. Appendix to Commissioner's [sic] Report," contains a copy of "His Majesty's Order in Council of the 18th of August, 1786," and "Extract of His Majesty's Instructions to His Excellency Guy Dorchester," of Aug. 23, 1786, a copy of Fawkener's letter of February 5, 1787, transmitting the Order-in-Council, as well as "Extracts from the Minutes of Council," relating to the investigation of the estates (1787–9). This and the "Reference" listed above would appear to be part of what was originally one lengthy appendix to the commissioners' report, but the documents have become separated. The "Appendice" is also in the manuscript collection of P.A.C.

Dalhousie Papers. Transcripts of these papers are in P.A.C. The papers are calendared in the Archives *Report* for 1938 (app. II), with an index at the end of the calendar.

G$^\text{I}$ Series. This series consists of dispatches, with enclosures, from the secretaries of state to the governors, or officers administering the province, from 1787 to 1841. These papers are calendared in Archives *Reports* for 1930, 1931, and 1932, with an index in the *Report* for 1932. The *Report* for 1938 (app. I) contains a calendar of stray dispatches which fill many gaps to be found in the series. These "strays" have been incorporated into the regular collection of dispatches where they have been placed according to dates.

Haldimand Papers. Copied by P.A.C. from the Haldimand Collection (British Museum), comprising 232 volumes. B–21–1 contains correspondence between General Amherst and R. Burton.

"Letter from The Chief Justice to His Excellency Lord Dorchester, 13 Dec. 1788," in file marked "Sir Guy Carleton," in P.A.C.

Macdonald Papers. Bound volumes of John A. Macdonald's papers are in the manuscript division of P.A.C. Volume XCIV of the papers is a miscellaneous collection (letters, pamphlets, newspaper clippings, a few petitions) dealing with the 1889 agitation over the Jesuits' Estates Act of 1888.

Minutes of the Council. For the period from the establishment of civil government in 1764 to the coming into force of the Quebec Act in 1775 there are three volumes entitled "Legislative Council." They record the executive as well as the legislative activities of the Council. Instead of being numbered, the volumes of the Council minutes are distinguished by capital letters, the three just mentioned being A, B, and C. Volumes D, E, and F are confined to the legislative activities of the Council from the summer of 1775 to the end of 1791, when the old province of Quebec passed out of existence. These volumes are paralleled by another series entitled "State Book" or "Privy Council," the volumes D to I containing the minutes of the Council as an executive body. This series has no volume A, B, or C because of the nature of the Legislative Council volumes A, B, and C. The Council minutes are located in P.A.C. but have not been calendared.

Murray Papers, II, Letter Book 1763–5. Copies of personal correspondence of General Murray, including those that relate to his recommendations of Père Roubaud. Transcripts in P.A.C. are from C.O. 42, I.

Q Series. This series consists of transcripts from the original papers in P.R.O. which, with certain exceptions, now form part of C.O. 42. The series comprises the official correspondence addressed to the Colonial Office by the governors, lieutenant-governors, and administrators of Quebec (later Lower Canada and Upper Canada) from 1760 to 1841. It relates to all subjects concerned with the political, social, economic, religious and military life of Canada. It includes miscellaneous correspondence from various officials and other persons, minutes and journals of the councils, memorials, petitions, returns, statistics, land grants, military reports, clergy questions and Indian affairs.

There are nearly 900 volumes in the entire series. Calendars have been made for the greater part of them. Those dealing especially with Quebec (and Lower Canada under the Constitutional Act of 1791) are calendared in appendices to P.A.C. *Reports* as follows: vols. 1–57 in the *Report* for 1890, pp. 1–325; 58–84 in the *Report* for 1891, pp. 1–200; 85–106 in the *Report* for 1892, pp. 153–285; 107–24 in the *Report* for 1893, pp. 1–119; 125–48 in the *Report* for 1896, pp. 1–252; 149–67 in the *Report* for 1897, pp. 253–395; 168–86 in the *Report* for 1898, pp. 397–580; 187–200 in the *Report* for 1899, pp. 581–713; 201–25 in the *Report* for 1900, pp. 715–912; 226–41 in the *Report* for 1901, pp. 913–1042; and 242–6 in the *Report* for 1902, pp. 1043–1109.

Some of the volumes of the series are so large that they have been bound in two or three separate parts, and some volumes have been inserted since the series was numbered. The volumes inserted later are designated by capital letters after the numbers. The originals of these supplementary volumes form part of the C.O. 43 series in P.R.O.

Q, volume I, is the same as C.O. 42, volume XXIV. The discrepancy in notation originated more than half a century ago when the first archivist of the Dominion, Dr. Douglas Brymner, had the transcripts made. At that time the present classification of the originals in P.R.O. had not been adopted.

Q. 50A, 50B, 50C, 50D, 50E, 50F, 50G: 1 and 2, and 50H are P.A.C. transcripts of the volumes C.O. 42: 74–81 inclusive. A brief indication of the contents of the Q volumes is given in the P.A.C. *Report* for 1890, pp. 292–3.

Shelburne Manuscripts. This collection in P.A.C. contains (pp. 30–6 of vol. LIX) a copy of "Thoughts upon the Ecclesiastical Establishment in Canada" by the Archbishop of York.

"Transcripts of the Minutes of the proceedings of the Commissioners for managing the Estates heretofore belonging to the late Order of Jesuits," in a file marked "Reports on Jesuits' Estates, 1790–1842," in P.A.C. The transcript covers the period from January 5, 1821, to March 27, 1822.

4. *Special Documents*

Desjardins' Manuscript. The use of Father Paul Desjardins' unpublished manuscript for volume III of his history of Collège Sainte-Marie was invaluable to the writer in the completion of chapters IX and X of this history of the estates question. In addition to Father Desjardins' judicious appraisal of events in the history of Collège Sainte-Marie, his published as well as unpublished work includes important documents.

Masson Papers. Rodrigue Masson's papers are in the possession of his grandson, Major Henri McKenzie Masson, Montreal. Major Masson generously assisted the writer in making copies of documents that relate to the role of the Lieutenant-Governor in the Jesuits' estates settlement.

B. Printed Material

Abstract of Proceedings in Council, relative to the Grant, to the late Jeffery Lord Amherst, of the Estates, belonging to the Jesuits, in Canada. This useful document (date and place of publication not indicated) is in the P.A.C. pamphlet collection.

CHRISTIE, ROBERT. *A History of the Late Province of Lower Canada*, 6 vols. Quebec and Montreal, 1848–55. Volume VI consists entirely of "Interesting Public Documents and Official Correspondence, Illustrative of, and Supplementary to the History of Lower Canada"—in large measure, the papers of Herman Witsius Ryland.

DOUGHTY, ARTHUR G., ed. *The Elgin-Grey Papers 1846–1852*, 4 vols. Ottawa: J. O. Patenaude, Printer to the King's Most Excellent Majesty, 1937.

DOUGHTY, ARTHUR G., and DUNCAN A. McARTHUR, eds. *Documents Relating to the Constitutional History of Canada, 1791–1818.* Ottawa: C. H. Parmelee, Printer to the King's Most Excellent Majesty, 1914.

KENNEDY, W. P. M., ed. *Statutes, Treaties and Documents of the Canadian Constitution, 1713–1929*, 2nd ed. Toronto: Oxford University Press, 1930.

LUCAS, C. P., ed. Lord Durham's *Report on the Affairs of British North America*. 3 vols. Oxford: Clarendon Press, 1912.

SHORTT, ADAM, and ARTHUR G. DOUGHTY, eds. *Documents Relating to the Constitutional History of Canada, 1759–1791.* 1 vol. in 2 parts. 2nd ed. Ottawa: J. de L. Taché, 1918.

TÊTU, MGR H. et L'ABBÉ C. O. GAGNON, eds. *Mandements, Lettres Pastorales et Circulaires des Evêques de Québec.* 4 vols. Quebec: Imprimerie Générale A. Coté et Cie., 1887–8.

THWAITES, REUBEN G., ed. *The Jesuit Relations and Allied Documents: Travels and Explorations of the Jesuit Missionaries in New France, 1610–1791.* 73 vols. Cleveland: The Burrows Brothers Company, Publishers, 1896–1901.

C. Government Publications

A Complete and Revised Edition of the Debate on the Jesuits' Estates in the House of Commons, Ottawa, March, 1889. Montreal: Printed by Eusèbe Senécal & Fils, 1889.

Acts of the Privy Council of England: Colonial Series, 1766–1783 (James Munro, ed.) vol. V. London: His Majesty's Stationery Office, 1912.

Debates of the House of Commons of the Dominion of Canada, annual volumes.

Débats de la Législature de la Province de Québec, annual volumes.

Journals of the House of Assembly of Lower Canada, annual volumes.

Journals of the House of Commons (Great Britain), annual volumes.

Journals of the House of Commons of the Dominion of Canada, annual volumes.

Journals of the House of Lords (Great Britain), annual volumes.

Journals of the Legislative Assembly of the Province of Canada, annual volumes.

Journals of the Legislative Assembly of the Province of Quebec, annual volumes.

Journals of the Legislative Council of the Province of Lower Canada, annual volumes.

Journals of the Legislative Council of the Province of Quebec, annual volumes.

Provincial Statutes of Canada, annual volumes.

Provincial Statutes of Lower Canada, annual volumes.

Sessional Papers of the Dominion of Canada, annual volumes.

Sessional Papers of the Province of Quebec, annual volumes.

D. Secondary Works

AUDET, LOUIS-PHILIPPE. *Le Système scolaire de la province de Québec.* 4 vols. Quebec: Les Editions de L'Erable and Les Presses universitaires Laval, 1950-2. Vols. III and IV deal particularly with the Royal Institution.

BRAUN, ANTOINE NICOLAS. *Mémoire sur les biens des Jésuites en Canada, par un Jésuite.* Montreal: C. O. Beauchemin & Valois, 1874. A pamphlet of 182 pages in the collection of P.A.C.

BURT, A. L. *A Short History of Canada for Americans.* Minneapolis: University of Minnesota Press, 1944.

—— *The Old Province of Quebec.* Minneapolis: University of Minnesota Press, 1933.

DESJARDINS, PAUL, S.J. *Le Collège Sainte-Marie de Montréal.* 2 vols. Montreal: Collège Sainte-Marie, 1940, 1945.

GARNEAU, FRANÇOIS XAVIER. *Histoire du Canada.* 9 vols. Montreal: Editions de L'Arbre, 1944–6. This eighth edition is inferior to the sixth, edited by M. Gabriel Hanotaux (Paris: Libraire Félix Alcan, 1920). The sixth edition is not indexed, however.

GÉRIN-LAJOIE, A. *Dix Ans au Canada de 1840 à 1850: histoire de l'établissement du gouvernement responsable.* Quebec: Typographie de L. J. Demers & Frère, Editeurs-propriétaires du "Canadien," 1888.

GROULX, L'ABBÉ LIONEL. *L'Enseignement français au Canada.* I. Montreal: Libraire d'Action Canadienne-Française, 1931.

HOPKINS, J. CASTELL. *Life and Work of the Rt. Hon. Sir John Thompson.* Toronto, London and Brantford: United Publishing Houses, 1895.

KENNEDY, W. P. M. *The Constitution of Canada.* London: Oxford University Press, 1922.

KINGSFORD, WILLIAM. *The History of Canada.* 10 vols. Toronto: Rowsell & Hutchison, 1887–98.

LEWIS, JOHN. *George Brown* (vol. VII of The Makers of Canada Series). London and Toronto: Oxford University Press, 1928.

MILLMAN, THOMAS R. *Jacob Mountain, First Lord Bishop of Quebec: A Study in Church and State 1793–1825.* Toronto: University of Toronto Press, 1947.

MUNRO, WILLIAM BENNETT. *The Seigniorial System in Canada.* New York: Longmans, Green and Company, 1907.

NEATBY, HILDA M. *The Administration of Justice under the Quebec Act.* Minneapolis: University of Minnesota Press, 1937.

PASTOR, LUDWIG, FREIHERR VON. *The History of the Popes from the Close of the Middle Ages.* Trans. E. F. Peeler. 40 vols. St. Louis, Missouri: B. Herder Book Company, 1913–53.

RANKE, LEOPOLD VON. *The History of the Popes during the Last Four Centuries.* 3 vols. London: George Bell & Sons, 1907.

RANKIN, A. *Jesuits' Estates in Canada, Public Property.* Montreal: J. C. Becket, 1850. A pamphlet of 134 pages in the collection of P.A.C.

ROCHEMONTEIX, CAMILLE DE. *Les Jésuites et la Nouvelle France au 18ᵉ Siècle.* 2 vols. Paris, 1906.

RUMILLY, ROBERT. *Monseigneur Laflèche et son temps.* Montreal: Editions B. D. Simpson, 1945.

—— *Histoire de la province de Québec.* 23 vols. Montreal: Editions Bernard Valiquette, 1940–51.

SAVAÈTE, ARTHUR. *Voix Canadiennes: vers l'abîme.* 12 vols. Paris: A. Savaète, 1908–22.

SHORTT, ADAM, and ARTHUR G. DOUGHTY, eds. *Canada and its Provinces.* 23 vols. Toronto: T. and A. Constable, 1914–17. Volume XXIII contains an excellent general index, a list of manuscript sources, bibliography for each of the chapters in the series, chronological outlines, and historical tables.

SKELTON, O. D. *The Life and Times of Sir Alexander Tilloch Galt.* Toronto: Oxford University Press, 1920.

SULTE, BENJAMIN. *Les Forges Saint Maurice* (Mélanges Historiques, VI). Montreal: G. Ducharme, 1920.

TÊTU, MGR HENRI. *Les Evêques de Québec.* Quebec: Narcisse S. Hardy, 1889.

TRUDEL, MARCEL. *L'Eglise canadienne sous le régime militaire, 1759–1764.* 2 vols. Quebec: Les Presses universitaires Laval, 1956–7.

VATIMESNIL, COMTE DE. *A Note, in addition to that of 1845, on the Jesuits' Estates.* Quebec: Frechette et Frère, 1847. A pamphlet of 21 pages in the collection of P.A.C.

—— *Memoir upon the Estates which the Jesuits Possessed in Canada, and the Objects to which these Estates Should be at Present Applied.* Montreal: Desbarats & Derbishire, Queen's Printers, 1845. A pamphlet of 39 pages in the collection of P.A.C.

WADE, MASON. *The French Canadians, 1760–1945.* London: Macmillan and Company Limited, 1955.

WILLISON, J. S. *Sir Wilfrid Laurier and the Liberal Party.* 2 vols. Toronto: George N. Morang and Company Limited, 1903.

E. ARTICLES

BELL, KENNETH. "Education, Secondary and University," *Canada and its Provinces* (Adam Shortt and Arthur G. Doughty, eds.), XVIII, Toronto: T. & A. Constable, 1914, pp. 345–402.

DECELLES, A. D. "Quebec under Confederation, 1867–1913," *Canada and its Provinces,* XV, pp. 167–215.

DESROSIERS, L'ABBÉ ADELARD. "French Education, 1763–1913," *Canada and its Provinces*, III, pp. 275–323.

PARMELEE, GEORGE W. "English Education," *Canada and its Provinces*, XVI, pp. 445–501.

POULIOT, LÉON. "Au sujet des 'Biens des Jésuites'," *Le Bulletin des Recherches historiques*, XLIV: 6 (June, 1938), pp. 173–5. Includes notes made by Father Turgeon when he visited with Mercier after the latter's return from Rome in 1888.

SHORTT, ADAM. "General Economic History, 1763–1841," *Canada and its Provinces*, IV, pp. 521–96.

F. UNPUBLISHED THESES

FRASER, BARBARA J. L. "The Political Career of Sir Hector Langevin." University of Toronto, M.A. thesis, 1959.

HEISLER, JOHN PHALEN. "Sir John Thompson, 1844–1894." University of Toronto, Ph.D. thesis, 1955.

LAPIERRE, LAURIER L. "Joseph Israel Tarte: A Dilemma in Canadian Politics (1874–1896)." University of Toronto, M.A. thesis, 1957.

NEATBY, H. BLAIR. "Laurier and a Liberal Quebec: A Study in Political Management." University of Toronto, Ph.D. thesis, 1956.

O'SULLIVAN, JOSEPH FRANCIS. "Dalton McCarthy and the Conservative Party, 1876–1896." University of Toronto, M.A. thesis, 1949.

G. REFERENCE WORKS

POLLEN, J. H. "Society of Jesus," *Catholic Encyclopedia*, XIV. New York: The Encyclopedia Press, 1913, pp. 81–110.

STEPHENS, H. M. "Jeffery Amherst," *Dictionary of National Biography*, I. London: Smith, Elder, and Company, 1885, pp. 357–9.

TANGUAY, L'ABBÉ CYPRION, ed. *Dictionnaire généalogique des familles canadiennes*. 7 vols. Montreal, 1871–90. Useful in the study of the title deeds for the Jesuits' estates.

INDEX